Mary Pat Henehan, DMin

Integrating
Spirit and Psyche
Using Women's Narratives
in Psychotherapy

The Haworth Pastoral Press®
An Imprint of The Haworth Press
New York • London • Oxford

Integrating Spirit and Psyche

Using Women's Narratives in Psychotherapy

THE HAWORTH PASTORAL PRESS
Religion and Mental Health
Harold G. Koenig, MD
Senior Editor

Integrating Spirit and Psyche
Using Women's Narratives in Psychotherapy

Mary Pat Henehan, DMin

The Haworth Pastoral Press®
An Imprint of The Haworth Press
New York • London • Oxford

Published by

The Haworth Pastoral Press®, an imprint of The Haworth Press, Inc., 10 Alice Street, Binghamton, NY 13904-1580.

PUBLISHER'S NOTE
Identities and circumstances of individuals discussed in this book have been changed to protect confidentiality.

The lines from "maggie and milly and molly and may," Copyright © 1956, 1984, 1991 by the Trustees for the E. E. Cummings Trust, from COMPLETE POEMS: 1904-1962 by E. E. Cummings, edited by George J. Firmage. Used by permission of Liveright Publishing Corporation.

Cover design by Lora Wiggins.

Library of Congress Cataloging-in-Publication Data

Henehan, Mary Pat.
　Integrating spirit and psyche : using women's narratives in psychotherapy / Mary Pat Henehan.
　　p. cm.
　Includes bibliographical references and index.
　ISBN 0-7890-1209-X (alk. paper)—ISBN 0-7890-1210-3 (soft)
　1. Feminist therapy. 2. Feminist psychology. 3. Women—Psychology. 4. Autobiography—Therapeutic use. 5. Storytelling—Therapeutic use. 6. Personal construct therapy. I. Title.
RC489.F45 H46 2002
616.89'14'082—dc21
　　　　　　　　　　　　　　　　　　　　　　　　　　　2002068536

For my mother, Rita C. Henehan
(1912-1997)

ABOUT THE AUTHOR

Mary Pat Henehan, DMin, is a licensed marriage and family therapist in private practice and a pastoral counselor. She is an approved supervisor with the American Association for Marriage and Family Therapy, and she chairs the State Committee for Supervision. Dr. Henehan is an adjunct assistant professor in the School of Public Health at Saint Louis University. She has over 35 years of experience in health care. Her research interests are in the areas of spirituality and health, mind/body issues, family violence, and parish nursing.

Dr. Henehan is a clinical member of the American Association for Marriage and Family Therapy, the American Association of Pastoral Counselors, the Employee Assistance Programs Association, the Association for Couples in Marriage Enrichment, and the Federation of Christian Ministers.

She has led numerous workshops locally and nationally on health and spirituality. This is her first book. Dr. Henehan lives in St. Louis with her husband, also an author.

CONTENTS

PART VI: WISE WOMEN

Preface

I began this book several years ago after I heard Isabel Allende on National Public Radio talking about how she felt her books in her belly. I too could say I felt this book in my belly and also in my bones. *Integrating Spirit and Psyche* began with the women's groups I facilitate. Some themes were expressed repeatedly: "I feel bad about myself." "I can't speak up at times." "I don't feel I have any rights." "I feel stupid." "I feel like I am bad." As therapy would progress, new narratives were expressed: "I do have a voice." "I am knowledgeable." "I like being who I am." and "I can work through this conflict."

Narrative therapy enhances my understanding of change and growth in clients and in myself. This therapeutic course takes into account the effect of discourse patterns or stories that constitute the self. Therapy then becomes the practice of externalizing these stories in favor of other alternative and/or preferred stories to enhance self-image. Narratives are present in individual psyches initially but are often subordinated to the dominant story. Usually, personal stories are supported by ideological practices circulating in a given culture. Sometimes counterplots to the dominant story form as individuals grow. New abilities develop that can be used to challenge destructive aspects of the dominant narrative. This approach to therapy does not view the person as the problem but rather views the problem as the internalization of certain ideas about the self that circulate in a given culture. For example, women may have derived their concept of what they should weigh from the dictates of their culture. This may lead them to have negative feelings about themselves if their weight does not fit within the perceived norms. Girls and women often feel as though they have less self-worth when they are at what is not considered their "ideal" weight.

As a writer and therapist, I encourage the people I work with to replace negative ideas they have about the self by using a deconstruction process. This book elaborates on those ideas and offers readers an opportunity to think about these ideas in their own lives. Each chapter concludes with reflection questions. Questions often open up space and allow the reader's story to develop. Reauthoring a story is primarily achieved through questioning. A deeper meaning for the reader is also created through this process. Writing responses to these reflection questions can result in reauthoring for the reader.

The narrative approach can be compared to tearing down an old house and building a new and improved one in its place. Energy abounds in creating the new space, drawing upon the experience of what worked in the old house and what did not. The process involves both destructive and constructive elements. The new house becomes the preferred narrative.

Drawing on the earlier example of weight issues, the preferred story might not include weight charts but rather a focus on the woman as a talented musician, a person who exercises regularly, or a woman who is developing a deeper inner life of beauty and creativity.

Imagination is a key element in constructing a new house. Being able to imagine what kind of flooring is desirable as well as how many windows, and being able to picture the placement of windows is essential in helping the process move forward. In like manner, the ability to tap into one's dreams is important in creating and developing one's new (preferred) narrative. This is the reauthoring process in a nutshell.

My clients inspired this book, along with the generations of women and women-to-be in my own family. My mother, Rita, who raised five children, helped parent two foster children, and worked through the trauma of sexual abuse. My grandmother, Catherine DeVry, who, in addition to raising a family and working outside the home, involved herself in politics in Chicago as a precinct captain—an indication of how highly she valued her newly won right to vote. My Aunt Venice, who while visiting her granddaughter, Amy, in Killeen, Texas, the day before Amy's wedding was murdered in Luby's Cafeteria by a women-hating mass murderer. My Aunt Mary, who served as an Army nurse in World War II during the bombing of Italy. Virginia, my mother-in-law, who bonds so affectionately with her grandchildren and great-grandchildren. Rita, my sister, who has had the strength to divorce and remarry. My sister, Sue, who balanced raising children with pursuing a career as a nurse in the emergency room and in cardiac care. Eryn, my niece, who generously gave a summer to work in Africa to help fight AIDS. My newest niece, Brigid Rose, who simply delights us all with her smiles and bright face. My sister-in-law, Suz, who homeschools her three sons and continues to make us all think about the treatment of Mother Earth. Another sister-in-law, Paddy, who has been a treasure in my brother's life. Finally, my sister-in-law Kay, who is faith filled and well connected to her three daughters and her six grandchildren.

This book is about narratives or stories that I have heard from women and stories from my own personal experience. The term *narrative* is used to mean thinking about our lives as stories and talking about what is meaningful and fulfilling. A narrative approach delineates the constructive and destructive dimensions of social realities. Women can rewrite their lives as they become aware of their stories.

The content of this book stresses the integration of psychological and spiritual elements. Women's stories need not be constrained by the past. The present is a time for women to come into their own, and the power of each woman's story will move us all forward.

I draw on spirituality in the book. By spirituality I mean the vital principle in men and women, awareness, animation, divine influence as an agency working in our hearts. The integration of spirit and psyche is vital for change.

By training, I am a marriage and family therapist, which means I spend a large amount of my time seeing individuals, couples, families, and groups in crisis. I also supervise students learning this profession, and I teach courses at Saint Louis University's School of Public Health and in the Department of Counseling and Family Therapy. I hear numerous stories and try to discern the positive and negative themes. Many people perpetuate their narrative's destructive elements because of a lack of awareness of their inner world. I hope that this book offers cause for reflection, for men and women alike, about the power of narrative, the resources that faith and health provide, and the hope of reauthoring that does and can take place in our lives.

Part I examines elements that enhance a sense of self. Parts II and III explore the destructive messages women receive from family and society: "You are helpless" in the face of violence and abuse, and "You are nobody." Part IV explores the new stories that are emerging from women, such as, "I am knowing"; "I can take credit"; and "I have a divine herstory." Part V elaborates on the wisdom and wildness of women. I use the term *wildness* to mean the untapped potential in women. When visiting a national park, one appreciates anew the "wildlife" present. I believe women have this wild dimension and that it is yet to be discovered. It is also about freedom and restructuring constraining beliefs. I hope this book will assist women in their journey toward greater freedom. Part VI examines the role of wise women in our lives and offers some spiritual practices to assist growth in various areas.

Michael White and David Epston (1990) summarize the process well in *Narrative Means to Therapeutic Ends,* when they say, "It is never the size of the step that a person takes that counts, but its direction."

The clinical narratives I use in this book have been altered to protect confidentiality. Fictitious names have been used, and other factual information has been changed.

I am very grateful to my clients, teachers, colleagues, and students with whom I have had the privilege of being in relationship.

Acknowledgments

To my husband, Jack Renard, PhD, for his support. And to Karen Caldwell, PhD, who provided special help and encouragement in undertaking this project.

Helpful comments and suggestions were made by a number of people who read the manuscript or portions of it at various stages of its development. I wish to thank: Virginia Renard; Joseph Pfeffer, PhD; Judy Miller, PhD; Tom Conran, PhD; Mike Ewing; Jo Gallagher; Terry Mulligan; Ethel Dimont; Josephine Goodman; Jerry Macklin; Connie Abeln; Caryl Simon; Joan Johnson; Jill Esrock; Steve and Kathryn Robbins; Corinne McAfee; Kay Uhles; Rod Fadem; Robert Nazarene; Julie Lotharius, PhD; George Pegues; Robert and Jessica Saigh; Michael Thornton; Anne-Marie Donovan; David Motherwell; Judy Rolfe; Jon Doolin; Barry Kepp; Alonzo Johnson; Gail Eisenhart; Elaine Payne; John Lowerison; Michael Tvanote; Whitney Howland; Cindy Fehmel; Chris Bauer; John Newmark; and Jane Gwaltney.

I am grateful to Rebecca Browne and Harold Koenig, MD, for guiding me to publication.

PART I:
ENHANCING THE SELF

Chapter 1

First- or Second-Class Citizens?

When through one woman a little more love and goodness, a little more light and truth come into the world, then that woman's life has had meaning.

Eulogy for Mary Jane Lublow
Father Delphs, *Prayer*

And God said, "Let there be light," and there was light.

Genesis 1:3*

In this, the twenty-first century, the oppression of women still exists. In fact, women worldwide are not yet considered equal to men. We need enlightenment and insight to change this situation. I draw on scripture for the support that we need to shed light on this timely issue. For instance, I explore how childlessness is used to devalue some women and how the dominant cultural group controls this perception. A review of law and financial compensation points out how the dominant cultural group controls the bigger picture for women today. Each chapter ends with reflection questions to assist the reader in the process of rewriting one's own story using constructive elements.

WOMEN WHO DO NOT HAVE CHILDREN

Mary Jane Lublow was a very important person in my life. She was like a second mother to me and to my brothers and sisters as we were growing up. Acting as a model for me, she showed how women could

---

*All scriptural quotations can be found in *The New American Bible* (1970). Trans. by the Catholic Biblical Association of America. Camden, NJ: Thomas Nelson Inc.

work and support themselves independent of a man. This was just one of the many lessons I learned from her. We called her "Auntie Mary Jane" because she took such an interest in our lives, attending ballet performances, basketball tournaments, and piano recitals. She communicated much love and care. She made us creative birthday party invitations in the shape of swimming goggles and ballet slippers. Mary Jane was my mother's friend, and a co-worker at Bell Telephone Company who advanced from operator to manager.

She did not have children. Some would consider her a second-class citizen or an "old maid." Women who do not have children are thought by some to be missing something. Mardy Ireland writes in *Reconceiving Women: Separating Motherhood from Female Identity:*

> Rather than viewing the woman who is not a mother as missing something, let us look instead for what is absent from our usual conceptions of womanhood. . . . Women who are not mothers are frequently described as women to be pitied (barren or unmarriageable), or as exceptional women.[1]

DOMINANT CULTURE

The pervasive American culture is a white, male-dominated system. In the United States, women are viewed as a minority group even though women outnumber men. Women of color must cope with the additional challenge of racism. Women often see themselves in a one-down position, and indeed that is where our culture puts them, although this is changing as more people speak out in support of equal rights. I have become more wary of placing myself in a one-down position. A male co-worker and I set up a time to meet about some common interests. As he was writing my name in his appointment book, he said, "I may forget and think you are a patient coming in for an evaluation." I heard and interpreted his statement as implying that he was one-up and I was one-down in this situation. Deciding to use humor to respond to him, I laughed and said, "I may need an evaluation by that time." I believed that I knew what was going on—first-class and second-class citizen dynamics. Awareness of these dynamics helps.

Change is a slow process. Not until 1920 did women win the battle for the right to vote. My grandmother lived through that period of history and was involved in politics. She viewed voting as a privilege that was difficult to obtain. Before the Nineteenth Amendment was passed, women were considered the property of their husbands.

As second-class citizens, women's talents are neither recognized nor validated by the male-dominated society. Nor do women give themselves credit. It is curious that Mary Ann Evans became a famous author by using the male pseudonym George Eliot, and dressing as a man. Mary Ann Evans was able to fool the public about her gender and succeed. Her books, including *Middlemarch* (1871-1872) and *Adam Bede* (1859), became classics because she disguised her femininity and fooled the dominant culture of her day.

The first woman to write and publish a book in the American colonies was Mary White Rowlandson. She was captured by the Wampanoag Indians in 1676. Rowlandson and her three children were among the twenty-four hostages taken from the settlement at Lancaster, Massachusetts. She was released after eighty-three days. She wrote about her experiences, and her book was published anonymously in Cambridge, Massachusetts in 1682, with an editorial apology for bringing a woman into "publick view." The narrative of the captivity and restoration of Mary Rowlandson went through fifteen editions by 1800.[2]

Think of the number of symphonies you have heard or listened to composed by women. Not until 1997 was I in the presence of a woman composer. At the National Women's Studies Association that year, Carolyn Bremer played a recording of an unpublished symphony she composed, titled *A Woman's Voice*. Often the dominant culture creates images that are gender biased. I had come to expect my symphony experience to be male dominated until I heard Carolyn Bremer's composition. Only then did I become aware that I had never heard a woman composer.

The music of the German Benedictine abbess Hildegarde of Bingen (1098-1179) lately has been rediscovered. She became famous for her prophecies and visions, which brought her consultations with the most powerful rulers of her day. She recorded her visions over a period of thirty years while also compiling treatises on medicine and natural history. Her *Symphony of the Harmony of Heavenly Revelations* is a collection of seventy-seven songs and one music drama.[3] These are only a few examples of talented women largely unrecognized in their times.

As women become first-class citizens, they will be free to express themselves in a variety of ways, such as writing and music, and they will be validated for their contributions. The culture suffers when women's gifts and the feminine side are buried.

Emotional Intelligence, by Daniel Goleman, illustrates the vital importance of feminine feelings and affect.[4] The growing violence in our culture is directly related to the devaluation of the emotional aspects of the personality by the dominant group. One important aspect of examining cultural violence is understanding the lack of legal protection for women.

LEGAL PROTECTION

The lack of legal protection for women is astounding. Because of the highly publicized murder of Nicole Brown Simpson in 1994, the world became more aware of the injustices done to abused women. The O. J. Simpson trials brought this hidden reality before us, with its relentless display of Nicole's battered face on television screens, in newspapers, and in magazines. For months, perhaps years, Nicole had hidden the grim photographic evidence in a safe deposit box, tucked away with the fear that her story might never be told. O. J. Simpson was eventually convicted of wrongful death in a civil suit. Defense lawyers argued to excuse domestic violence; the attitude that "boys will be boys" prevailed.

One woman found the decision in the O. J. Simpson criminal trial so upsetting that it became a factor in her attempt to take her own life. She did not succeed and instead lived to tell of the great hopelessness she felt for women the day the announcement of his acquittal was broadcast across the world.

The overwhelming number of lawmakers in our society are males. However, a study on state legislatures, conducted in 1992 by the Center for the American Woman and Politics (CAWP) at Rutgers University and Debra Dodson (who did the surveys), found that when women are elected they reshape the public agenda, helping women more than their male colleagues do. Family caretaking issues are critical for divorced women, mothers of small children, women of color, the elderly (most of whom are women), and other groups who do not have the power to make laws and thus are doubly burdened.[5] Not only must they deal with the responsibility to care for their families, they must do so without necessary resources.

In the state of Missouri, positive changes are being made as women are elected to the U.S. Senate. Some women senators supported a policy to track homicides connected to domestic violence in the state. Most female murder victims in the United States are victims of domestic violence. Some women are protected in Missouri, but many are not. The *St. Louis Post-Dispatch* reported that in the state of Missouri in 1997, 4,475 women and 5,223 children were able to find shelter, yet 7,367 victims were turned away. Perhaps women are not protected because they are viewed as second-class citizens.[6] Research suggests that wife beating results in more injuries requiring medical treatment than auto accidents, rapes, and muggings combined.

The statistics in the United States are alarming. Every nine seconds a woman is physically abused by her husband.[7] Women are twice as likely as men to be killed by their partner or spouse, yet women (generally battered for years) who murder their husbands are often given longer sentences than those received by men who murder their wives.[8]

Significant problems exist in the United States, but women are valued even less in other countries, such as China, where there is a common practice of leaving unwanted baby girls in marketplaces. If the baby is fortunate, she is found by orphanage staff and cared for, or she may be adopted by a foreign family. From my practice as a marriage and family therapist, I see families who adopt children from foreign lands where baby girls are unvalued. Overall, these children seem to be thriving, but many have nightmares and flashbacks, becoming temporarily inconsolable. The normal attachment process was disrupted for these children at the time of abandonment by the biological parent, causing trauma that may persist indefinitely.

Karin Evans, who adopted a daughter from China, documented her experience in *The Lost Daughters of China: Abandoned Girls, Their Journey to America, and the Search for a Missing Past*. She casts light on the age-old cultural preference for boys.[9] Evans tells of the dire straits of some Chinese orphanages. A friend of hers who adopted overseas was handed a baby girl in the hotel they were staying at in the north of China. She had to undress the baby, redress her in the clothes she had brought, and return the original clothes to the orphanage caretakers. There are more than 22,000 children—all born in China, nearly all of them girls—that have been brought to the United States.[10]

FINANCIAL COMPENSATION AND SUCCESS

Men are twice as likely to hold leadership positions as women are. When I was vice president of mission at DePaul Health Center in St. Louis, Missouri, I experienced the gender gap firsthand. I served on an executive council with nine other executives; only one of those nine was a woman. In addition, the women on the council did not receive financial compensation equal to that of the men, even though the women carried the same or even greater workloads. For instance, the vice president of nursing had half of the total staff of the hospital under her responsibility. Inequities exist on the local, state, and national levels. The gap between the salaries of men and women increased again with the U.S. Census report of 1997. In two-parent families, men do about one-third of the household work and less child care even when both parents work at outside jobs.[11]

To look at the matter another way, consider women's anxiety levels and guilt about ambitious striving. I often see clients who want a better job but are waiting for someone else to believe in them and tell them they have a chance of advancing. I try to challenge their thinking and ask, "What do you believe about yourself and your abilities?"

I have to admit it is not easy for me to put myself forward either. Recently I asked for a raise. Afterward I realized that I was worried that I would be judged negatively. I presented my request as a social justice issue of fair reimbursement, and it was granted.

Harriet Goldhor Lerner, in *Women in Therapy,* says it well: "Women fear that they will pay dearly for their accomplishments. They frequently equate success, or the very wish for it, with loss of femininity and attractiveness, loss of significant relationships, loss of health."[12] Successful women need a strong support system to rework these all-too-common destructive beliefs regarding their accomplishments.

I received a call from Nancy, a former client, who had moved to New Mexico. She was very unhappy in a job she had taken there. Nancy called me to discuss leaving the job that she did not like and to get some coaching on finding a job she would find more pleasant. She struggled with the conflict over going it alone or getting the support she needed. When she began suffering back pain she felt that it might be related to her being unhappy at work, and so she sought consultation. It was a painful time for her as she let go of a destructive work setting and harmful beliefs about herself as a failure. Finally Nancy chose a place that became a nurturing workspace. She worked well with her supervisor and was able to progress toward accomplishing her goals of working with victims of child abuse. In time, she became more comfortable, realizing that she had useful talents. She felt more confident in her new job setting, and her back pain went away.

Irene Stiver puts it another way in *Women's Growth in Connection:* "Some women experience so much anxiety about reentering the work arena that they do not try to get a job, even though they may have a strong interest in doing something that would use their talents and abilities."[13]

Many women I see are stressed by a number of factors. Situational depression occurs when women are abandoned by husbands who found younger women. Dissolving a relationship of many years and doing the emotional work of separation takes a lot of energy.

Sociologist Arlie Russell Hochschild documents moving interviews in her research project that became a best-seller. In *The Time Bind: When Work Becomes Home and Home Becomes Work,* she interviews some single-parent families, mostly women, who struggle to pay for child care, earn a fair wage, and deal with the emotional work of divorce, which is often an isolating experience.[14]

On the positive side, support for the success of women is emerging. *Nine and Counting: Women of the Senate* documents the support U.S. Senator Barbara Mikulski from Maryland gives to new women senators. Strong, unpretentious, a strategist, and a coalition builder, she is known as the "dean" of women in the senate. She tells them, "Stick with me; you'll have a future."[15] She coaches newcomers in the tough realities and struggles of the male-dominated senate. The question still needs to be asked: Why did we have only nine women senators in the year 2000, and only thirteen in 2001?

Other themes could be developed involving first- and second-class citizens, so as you think about the reflection questions you may want to add your own themes and elaborate on them. Take the time to reflect. Change happens when we process.

REFLECTION QUESTIONS

1. What comes to mind when you think about being a first-class citizen? Use your imagination. You may think about situations in which you would be free from worry. What comes to mind when you think about being a second-class citizen? What feelings go along with being treated as a second-class citizen? Give examples of feeling dismissed, talked down to, or humiliated by someone.
2. Name three people who treat you as a first-class citizen. Name three people who treat you as a second-class citizen. Is there any change you can make in your interactions with the people who treat you like a second-class citizen?
3. List three ways you express yourself. Name three women artists you admire.
4. How do you feel about being successful? List three fears concerning success. Name three ways you celebrate your successes.
5. Name any injustices you feel in your work and/or home life.
6. Compose three affirmations for yourself, such as, "I can use my talents and be happy being successful."
7. Why do you think we had only thirteen women senators in 2001?

Chapter 2

Self in Context

Nobody sees a flower—really—it is so small it takes time—we haven't the time—and to see takes time, like to have a friend takes time.

Georgia O'Keeffe
"About Myself" (1939)

Nothing in life is more wonderful than faith—the one great moving force which we can neither weigh in the balance nor test in the crucible . . . mysterious, indefinable, known only by its effects, faith pours out an unfailing stream of energy.

Sir William Osler
"The Faith that Heals"

As women are considered second-class citizens by the dominant culture, the next step is to look at women in some alternative ways. Georgia O'Keeffe had the creativity to paint a flower with fresh new eyes. That is our challenge as we look at befriending ourselves: to see with fresh eyes. I will explore a woman's sense of self through four areas: (1) establishment of self-esteem and spirituality—as Sir William Osler has pointed out, spirituality and faith are an important source of energy; (2) growth and development in women; (3) research in female intelligence; and (4) some practical suggestions to assist in growth of the self. Stories flow from soul or self.

SELF-ESTEEM AND SPIRITUALITY

Self-esteem is a key building block for healthy self-confidence in both children and adults. Virginia Satir presents ideas one has about oneself as "self-worth." She found in her practice of treating troubled families that the solution was the same: treat low self-esteem. She noticed the following in all troubled families:

- Self-worth was low.
- Communication was indirect, vague, and not really honest.
- Rules were rigid, inhuman, nonnegotiable, and everlasting.
- The family's link to society was fearful, placating, and blaming.

She saw a different pattern in vital nurturing families:

- Self-worth was high.
- Communication was direct, clear, specific, and honest.
- Rules were flexible, human, appropriate, and subject to change.
- The link to society was open and hopeful and was based on choice.[1]

Satir believed that these differences rested on new learning, new awareness, and a change in consciousness.

Many people have misconceptions about the word *self.* I use the word self to mean the unique being that each person is. To some it means selfishness, self-centeredness, and a lack of consideration for others. Self is defined as (1) a person referred to with respect for complete individuality, and (2) the uniting principle, as a soul. It includes the spiritual and psychological self.

Spirituality enhances the sense of self in these ways:

- It provides a sense of inner peace and harmony.
- It provides a creative energy that is constant yet changing.
- Participation in the fullness of life occurs because it gives meaning, value, and direction to all human concerns.
- It stimulates a search for meaning in life.
- It creates a sense of relatedness to dimensions that transcends the self in such a way that it increases self-esteem and empowers the individual.[2]

Spirituality keeps us balanced and focused. Psychology helps us understand ourselves and the means by which we can continue to grow and enrich our lives.

GROWTH AND DEVELOPMENT

Joan Borysenko updates the traditional concepts of "maid," "mother," and "crone."[3] For instance, the maiden years have gotten progressively shorter due to electricity and the stimulation of the brain's pineal gland, bringing on puberty several years earlier than in the nineteenth century. In the days before electric lighting, the mean age for puberty was fourteen or fifteen. Now it is between eleven and twelve years of age. The psychological phases that women go through are better described as (1) childhood and adolescence, (2) guardianship, and (3) elder.

1. *Childhood and adolescence (birth to age 21):* In the past a male model of development, that of independence and autonomy as the norm to healthy adulthood, has been imposed on girls. Carol Gilligan challenged that notion and said girls develop differently; relationality is key.[4] Adolescence is a time to find one's identity and one's voice. *Little Voice,* a movie, portrays this point well. Jane Horrocks plays a painfully introverted teen who can express herself only through the voices and songs of Judy Garland and other celebrities. When she finally finds her own voice, the viewer feels the surge of joy that the character has at last come into her own sense of self. She becomes the bird set free of its cage.[5]

2. *Guardianship (ages 21 to 49):* Love relationships take center stage during these years. Today the median age at which a woman first gives birth is twenty-six in the United States. Emotionally healthy mothers are unconditionally loving toward their newborns. The guardian keeps the circle of life whole. She is a peacekeeper but with the power to tell the truth. The classic story *Little Women* illustrates this guardianship role. Marmee, the mother, is left to raise four daughters when her husband goes off to war. Susan Sarandon, who plays Marmee in the 1994 movie version of Louisa May Alcott's story, demonstrates the power of nurturance and affection for each of her unique daughters—spirited Jo, conservative Meg, fragile Beth, and romantic Amy.[6]

3. *Elder (ages 50 to 100+):* Women are often beautiful, savvy, and wise. They impart values that support and encourage the growth

of others and the preservation of life.[7] The character of Mother Joe portrays this role in the African-American film *Soul Food* (1997). She wisely keeps the family together with her weekly Sunday dinners, then hands over this role to the next generation at the time of her death.[8]

Integrating the psychological and the spiritual aspects of the human person is essential to a holistic approach. In therapy, integration is a great asset to healing.[9] It is the journey into spirituality that manifests itself through compassionate listening between a family and its members, and the therapist.[10]

Examining how we understand God, and any correlations between our understanding and the main caregivers in our life, is important. For example, a noninvolved God in our experience might correlate with a detached parent.

Feminists have long lamented the accepted traditional attitude of ignoring emotional development. I refer to self as connection with the core of one's own being and an interdependent connection with others. Carter and McGoldrick suggest that skills in human interdependence lead to maturity in the following ways for the adult woman when she:

- Participates in cooperative activities of many kinds at home, at work, and at play
- Expresses a full range of emotions and allows this range in others
- Expresses differences of belief or opinions to others without attacking them or becoming defensive
- Relates with openness, curiosity, tolerance, and respect to people who are different and is comfortable with diversity
- Nurtures, cares for, and mentors others
- Accepts the help and mentoring of others[11]

As we journey through life with respect and love in our relationships, we gain wisdom. Borysenko discusses that studies demonstrate the truth that women continue to develop their strengths and actually bloom, rather than fade, with the advent of midlife.[12] Older women often possess the power to tell the truth and, when necessary, be a warrior for justice. I use the feminine aspects of warrior, which are the healing and transformative powers, versus the masculine aspects of warrior, which often are characterized by aggression and violence. Situations improve through respect, understanding, and love—

and rarely through war and violence. I do not want to oversimplify the notions of feminine and masculine warriors; however, the focus of this book does not allow for an in-depth examination of these concepts.

RESEARCH

Women who are conditioned by academia to believe in a single track of logic can end up feeling stupid because they have other approaches to truth. Often a male model of knowing has been applied to women. Women value relationships and dialogue more than debate.[13] Academia stresses having an idea, developing that idea to defend a position, and developing an argument to support that position (male model). Women tend to have more of a discussion approach to ideas and thoughts than a debate approach. When I watch the public television program *Firing Line,* I know that my approach to discussion is quite different from the model portrayed by the participants in that political forum. The model portrayed is very male, adversarial, and argumentative in nature. Women's ways of knowing are still being examined.

Monica McGoldrick and Betty Carter write about the research done on different kinds of intelligence:

- *Emotional intelligence:* the ability to control impulses, to have empathy with others, and conduct responsible social, interpersonal, and intimate relationships
- *Spatial intelligence:* the ability to find one's way around
- *Musical intelligence:* the ability to perceive rhythm and pitch
- *Bodily kinesthetic intelligence:* the gift of fine motor skills as seen in a surgeon, athlete, or dancer
- *Interpersonal intelligence:* the ability to understand others
- *Intrapersonal intelligence:* the ability to understand oneself and to gain insight
- *Artistic intelligence:* the ability to connect words, color, materials, music, and space in interesting and unique ways, and to appreciate beauty[14]

To this I would add *spiritual intelligence:* the ability to find meaning and purpose in life, to have meditation/prayer skills, to be in communion with a higher power, to have a sense of social justice, to have a belief system that guides decisions, and to be active in a faith community.

Learning is a lifelong process, and we need affirmation for all ways of expressing the self. I find this concept of multiple intelligences helpful. I saw a young woman who had been struggling with depressed feelings because her grades had dropped, resulting in her labeling herself as stupid. She had an A average in the beginning of her sophomore year. During that year change began to occur when she stopped focusing on her struggle with one course in history and began implementing her interpersonal skills. She asked for help from other students doing well in the history course, who assisted my client in improving her grades. She gradually felt lighter. She loves to talk on the phone and has recently used her skills in developing constructive relationships.

Some research done by the American Association of University Women reveals that the most evaded topic in schools is the issue of gender and power. If you are feeling some resistance in examining these issues, so is the rest of U.S. society.

PRACTICAL WAYS TO PROMOTE GROWTH OF THE SELF

Julia Cameron offers a practical way of promoting the growth of the self.[15] She describes a tool she calls "morning pages." These are explained in greater detail in her book, *The Artist's Way.* One of the biggest obstacles to growth is the inner critic. Cameron suggests writing down your stream of consciousness in longhand when you first wake up in the morning. She insists on three pages. You may be surprised at the thoughts and feelings that come pouring out. Cameron sees this tool as an important way to clear and focus the mind. If you have self-defeating thoughts, these pages will bring these thoughts into the open so you can talk back to them. The practice of writing morning pages allows you to stand back and observe your own inner process. They can give you insight and a way to understand yourself.

I have used morning pages for the past few years and find that writing first thing in the morning is a way to process my thoughts and feelings. This exercise increases awareness; I can pick up on any defeatist attitudes, and I am less likely to sabotage my own successes. The writing of morning pages also frees up my self-expression. This process encourages me to look inside myself and own my feelings.

In addition to the practice of morning pages, an examination of gender roles can also bring about positive change in families. Women have many choices today. Awareness of roles we play and those we do not want to play is essential.

Equality for women is a difficult issue. I grew up between two brothers, which had advantages and disadvantages. The advantages were that I learned to be comfortable around men. When I was an administrator, I had good relationships with my male colleagues. I liked my brothers because they challenged me. We used to play basketball in our driveway; I held my own in scoring points.

The disadvantage was that more opportunities were given to them because they were male. My two brothers administered my parents' financial trust. I felt that I had equal abilities, but it was a gender issue. In a majority of families men handle the finances and women become the caregivers.

Now a number of factors are making female caregiving impractical for families. More than half of all women ages forty-five to sixty-four are working full-time. Nurturing roles in families therefore need to be assumed by both men and women. Some theorists believe that learned gender roles change throughout life. Men and women long to express the unexpressed side of their being. Women often grow in becoming more assertive and men grow in expressing their nurturing side. The caring of elders in our families need not be assigned solely to women.[16]

REFLECTION QUESTIONS

1. What keeps your self-esteem high? What brings your self-esteem down? Can you make changes to increase your self-esteem? Is your communication direct? If no, why not?
2. Breathing with awareness can help us relax and slow down. Some women are busy all the time and do not stop to be aware of the self. Do you appreciate the pattern of your breathing? Place one hand on your abdomen and feel the rhythm of the

movement of your muscles. Become aware of where in your body you feel tension as you breathe in and out. Let go of the tension.

3. What kinds of intelligences do you feel you have? (For example, I am aware that I have bodily kinesthetic intelligence. I recently participated in some sporting events and won medals in basketball, swimming, and broad jump.) Describe some ways you express your variety of intelligences.

4. Name three people who take power from you and to whom you surrender this power. Name three people who empower you. Call one of them and spend some time with him or her.

5. Circle six words that indicate how you understand a higher power or God.[17]

judgmental	negative
cruel	caring
loving	compassionate
distant	imaginary
absent	rigid
nonexistent	trustworthy
strict	predictable
purposeful	nonattentive
indifferent	unreal
disengaged	fanciful
healing	gentle

If you could not find six words, create your own description of your understanding of your higher power or God. Are there correlations in the adjectives you use to describe God and your caregivers?

6. Try writing morning pages for a week. Struggle with your inner critic. Write what the critic is saying and how you can respond. (For example: [Inner critic] "You can't teach." [Your response] "Why would you say such a thing? I have been teaching for years and students have told me how I have helped them. Get lost!")

7. What blocks to growth did you discover in writing your morning pages?

8. Women are typically unrecognized in history. You may find it helpful to outline all the unappreciated work your mother, aunts, sisters, grandmothers, and sisters-in-law did and do, emphasizing their courage, abilities, hard work, and strength.

9. Do you feel free to ask both men and women in your family to assist with nurturance in the family system? Can you elaborate on your answer?

10. Describe the gender role you played in your family while growing up. Do you play that role now? Do you want to?

Chapter 3

Ancient and Ancestral Woman

Lost in the present: have we forgotten how to remember?

Michael Ventura
"The Mission of Memory"

The closest friends I have made all through life have been people who also grew up close to a loved and loving grandmother or grandfather.

Margaret Mead

In Chapter 2 we explored spirituality and self-esteem, the ways women know and develop, and some practical ways to be aware of ourselves and of our images of a higher power. In this section, I explore (1) the role of Athena, one of the Greek goddesses, daughter of Zeus; (2) family systems and the stories about the women who went before us; (3) the changing place of women in the countries of South Africa, the United States, and India.

Michael Ventura points out the role of memory in an article in *The Family Therapy Networker*.[1] Memory revives those who have gone before us—our parents, a teacher, a deceased friend. Life is really made of memories. Ancient archetypes are also a part of our memory process. Years ago I studied *The Odyssey* and Greek mythology. My visit to Greece brought back some of the memories of these stories.

GREEK GODDESS ATHENA

I was on a Mediterranean tour of ancient cities—Florence, Pompeii, Venice, Athens, Ephesus, and Istanbul. One of my favorite places was Athens. Seeing the Acropolis is a memory that is forever etched in my mind. Greek mythology has been preserved through the writings of Homer. His epic works *The Iliad* and *The Odyssey* date from the middle of the eighth century B.C.E. Heroic tales were originally sung to the kings by the bards (fourteenth through eleventh centuries B.C.E.), then in the tenth century B.C.E. epic poetry emerged as a literary form. The transmission of the Homeric poems acquired great importance in the city of Athens in the sixth century B.C.E. Every four years they celebrated a major festival in honor of Athena. It was called the Panathenaia and they recited Homeric poems at a feast. There are visual records of this history in Attic Art, as well as in the north frieze of the Parthenon where one can see horsemen in the Panathenaic procession.

Citizens had great reverence for their patroness, Athena, one of the daughters of Zeus. The artists through the centuries portrayed her protecting the citizens of Athens. She is often portrayed in heroic art guarding the Athenians in battle and ensuring victory.[2]

Being in the midst of all the history at the Acropolis, I recalled my sense of pride in Athena and my feeling that the feminine was valued there. The Caryatids (see Figure 3.1.) are one of my favorite sculptures of women. The columnlike women hold up the structure of the temple with such grace and beauty. I believe the spirit of the goddess is much needed in today's scientific world. Twenty-first-century people need to be cared for, watched after, and protected just as the Athenians did. The cosmos, in Greek thought, was equally shared by male and female powers. I experienced the Acropolis as a celebration of the best of humanity—the spirit and the divine. Greece and the whole Mediterranean world have strong goddess roots.

Research is now revealing the importance of goddesses. Layne Redmond's *When the Drummers Were Women: A Spiritual History of Rhythm* discusses how for thousands of years people throughout the Mediterranean world worshiped goddesses.[3] At the heart of the worship was a frame drum that was used to reconstruct the rhythmic dance of the cosmos—the progression of the seasons, the cycles of the moon, and the growth and fruition of the crops. Layne Redmond's research is revealing because drumming has traditionally been associated with male bonding and has been presented as a male activity. Once again, women have been overlooked as the primary agents in creating worship ceremonies.

When Joseph Campbell was interviewed by Bill Moyers for the video *Love and the Goddess*, Campbell bluntly said, "Christianity

FIGURE 3.1. Acropolis, The Caryatids, Athens, Greece, 1999. Photo by author.

wiped out an appreciation of the goddess." The new dominant Christian culture empowered men and identified the goddess with paganism.[4] The original meaning of the term *pagan* was a person who lived in the country; no harsh judgment was attached to the word. It is time to bring back the goddess and let her enlighten our lives again.

Jean Shinoda Bolen writes about her experience with women seeking therapy to learn how to be better protagonists or heroines in their own life stories. She presents us with images of women—provided by the Greek goddesses—that have stayed alive in the human imagination for over 3,000 years.[5]

FAMILY SYSTEMS

It takes a whole people to create history. One person alone can retain only fragments. It takes shared memory to create history. Talk with family members to piece together your family history, especially the lives and roles of the women.

A tool I use in my marriage and family therapy practice is a genogram, or a family diagram of three generations. The genogram displays information about family members, their relationships, and their communication patterns. For example, chemical addiction can be genetic (for a sample genogram format, see Figure 3.2). The half-shaded circles (females) and squares (males) represent individuals' struggle with substance abuse. A slash across the line connecting spouses represents separation or divorce. The family diagram can lead to understanding emotional issues. Questions such as the following may assist in gaining understanding of emotionally related family dynamics:

1. How will the family members accommodate diverse beliefs (Catholicism and Judaism, in this instance)? Will both parties feel respected?
2. How will emotions be talked about regarding the divorce?
3. Is Tom's addictive behavior a family pattern? Are drugs used to numb feelings?
4. Is Tom's grandfather's high blood pressure a way to cope with stress? Is it mind-body related? Is my body carrying stress? In which organ? Do any members in the family model express their feelings with words? Has anyone been in a recovery program?

The genogram points out patterns that people can choose to repeat or to reconstruct.

I recall that my great-grandfather moved in with us when I was about eight years old. I remember him very well, and his stories about the Chicago fire, but I do not remember him telling stories about his wife. She remains unknown to me except through my connection with her daughter, my maternal grandmother, Catherine DeVry.

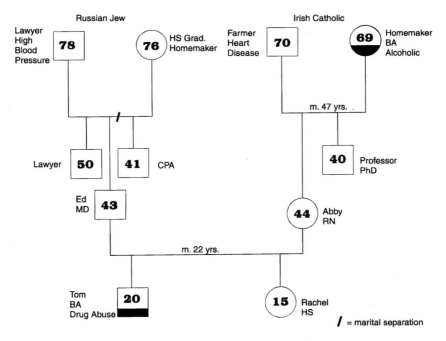

Russian Jew | Irish Catholic

Lawyer
High
Blood
Pressure **78**

76 HS Grad.
Homemaker

Farmer
Heart
Disease **70**

69 Homemaker
BA
Alcoholic

m. 47 yrs.

Lawyer **50** | **41** CPA

40 Professor
PhD

Ed
MD **43**

44 Abby
RN

m. 22 yrs.

Tom
BA **20**
Drug Abuse

15 Rachel
HS

/ = marital separation

FIGURE 3.2. The genogram is used to diagram the family system; it provides data about openness or closedness in each relationship. Emotionality and patterns are examined in Tom and Rachel's family system. Note addictions can be passed on from generation to generation, unless treated.

A similar problem exists on my dad's side of the family. I know the name of my grandmother Henehan's father but not the name of her mother. I recently called my Uncle Bernie to see if he could fill in the blank for me, and he could not. Research does pay off; I did eventually find out that my great-grandmother's name was Mary Tanzey.

A real joy for me was to do some research on my mother's side of the family. My mother liked to describe her favorite grandmother, Georgine Stieglitz DeVry, as one who "was cultured, enjoyed music, and liked art." I began to be curious about her, leading me to open my great-grandmother's prayer book given to me by my mother. I found a slip of paper I had not noticed before. The paper said in Latin:

> The confession and communion for Easter tide in the parish Church of Saint John the Baptist in Kitzingen, 1859

I immediately got a map out and I was thrilled when I found my great-grandmother's town in Germany. I imagined what it must have been like for her to travel by boat to the United States. I found her marriage certificate confirming the date she was married in New Jersey—1868. A little persistent digging may yield more surprise memories. The past helps root us in the present.

Having Irish culture as a background on both my mother's and father's sides of the family, I am aware of the strong ancient tradition in Irish legend that celebrates Irish women as formidable, tenacious, and powerful rulers.[6] Brigid of the fifth century was an abbess and had the authority of a bishop, running the monastery of her time, governing both women and men. This tradition must be combined with an awareness of the 900-year history of oppression in Ireland, which was focused on Irish men who were systematically deprived of any sense of power, and who often turned to drink to blot out their pain. Individual men and women give birth to liberation, as do whole countries.

CHANGING PLACE OF WOMEN

In general, the place of women is improving throughout the world. A recent PBS documentary titled "A Woman's Place," discusses the changing situation of women in South Africa, the United States, and India.[7] The documentary reviews ancient messages and customs: women are subservient; men make the laws; men are superior to women; only men have authority; and women have no right to inheritance. Legal change is often the first step. In South Africa, the new constitution clearly states that women have equality. Male descendants alone had been the only gender recognized in the family trees in cases of inheritance laws in South Africa. Currently, women are enlightened to their new status through education and a strategy to work with the chiefs for grassroots change.

Stateside, U.S. legislators recently declared domestic violence a crime. Domestic violence represents present cultural assumptions that men and women are unequal, a subject discussed in "A Woman's Place." Minnesotan lawyer Mary Asmus began to examine the problem of women victims failing to speak out in court. The system did not allow for the reality that battered women remain under the control of those who abuse them. Most battered women cannot talk openly about their situation without experiencing severe consequences. The legal system is based on persons having a voice and being able to speak freely about their situation. Mary Asmus developed a strategy to allow "hearsay" in court cases of domestic violence. Police and members of the community could testify as hearsay. Even with innovation, however, it remains difficult to prosecute domestic violence cases.

The situation is far from good in India as well. Women are often blamed for divorce in India. Humiliation of women is a norm, especially due to failed marriages. The presence of women lawyers has helped to change some of the negative customs. Indian women do not enjoy the right to property. Husbands do have to provide shelter for their wives, and a clever woman lawyer can use this in a woman's best interest.[8] Women can demand a housing plan as part of the divorce proceedings.

The place of women is being challenged all over the world. Some positive changes are happening. Laws are not static, and interventions on the behalf of women are needed. Answer the following questions to consider some of these issues in greater detail.

REFLECTION QUESTIONS

1. Can you relate to the ancient archetype of the goddess? In what way is this meaningful?
2. Have you experienced women musicians and other women artists? Describe.
3. What family stories do you recall about your grandmothers and great-grandmothers?
4. Look around your home. What reminds you of the past? Is there a table, vase, bowl, or image that was handed down to you from a family member? Write about that piece and examine it. Does it have a date attached or other inscription?
5. Write an autobiography. Knowing our history enriches the present. Start with writing about a period of five years that come to mind. For example, after my father died, my mother moved to St. Louis in 1992 and lived there until her death in 1997. I can recall and write about a lot regarding this time period.

6. Make a genogram of your three-generational family. Do you notice any patterns? Are there patterns you like and patterns you want to change? What roles have women played in your family history?

7. How do you perceive the role of women in different cultures? Do you recall any sayings or proverbs about the status of women (such as the Indian proverb, "Virtuous is the girl who suffers and dies without a sound")?

8. What educational programs do you think are needed to benefit women and girls?

Chapter 4

Women's Spirituality

From a spiritual vantage point our major life task is much larger than making money, finding a mate, having a career, raising children, looking beautiful, achieving psychological health, or defying aging, illness, and death. It is a recognition of the sacred in daily life—a deep gratitude for the wonders of the world and the delicate web of inter-connectedness between people, nature and things—a recognition that true intimacy based on respect and love is the measure of a life well lived.

Joan Borysenko
A Woman's Book of Life

All of us must renew our own sense of spirituality and work to live up to its expectations and values.

Hillary Rodham Clinton
It Takes a Village

One who listened was a woman named Lydia, a dealer in purple goods from the town of Thyatira. She already reverenced God, and the Lord opened her heart . . .

Acts of the Apostles 16:14

In Chapter 3, I explored how women have been invisible in history, how the goddess was labeled a pagan, and how our ancestors' stories are unknown to us. In this chapter, I explore how women's spirituality is restricted by past roles and by negative attitudes about women. There are glimmers of hope: women have always had an innate appreciation for the importance of connections between people. Values have been examined throughout time; in the Acts of the Apostles,

Lydia is held up as a role model in the early faith community. More now than ever, leadership positions are becoming more available to women.

DEFINITIONS OF SPIRITUALITY

I feel several perspectives are helpful when considering the definitions of spirituality:

1. Spirituality is defined as the actualization of the human capacity to be spiritual. Some feel that we are all born with soul, and created in the image and likeness of God.
2. Spirituality embraces all of life, not just methods of prayer and the practice of virtue.
3. Religion and spirituality may or may not be the same. Religion deals with a creed and the practices which follow from that creed. Spirituality deals with total human development. It is about connectedness with the self, with the other, and with the sacred as experienced by the individual. Spirituality is the cultivation of soul in men and women, awareness, animation, and divine influence as an agency working in the hearts of men and women. It can mean courage, vigor, and firmness of intent.
4. Recovery from addictions has employed spirituality in the healing process with great success. L. Jampolsky states that at the core of a fear-based addictive thought process is the belief that the individual is inadequate and needs something outside herself to make her whole. A rediscovery of spirituality can help correct this flawed belief system and replace it with the belief that the natural state of a person is to feel whole, peaceful, and content.[1]
5. Jung describes spirituality as a journey toward integration: a journey to individuation (becoming your own person), a journey to the center.[2]
6. Spirituality is about evolution as the world of people becomes more loving and caring. Transforming the planet is a goal by releasing the playful, joyful energy that pulsates in all beings.[3]

CONSTRICTIONS OF THE PAST

Why focus on women's spirituality? In most religions the Word of God is preached by men and is interpreted by men. Some aspects of spirituality need to come out of the female experience, such as possessing a sense of Mother Earth's beauty. Because all people have the capacity to be spiritual, yet we hear only from men in most religions (who constitute less than half of the human population), we experience a terrible loss and lack of perspective. A patristic saying, "The glory of God is humanity fully alive,"[4] is a challenge to change the status of women who are only "partially alive."

Marija Gimbutas, a professor of European archaeology at the University of California at Los Angeles, describes "Old Europe," dating back at least 5,000 years before the rise of male religions, as matrifocal. This culture worshiped the Great Goddess. It was a peaceful, art-loving, and a sea- and earthbound culture. Evidence gleaned from the burial sites shows an egalitarian society that was destroyed by the invasion of horse-riding Indo-European peoples from the northeast. The invaders were patrifocal, mobile, warlike, and indifferent to art. These invaders considered themselves superior because of their ability to conquer the earlier settlers who worshiped the Great Goddess. Many names, such as Astarte, Isis, and Au Set, were given to the feminine life force deeply connected to nature and fertility. The snake, the dove, the tree, and the moon were her sacred symbols.[5]

Appreciating diversity gives us a fuller picture of spirituality. Goddess worship as described had positive fruits for the culture, such as peace. The diversity of the Greek goddesses who have lived in the imagination of human beings for over 3,000 years inspires us.

Native Americans also have a lot to teach us about the Great Spirit, and the sacred and feminine in nature. I have always appreciated the meaning Native Americans give the earth; their dances seem to discover the heartbeat of the god or the goddess in the earth. David Leeming reminds us that the great goddess archetype is firmly established in Native American mythology, and she is nearly always a nurturing earth mother.[6] My husband and I had the privilege of attending a Native American dance ceremony in New Mexico at the invitation of David and Pam Leeming and the Pueblo community. The dances performed expressed the gratitude of the community for a good harvest that season.

Spirituality is about life experience and the holy. The tender experience of a nursing infant at his or her mother's breast is sacred. Virginia Satir feels spirituality is a basic concept, similar to most Native American cultures. She included a chapter on spirituality in her revised book, *The New Peoplemaking,* saying, "For me, seeds and birth are spirituality in action."[7]

Diversity is an issue in religious organizations. Why are women not represented in policymaking positions in major religious groups? Early in Judeo-Christian history, women developed a sense of sacral unworthiness. Not only could they not be ordained, but they were not allowed a place in the sanctuary. For example, women are not allowed to share their thoughts on the Word of God in a public setting by giving a sermon at a Catholic Mass. In the orthodox tradition, Jewish women are not allowed to read from the Torah.

Some religious groups have projected onto women evil and negativity. The book of Hosea in the Hebrew Bible supplies the often-used metaphor of the "unfaithful wife, the harlot" (Hosea 3:1-3). This image is also used to support the faithfulness of God: we have a God who never gives up on us even if we are like the harlot, i.e., the worst of the worst. Women need to reflect on Scripture with their experience and to understand that God should be a positive influence on their lives. I once knew a woman who believed that God was responsible for her bone pain. When she realized her suffering was a misfortune, she began to get better. She changed her image of God also. God was no longer out to get her, nor was God responsible for her pain.

Shekhinah is a Hebrew term used in rabbinic literature for numinous immanence of God in the world.[8] The term can be found in the Targum or the Aramaic translation of the Bible that dates back to the first century (C.E.). *Shekhinah* alludes to the ark of the covenant and this passage in Numbers:

> Whenever the ark set out, Moses would say,
>   "Arise, O Lord, that your enemies may be scattered,
>   and those who hate you may flee before you."
> And when it came to rest, he would say,
>   "Return, O Lord, you who ride upon the clouds,
>   to the troops of Israel." (Numbers 10: 35-36)

Shekhinah is used by feminist writers as a way to expand the notion of God to include the feminine aspects of God. David danced when he welcomed the ark of the covenant back to Jerusalem. I consider *shekhinah* a return to celebration and dance.

In the New Testament, in the Gospel of Luke (7:37), a reference is made to a woman: "she is known in the town to be a sinner." Jesus does not buy into the negative projection and holds up this woman's warmth and hospitality as an example to all. In reading the Scripture, remember all books were authored by men.

Another area that is mostly controlled by men is the liturgical calendar. Change is needed to expand the number of women in the church calendar of, for example, Roman Catholics. The names and narratives of men are heard and remembered in Catholic liturgical assemblies far more often than women. Out of the church calendar year, there are only forty-one commemorations of women, and twelve of those are Marian related, such as the Assumption of Mary. In addition to the lack of women role models is the limited variety of female images presented. Often virgin, martyr, and member of a religious order are the main categories of women acknowledged.[9] Holiness presented in this constricted way may result in loss of women in church membership. Other important models of holiness that are lacking include educators, parents, couples, counselors, and social reformers.

Negative projections by the dominant group are very destructive. European witch burning was a prime example of this destruction. Starting in 1484, as many as several million people were put to death for witchcraft during a 300-year period, the greater number of which were women. The pope authorized this witch-hunt in 1484 with a Papal Bull.[10] Anne Llewellyn Barstow states that an analysis of violence, such as that which occurred during the witch-hunts, exposes sexual terror and brutality, a topic too little discussed.[11]

Spirituality is at the core of our value system. Negative projections can lead to a devaluation of women and, taken to the extreme, violence. Violence, a disregard for what is human and precious, the overwhelming pace of change in our society—all require us to examine our roots and our values. Disturbing statistics about abuse of women in our culture are published in daily newspapers. Violence will occur in at least two-thirds of all marriages.[12] Violence in families and now in schools, synagogues, and churches has become an accepted tragedy.

Examining our core value system is difficult work. Letting go of values that are no longer meaningful can bring forth emotions we have struggled against for most of our lives: helplessness, rage, and despair. Stripping away layers of encultured patriarchal values that exclude women and keep them invisible and changing beliefs are disruptive actions we can take.[13]

There is a renewed interest in spirituality. Several popular magazines have featured articles on spirituality, including *Newsweek* on the mystery of prayer,[14] *Time* on faith and healing,[15] and *McCall's* on spirituality, a piece written by Joan Lunden.[16] Materialism has left many people feeling empty. Advertisements have added to this emptiness. Beautiful women are often used in ads to sell cars, alcohol, or cigarettes. Objectification is destructive to society and especially to women.

Images of women in the media can set the stage for advertisement, pornography, and violence. Centerfolds and silhouettes of nude women on mud flaps can instruct society in subtle ways—women have a body that complies uncomplainingly no matter what you do to it. The link between pornography and violence is well established. An FBI study of seventy-six serial killers determined pornography to be the primary "sexual interest" of 81 percent of them. Ted Bundy—who fits the common profile of serial killers, white men who target women as victims—confessed that pornography was linked to his becoming a serial killer.[17] Pornography has different levels of destructive messages that influence the relationships between people, but the disturbing aspect of pornography is that people can be treated as playthings and forced into submission—the opposite of treating another person with respect and freedom.

Violence in entertainment is commonplace. The 1991 movie *The Fisher King* has a scene of a mass killing. The Killeen, Texas, killings in 1991 in Luby's Cafeteria can be connected with this movie. A movie ticket for this film was found in the killer's pocket. *The Fisher King,* some might say, is not a violent film but a spiritual film. The insertion of violent scenes has an influential power that society has not fully examined.

Examining some images of women in the theater can be depressing. "The tenets of the women's movement have not taken hold," says Deb Margolin, a Yale faculty instructor in theater. She believes judgments are made on every woman who goes on stage: "Am I seen as fat?" or "Am I seen as a slut?" True equality and female self-acceptance have not yet taken hold in the theater, as is the case in so many other arenas.[18]

RECONSTRUCTION OF EQUALITY NEEDED IN SPIRITUALITY

Spirituality is a healing resource for both men and women. I think this reconstruction can occur in two ways: (1) reclaiming our stories and seeing them as sacred and (2) reflecting on what we can control and what we cannot.

We can approach the study of spirituality by looking into the lives of women we admire—people of faith are like a stained glass window portraying God's grace and love. Figure 4.1. is a picture I took of a stained glass window dedicated to Elizabeth Ann Seton. The statue was erected in the chapel built in Emmitsburg, Maryland. Here Seton began the first integrated school for girls, Saint Joseph's Academy. In addition to being a leader, she had great devotion to her friends. Friendship was a sacrament to her. It was her delight, her support, her stepping stone to sanctity. She was the first American woman canonized by Rome. For more on learning about spirituality by examining the lives of women, see Chapter 15.

Reclaiming Our Sacred Stories

Merle Jordan states that we must become fully aware of internalized authorities which may be functioning as a supreme power in our lives. We need to be conscious of both the hurtful authorities and the respectful and gracious ones. Merle Jordan describes how he heard his father's critical voice speaking to him as he tried to write his book. "You can't do it. It will fail. You are stupid. . . . You are incapable." Then Jordan states his reconstruction of his story: "My father's definition of me is not my only identity. Does he carry more weight than God's evaluation of me?" Jordan uses humor to say, "Perhaps it is the nonbook which I dedicate to him."[19] There is value in examining the voices of nagging negativity and believing in a new creation. You might try writing your spiritual autobiography.

FIGURE 4.1. Stained glass window of Elizabeth Ann Seton, shrine, Emmitsburg, Maryland. Photo by author.

Parenting can be a time for recreating stories. I saw a mother, Sally, who had been having recurring dreams about her childhood. She would prepare to teach a class but would not be ready. She would feel as though someone were chasing her and she could not get away. As we reflected together on her story of dreams, she became aware of self-defeating behaviors and how out of control she felt. Her mother did not give her much support growing up, and she felt her brothers got more of her mother's attention.

Sally began to realize in our session that she wanted to get to know her daughters. They were still young enough for her to accomplish that. Having used drugs in the past, she had created a destructive way of coping. Sally had to face the fact that drug use was not the answer. She had to review her life and develop constructive strategies. This would help her relate to her daughters and create a workable relationship with each of them.

Listening to Sally's concerns about parenting her daughters was a very spiritual experience. She demonstrated how she sings to Annie in the car, "Old MacDonald had a farm, E-I-E-I-O, and on this farm he had a—" and Annie responds joyfully with her imagined animal on the farm, "goat." Sally and Annie reminded me of an article I had read about parenting as a "charism"—a gift of the spirit bestowed on people for the sake of building up the community.[20] Sally also talked about how demanding it was for her to work, raise her daughters, and work out conflicts with her husband. She found her faith a great support in all these challenges.

Reflecting on Control Factors

Self-awareness brings one to the reality of being human and to recognize our inability to control another person. Our energy is wasted when we focus on how others can change. Some people try to impose their will on the universe and then wonder why they are frustrated and stressed. Spirituality is about our own willingness to change and be in a state of conversion.

Spirituality helps keep our lives in balance and assists us in discerning our needs and desires. In talking with women who struggle with addictions, it becomes clear that they focus on something external to themselves. They believe they need a drug or other "fixes" such as shopping or gambling as if their very lives depended on it.

Inner work is an important factor in reconstructing issues of control. Surrender to a higher power often helps a person regain peace. Addictions are spiritual diseases and recovery brings about spiritual growth. Reconstruction brings back "soul."

Following are some questions and statements for you to think about as you get in touch with your inner spirituality.

REFLECTION QUESTIONS

1. What values do you live by, such as love, respect, and empathy? How do these values influence your behavior?

2. Do you believe in your contributions to society? What do you see yourself contributing?

3. How do you image God or a higher power? What are some stepping-stones in your spiritual journey?

4. Draw a circle of life using circles for significant people and squares for events that have meaning. Your circle of life is a picture of grace and how God often works through people and events in our lives. For instance, a person close to her mother would draw a circle representing herself and another circle for a supportive friend. Color in meaning: red could mean care and love, and green could mean hope.

5. Pray with Psalm 131:2: "You have stilled and quieted my Soul, O God, like a weaned child on its mother's lap."

6. Take a walk with a friend and share the sights and sounds of Mother Earth as you experience them. Take time to touch the earth and to feel the textures of your natural surroundings. Let your five senses be open to nature.

7. Do you make a connection between dance and prayer? Do you see your body as a sacred vessel?

8. Do you experience outrage at how images of women's bodies are portrayed in the media and in our culture?

9. Name what you can control and what you cannot. For example, I can control my decision to exercise today, but I cannot control the forecast for rainy weather today, which could tempt me to not exercise. Or I can control my decision to attend an Al-Anon meeting and work the twelve steps for my

peace of mind but I cannot control whether my spouse decides to give up drinking.

10. How do past or present spiritual beliefs contribute or block healing and growth?
11. Is believing in a higher power a source of healing and peace for you?

PART II:
DISCREDITING NEGATIVE FAMILY SCRIPTS

Chapter 5

Men Are the Smart Ones

One hundred women are not worth a single testicle.

Confucius

Simone Weil is probably one of the best published enigmas of this century.

Phyllis Zagano
Woman to Woman

Women need to affirm their power and intelligence.

Charlotte Kasl
In *Addictions and Spirituality*

In Chapter 4, I examined the need for women to claim their rightful place in spirituality. In this chapter, I explore destructive cultural messages regarding women's intellect.

HISTORY

Examining the messages that young women receive as they mature is essential to being aware of the effects of these messages. Confucius (551-479 B.C.E.) lived a long time ago but his thoughts about male entitlement and devaluation of women still remain. Affirmation of the female intellect is progressing but has a long way to go. Phyllis Zagano and Charlotte Kasl, two women writers of our times, remind us of this fact in the quotes that opened this chapter.

Early American history presents us with the powerful story of Anne M. Hutchinson (1591-1643), the first woman to start a religious sect. She founded the antinomian party, which maintained that Christians were free from moral law by virtue of grace as set forth in the gospel. Her home was the meeting place of seventy-five Puritans (men and women). They met to discuss secular and theological matters. Anne Hutchinson was tried and convicted of heresy because she claimed to have experienced divine revelation. The judge said she had assumed postures to which only men were entitled. She stood for independent thought, and was convicted of heresy and sedition by the general court of the Massachusetts Colony. She was also excommunicated by the Boston Anglican Church and banished.[1]

Simone Weil (1909-1943), a philosophical genius who excelled in her academic work, had a commitment to social justice. Desiring solidarity with the poor, she left the academic world to serve the unemployed at Le Puy, France. She was of Jewish descent but also was deeply attracted to the Eucharist. She was trained as an intellectual but wrote from her heart, weaving the theme of "waiting for God" throughout her writing.[2] Yet she is not widely known. As I read her life story, and how deeply she expressed herself, I could not help but wonder if she had access to any arena in which to use her genius.

Reading accounts of the history of women at Saint Louis University, I was appalled to learn that no women professors were granted tenure until the 1960s. The Vatican frowned upon women studying at the College of Arts and Sciences, and the university had to report to the Vatican their statistics for enrollment of men and women. Many women enrolled in the school of education, thus the university was able to avoid the Vatican's negative attitude about educating women.

Maryville College, Webster University, and Fontbonne College in Saint Louis, Missouri were first started by religious women as corporate colleges of Saint Louis University where faculty were shared until accreditation was obtained.

This attitude that women are "not as competent as men" is common at public universities also.

THEORY AND GENDER

Family therapy and psychotherapy are ways to bring about greater freedom in the thought process. However, the theoretical models that many therapists work from are male based and biased. Harriet G. Lerner believes the most serious accusation against traditional psychotherapy is that in subtle but powerful ways it may lead women to conform to male definitions of femininity and may discourage rebellion from the "feminine role" by interpreting such rebellion as pathological.[3] Nancy Chodorow challenges traditional thinking and more specifically Freud's view of women as genitally defective. The dominance of the father is no longer valid. Equality of both parents should be stressed.[4] Jessica Benjamin also calls for gender balance when she asks, in reference to the Oedipal complex,

> Why must a patriarchal father supersede and depose the mother? If the struggle between paternal and maternal power ends in the paternal victory, the outcome belies the victor's claim that the loser, the mother, is too dangerous and powerful to coexist with. Rather, it would seem that the evocation of woman's danger is an age-old myth which legitimates her subordination.[5]

Judith Avis made a presentation titled *Family Narratives and Gender* at the 1991 American Association of Marriage and Family Therapy meeting in Chicago. She shared her own story about growing up believing she was not smart enough, even though she got all As at school.

Women are taught in subtle ways to stop speaking their truths. Charlotte Kasl made this point:

> At some level that if I asserted my truths, I risked being called a troublemaker, a bitch, or a man hater, the names used to keep women in their place. Freire's writing helped me to see that what we call codedendency is the double bind of women's oppression, which manifests itself in an addiction to security. Women are taught a lie, become immersed in that lie, and then feel incapable of running the risks it takes to extricate themselves.[6]

She was influenced by the writing of Paulo Freire (1921-1997), author of the *Pedagogy of the Oppressed* (1972). Kasl writes that Freire gave voice to her inner struggle, that of pitting our authentic self against that of the false self that society demands. She made the connection between her depression and giving up her power of choice, becoming passive, and looking to her husband as the wise one. For example, she begins her sixteen steps for discovery and empowerment:

We affirm we have the power to take charge of our lives and stop being dependent on substances or other people for our self-esteem and security.[7]

She questioned how the twelve-step program was structured to meet women's needs. Listening to her own truth, she eventually proposed a new twelve-step model for recovery from addiction adapted for women. She writes that men need to be sad, vulnerable, and afraid, and women need to affirm their power and intelligence.

MY STORY

I grew up between two brothers. I recall being "teased" about being a dumb blonde. I inherited this negative label in the name of humor and what I think they truly believed about women at that time. My brothers attended Loyola Academy and I went to Marywood School for Ladies. My identity in the family was the big sister and caregiver for the younger children. My brother Brian was known as "the brain" in the family. My brother Tom was "the football hero."

I have spent a lot of time proving my brothers wrong. I have completed two master's degrees and a doctoral program. I was able to take a negative and reframe it into a positive force in my life. Yet I worry that young women might still be receiving these negative messages about themselves. I was impressed with a ritual developed for young women going off to college, a ritual that affirmed their intellectual development in *Sisters of the Thirteen Moons*. It begins emphasizing the need for families to give their young women positive messages:

A girl's intellectual development is as important as her physical and spiritual development, but too often it goes ignored as we celebrate milestones in our lives. This ritual is an attempt by families to celebrate their daughters' beginnings in school. We know that educational settings are often inhospitable to girls, paying more attention to boys, setting aside greater resources for them and rewarding them more often. We want to send our daughters off to school armed with self-confidence and determination and a passion for learning.[8]

I used this ritual with families and with my nieces. I recommend you consider using such a ritual to support young women you know. The ritual includes a reading describing the success of a girl overcoming obstacles, such as *The Little Engine That Could* by Watty Piper, *Salt Hands* by Jane Chelsea Aragon, *My Mama Sings* by Jeanne Whitehouse Peterson, or *Music, Music for Everyone* by Vera Williams. The young woman personalizes the story and talks about a task she accomplished and the family affirms her. A blessing follows with the presentation of a small gift, something she can take with her to remind her of the reassurance she experiences in the ritual. It might be a bracelet, a stone to put in her pocket, or a key ring. Everyone present might touch the gift as a sign of connection. The ritual could end with a song that is a favorite of the young woman or the family. I like to use the song "Family Hands" by Mary Chapin Carpenter; it can be found on the *Hometown Girl* album.

I know that my father encouraged me in the use of my intelligence. He was a lawyer and had a natural appreciation for thinking. He would talk fondly of my grandmother, Ellen Henehan, how she would read the classics to him as a child, such as Charles Dickens, and the works of Nobel prizewinner Rudyard Kipling. My dad loved the writings of Shakespeare and C. S. Lewis. I also fondly recall my dad reading the Scriptures to us as a family during Lent. My husband and I have carried on this ritual of reading the Scriptures together after breakfast.

CLINICAL THEMES

One woman expressed a theme often voiced by clients: "I feel dumb even though I know I am not." This attitude relates to what I discussed earlier: women are treated as second-class citizens. Knowledge is power. Becoming a first-class citizen means they must recognize their intellectual worth.

With many couples I see in therapy, the wife struggles to be informed of the couple's financial situations. One woman, May, was feeling a lot of anger about the lack of mutuality and equality in the couple's decision making. Her husband, John, decided to use their credit card and as a result incurred finance charges. May was not comfortable with this because she thought they had agreed to not incur finance charges, yet felt she had no voice. As we talked about it, John could say, "Yes, I do want to hear your concerns and have you participate in the decisions." John began to make progress in hearing May, not "stonewalling" her. They both moved to a mutual sharing of power through the therapy. May had sworn before she had married not to be a woman who knew nothing about her financial situation; she now became resolute to not slip into the "stupid woman" position.

The more I work with couples in therapy, the more I see the destructiveness in this belief about women. In conversation with her husband, another woman, Judy, was able to confront and clarify that she too felt she was being treated as if she were stupid. Perhaps she falsely attributed this attitude to her husband, Ralph, but it was important to clear the air on this misunderstanding. After they talked about it, Ralph agreed to talk more openly about their finances. They were able to make some positive changes to get out of debt.

KNOWING, POWER, AND SEXUALITY

Textbooks are improving, but many women have been exposed to a greater number of heroes in stories than heroines. The hero's journey is a universal theme; it is our challenge to broaden the definition and process of journey so women know it includes them. Myths often include important truths about the human condition. Carnes states, "The struggles to break free from rigid, soul-stifling rules, develop a relationship with God, and express one's unique identity are universal."[9]

In Carol Gilligan's research on adolescent girls and their learning process she found that young women often say, "I don't know." The frequency of the use of the phase increased as the girls advanced through their schooling. Of course, this phrase can be a sign of wisdom as it is right to admit to many things we do not know, but in Gilligan's study it was more often related to giving away the power to know. Gilligan found that the culture the young women live in almost demands that they present themselves as "not knowing."[10]

Clarissa Pinkola Estes challenges women to reclaim their intuition as a powerful way to know. She says to reclaim intuition we have to let go of the ever-sweet and all-too-good mother. As the all-too-good-mother dies (the part that has to please everyone and take care of everyone at her own expense), the new woman is born who can set limits, say no, and protect the self. Intuitive powers have been a buried blessing in women, but Estes believes that nothing is ever lost in the psyche; this power can be reclaimed. Intuition gives us "lightening-fast inner seeing, inner hearing, inner sensing, and inner knowing."[11]

Mary Rose D'Angelo presents us with the following in her chapter on "Veils, Virgins, and the Tongues of Men and Angels: Women's Heads in Early Christianity":

> For early Christian men, as it seems, for men of antiquity in general, women's heads were indeed sexual members, and at least two of these men, Paul and Tertullian, expended much thought and no little ink in efforts to enforce the sexual character of women's heads. . . . But for the most part, the women of early Christianity are visible to later generations only through the eroticizing veil of the male gaze.[12]

Paul, in his letter to the Corinthians (1 Cor. 11: 2-16), refers to the need for women at worship to cover their heads. D'Angelo concludes that the veil confesses a woman's sense of submission to men and her sense of deficiency.

Artemis, the Greek goddess of nature and the hunt, often pictured with a bow and arrow, is an image that reminds us of the task to reclaim our minds. This fragment of Diana, as the Romans knew her, the sculpture *Running Artemis,* is extremely beautiful (see Figure 5.1). The torso expresses such vitality and active movement. Just think what we could experience if she were complete, if we could see her face and eyes.

Women are challenged to reclaim their minds and appreciate what happens when this is done and when it is not done. I believe that when girls and women stay in the old pattern of "not knowing," it has the following consequences:

1. They suffer from low self-esteem.
2. They are troubled by external demands instead of being able to tap into their own resources.
3. They participate in uninteresting and destructive relationships.
4. They avoid conflict and the resolution of differences.
5. They lack planning skills.
6. They are frightened by challenges and lack development.

FIGURE 5.1. *Running Artemis* from the Hellenistic period, marble sculpture. Note the beauty and grace of the female's torso. Saint Louis Art Museum, Purchase.

When women and girls claim their minds, the following occurs:

1. They have confidence in their abilities.
2. They have vitality and spark.
3. They develop the ability to surround themselves with people who build constructive relationships.
4. They can negotiate with ease.
5. They gain skills to plan for the future.
6. They experience the enjoyment of the challenges of lifelong learning.

An examination of the influences of negative messages to women helps develop awareness. There have always been women who have rejected cultural messages surrounding women's intellect and other issues. Harriet Beecher Stowe, in *Uncle Tom's Cabin,* wrote a critical portrayal of slavery (see Figure 5.2). After the publication of Stowe's first book in 1852, she became the most popular writer of her time. She went on to write nine other books, influencing the writing of Mark Twain with her use of literary realism.

REFLECTION QUESTIONS

1. What are some ways that you have been smart in the last three years? Discuss a decision you made of which you are proud.
2. Are there women you know who have been frustrated by not having a venue in which to use their intellectual skills?
3. Are there any destructive messages you learned about men and women in your family? Refocus the negative message into a positive statement. For example, from "Women don't need an education" to "Women are as equally deserving of an education as are men."
4. How much did your family emphasize developing your mind? (Consider spoken and unspoken messages.)
5. How successful did your family expect you to be with thinking and critical reasoning skills?
6. How are books treated in your home?

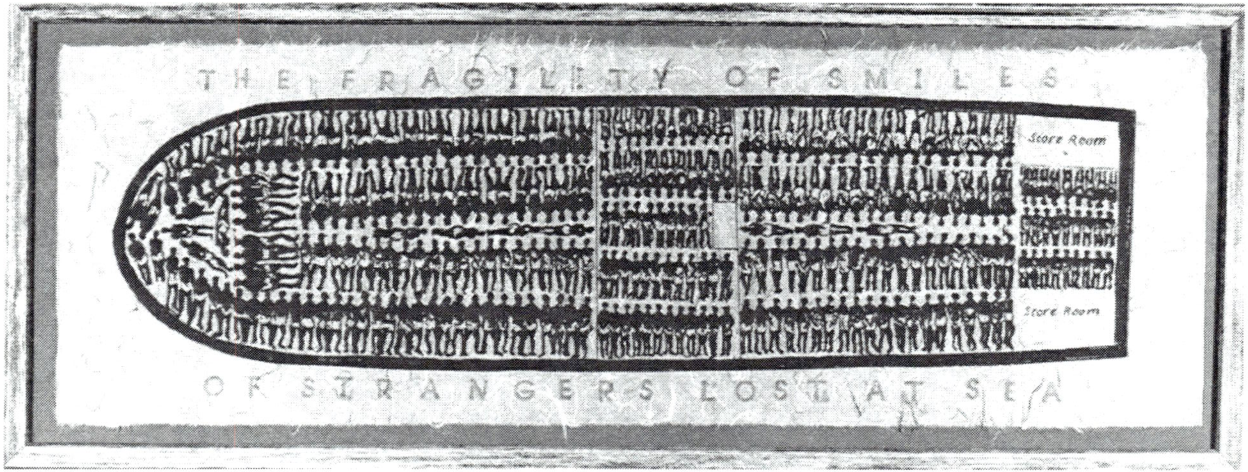

FIGURE 5.2. Screen print, "The Fragility of Smiles (of Strangers Lost at Sea)" by Betye Saar (1998) showing the realities of slaves chained in place, removed from family. The Saint Louis Art Museum, Museum Minority Artists Purchase Fund.

7. Keep a journal noting the books you have read, continuing education programs you have attended, and what you learned from everyday life.
8. Rewrite a story, making yourself the heroine.
9. Remembering the example of women covering their heads as a practice to symbolize their submissiveness, are there any practices that you are aware of that have denigrated women's minds?
10. Have you or can you use your intelligence to develop your knowledge of finances?
11. Can you think of ways in which you used your intuition in the last month? Were there times you held back from acting on your intuition? Why or why not?
12. Are there ways today in which heads of women are eroticized? Did you ever wonder why women wear makeup?
13. Is there anything that you need more confidence in (for example, using a computer)?
14. Do you take responsibility for using your intellect?
15. Name three women authors you have admired over the years.

Chapter 6

She Is Ill

It does not matter how long we have had negative patterns, or an illness, or a rotten relationship, or a lack of finances, or self-hatred, we can begin to make changes today.

Louise L. Hay
Heal Your Body

The more important stories are those that are enacted by our bodies, more than those we simply tell or write for others.

James and Melissa Griffith
The Body Speaks

Chapter 5 examined ways to free the minds of women from negative family and cultural messages. This chapter explores negative family messages women receive regarding illness and how illness may be caused by some family dynamics, such as the historical practice of foot binding. Louise Hay reminds us of the possibility of change in the midst of negative circumstances. Our bodies are an important source of information. James and Melissa Griffith encourage us to continue to be aware of the stories our bodies enact.

PATHOLOGY AND WOMEN

More women than men seek mental health services. Women experience more depression and marital dissatisfaction than do men.[1] Women in traditional marital relationships have poorer physical health, lower self-esteem, less autonomy, and poorer marital adjustment than women in relationships based on mutuality and gender equality.[2]

An example from my own family is my mother who had high blood pressure, diabetes, depression, and breast cancer. My mother was often very angry with my father but did not express her anger. She would say, "It is better for me to bite my tongue." I am now convinced that a connection exists between unexpressed emotion and bodily illness. Women are more susceptible to illness because they are not encouraged to express themselves honestly. Women are overly careful about others' feelings and thus hold back their own.

At every American Association of Marriage and Family Therapists' meeting, a master therapist meets with a local therapist and a family for teaching purposes. Two famous family therapists of the Milan school, Luigi Boscolo and Gianfranco Cecchin, consulted at the 1987 conference of marriage and family therapists. The family consisted of a mother, a father, and a daughter. Tina, the daughter, was experiencing delusions. As I observed the consultation session it became clear that the women in the family carried the pathology. The mother had colon cancer. Tina was diagnosed with manic-depression, a disease the paternal grandfather had. I began asking myself why the females were the sick ones in the family.

Females tend to be the emotional center of family life, and this may well put them at higher risk for stress. Women do more than men at home and they expend more energy on family concerns. Almost one fifth of women aged fifty-five to fifty-nine provide in-home care to an elderly relative. Over half of women with one surviving parent can expect to become that parent's caregiver.[3]

DANCE/MOVEMENT

Dance and movement are holistic personal expressions that diminish stress and provide healing. Serene Lim teaches alternative therapies to medical students in Australia. She suggests proper movement to heal back problems and stress-related disorders. She highly recommends the use of the Alexander technique,[4] which consists of:

- Becoming aware of how we are moving
- Changing old destructive habits, such as carrying our heads forward thus throwing us out of balance

- Improving the natural curves of the spine (Lengthening the spine in movement and at rest is one of the goals of this technique; maintaining the poise of the head is key.)

Performing arts groups use movement therapies to strengthen their performances, as well as a way to prevent illness.

I thought of the power of dance as an expression of emotion when I saw an all-female production company, the Gash/Voigt Dance Theater, present a wonderful program titled "Weaving the World Through the Eyes of Women." American, Turkish, and Greek dance companies collaborated to produce art that went beyond the history of countries with differences and, in the case of Greece and Turkey, long adversarial relationships. Art transcends politics. "Scenes from Women's Madness" was a number danced by the Greek dance company. Three women danced their "madness" expressing the ability to protect oneself from the violation of innocence, the knowledge of the social condition of women, the treason, the abandonment, and the existential chaos of their children's death. The dance company depicted scenes of women's madness inspired by literary figures such as Shakespeare's Ophelia, and Medea and other Greek mythic figures. Medea was the sorceress who assisted Jason and the Argonauts in attaining the Golden Fleece in the Greek tragedy written in 431 B.C.E. by Euripides.

Joyce McDougall demonstrates in *Theaters of the Mind* how psychological distress manifests itself through psychosomatic realities.[5] She makes several observations and hypotheses about the sequence of mind/body events including:

- "Certain allergic, gastric, cardiac, and other such reactions may be somatic expressions of an attempt to protect oneself against truly archaic libidinal and narcissistic longings that are felt to be life threatening, much as a small infant might experience the threat of death."
- The psyche sends primitive messages to the body warning of imminent danger.
- These primitive messages may be manifested through stress responses such as increased pulse and elevated blood pressure. Depressed mood may occur.

CHINESE FAMILY MESSAGES TO WOMEN

The documentary movie *Small Happiness: Women of a Chinese Village* provides us with some rare interviews showing dynamics between men and women. It was filmed in 1981 and 1982. The title of the film reflects a common Chinese saying, "A boy is a big happiness and a girl is a small happiness." Often in China, women who have had only daughters are considered to be "childless." One woman talked about being sold by her father, and also engaging in infanticide due to the lack of food. She had to kill her daughter because there was not enough food to go around. The strength and the suffering portrayed in the film is moving. The pain caused by foot binding was discussed by a woman who had been subjected to the practice. She showed how her toes were curled under, leaving only the big toe straight. Girls were taught to be ashamed of big feet from an early age. She had experienced the pain of the practice and the sores resulting from it. (See Chapter 8 for more on foot binding.) A man interviewed laughingly said, "If your wife argued with you, just step on her foot and she would sit down immediately." Arranged marriages were the practice in China until 1949.[6]

ILLNESS RESULTING FROM A LACK OF VOICE

In *Reviving Ophelia: Saving the Selves of Adolescent Girls* (1994), Mary Pipher concludes that young women who develop a voice (freedom to express their thoughts and feelings) will experience less depression, bulemia, and anorexia.[7] She believes that if parents tell their children, "You don't have to gratify every impulse," yet the culture does not back up this attitude, then this dynamic causes teens to be confused and conflicted. I see this happening in my practice. A young woman named Heather came in suffering from depression and began talking about the problems she was experiencing in her relationships. She admitted to drinking too much as a way of coping with rejection. Heather voiced to me what upset her, and soon some of her depressive symptoms went away. She realized drinking too much and experimenting with drugs solved nothing and instead stifled her ability to voice her real concerns. The friends she hung around with were important in determining whether her addictive behavior would heal or not. Peer pressure can cause a relapse. The culture of the school is key. Schools need to teach emotional intelligence to both boys and girls. It has been shown that women and young girls who develop a voice have a lower incidence of depression.

Lilyan Wilder writes in *7 Steps to Fearless Speaking* that it is important to love your voice. She encourages people to tape their voices, begin to accept their voices, and work toward improving them. Surrounding themselves with good, full, vibrant sounds helps and improves voice quality. She also suggests asking the question: Who are the people that have voices you admire? Oprah Winfrey? James Earl Jones? Wilder believes the more you listen to good sound, the more that sound resonates through your body, and will help bring out the richness of your own voice.[8]

James and Melissa Griffith look at mind-body issues in another way in their book, *The Body Speaks: Therapeutic Dialogues for Mind-Body Problems*. Emotions are the body's dynamic dispositions for action. Fear readies the body to flee; anger prepares the body to attack; and sadness disposes the body to search for what was lost. Emotional posture is a way of explaining how life narratives contribute to the endurance of unspeakable dilemmas. For example, a little girl, Rose, grows up during her mother's three marriages. She witnesses men beating her mother and lives in homes where there is little protection offered to women and children. Rose's self-narratives lead her to camouflage her terror from family and acquaintances because she feels no one will respond protectively to her. Rose becomes a tense and sickly child.[9] Mental health providers need to pay more attention to the emotional postures of clients to facilitate expression of feelings for healing to occur.

American culture puts pressure on women to be thin. Our cultural ideal, the fashion model, weighs 17 percent less than the average American woman. Anorexia nervosa and bulimia are on the rise and are ten times more likely to occur in females than in males.[10] Having a healthy sense of self as well as having the skills to express one's thoughts and feelings can help prevent disease.

ANGER AND GENDER

Girls and boys receive different messages about anger, few of them helpful. Traditionally, girls have been warned against being angry and are taught instead to be peacemakers and approval seekers. They end up suppressing anger and managing the emotional lives of others. As a result, girls may not learn confrontation skills. Harriet Goldhor Lerner claims in *Women in Therapy* that women have a special difficulty expressing anger effectively and directly.[11]

June Crawford, Susan Kippax, Jenny Onyx, Una Gault, and Pam Benton found extensive differences in both the expression of anger and the result of its expression among women. These researchers found that "women's anger was usually an expression of frustration and powerlessness, believing that a person with power did not have to be angry."[12]

Carol Tavris takes another perspective regarding anger management. Obsessing about a divorce may not bring about growth. She found women who grew from a divorce had an active social life, and they did not dwell on matters relating to their ex-spouse. Self-help groups can often be healing. Marion Jacob, a clinical psychologist at UCLA, advises her clients to write down every negative thought they have in the course of a day so they can recognize their inner dialogue and how it contributes to their anger. The point is to take accurate stock of the positive things in our lives.[13] (For more on anger see Chapter 11.)

In conclusion, women often bear the symptoms of the emotional system in the family. Illness must be seen in connection to the big picture of the relationships in the whole family. A genogram can be helpful in this regard (see Figure 3.1). Women need to voice their feelings and thoughts so their bodies do not carry the negative effects of repression, often causing sickness or lack of well-being.

REFLECTION QUESTIONS

1. Have you ever been labeled negatively? Describe the experience.
2. What illnesses are a part of your family history? Do you notice any patterns?
3. When you are under stress, what parts of your body manifest it? (Common problems include pain in the back, stomach, or head.)

4. Can you express your anger directly? Do you relate anger to powerlessness and frustration?
5. Do you reject parts of your body? For example, feet, chin, or hair? Is your rejection connected with messages from your family?
6. How do you feel about your voice? Tape it and listen to it; learn to love your voice.
7. Who are your favorite voices? Listen to some of them this week.
8. In what ways did your family encourage you to take initiative?
9. Recall signs of strength and health you felt in your family.
10. Look for signs of strength and personal power that you feel today. For example, you may have ended a relationship that was draining your energy.
11. Can dance be an expression of madness for you? Try movement as an expression of feelings.
12. Write down your negative thoughts. Do you see any anger in the thoughts you wrote down?
13. Take stock of the positive things in your life. Write down five positive areas of your life.

Chapter 7

Be Sacrificial and Silent

Silence is the best ornament of a woman.

English proverb

Only a shameful wife takes her husband to court.

Ugandan proverb

A woman's place is at her husband's feet.

Indian proverb

These proverbs obviously do not fit women anymore, yet proverbs are a traditional way to propagate beliefs. Surrounded by such messages, we grow up well versed in these beliefs and the expectations society has for us in terms of our attitudes and behavior. In time, these messages can become proven wisdom and create a conditioning of our thoughts and ideas about life.

Mental health professionals sometimes have wrongly characterized females as having more masochistic tendencies than males. Some would say it is their virtue—to sacrifice their needs for the sake of others. This concept of silent suffering relates to the idea in Chapter 6, "She Is Ill"—that continuous denial of needs leads to physical illness. This is one aspect of a complex issue.

Many women have been expected to be sacrificial and silent. Following is an example from my own family. Two years ago, our family gathered at my sister's home in Michigan; I was aware of the difference in the expectations of others toward me and toward my brother. I was to help in the kitchen and not expected to have much fun. If I did not, I had the feeling that I would be judged as not helping enough. Conversely, I noticed my brother never helped to clear the table or with meal preparation, nor was he expected to do so. My husband and

I were able to talk together about this. He noticed the same gender roles at work. In our marriage we have made conscious choices to experience daily life differently. For example, we both cook and do dishes, and we share the cleaning chores.

TWO STANDARDS

Kathy Weingarten agrees with my personal feeling that two standards exist—one for men and one for women. She writes in *The Mother's Voice: Strengthening Intimacy in Families:*

> A good mother is selfless and a bad mother is selfish. . . . Above all, I have feared finding myself on the selfish side of the split. Oddly, I cannot imagine these categories applying to fathers. Fathers may behave in all kinds of ways, but the idea that influences me seems to exempt them from the selfish/selfless tags.[1]

In addition, Weingarten challenges the glorification of the selfless love of the mother in the children's classic, *The Giving Tree* by Shel Silverstein.[2] The story is told from the perspective of the young boy who takes and takes and takes from his "mother," the tree. She gives everything to make the boy happy. First, she gives her leaves out of which he makes a crown for playing king of the forest. He climbs in her branches to swing and eat her apples. He sleeps in her shade. Finally, as the boy gets older he needs money. She gives her apples to be sold for his profit, her branches so he can build a home, her trunk for a boat. Finally, her stump is used as a place where he can sit.

Weingarten wonders how different the story would read if also an account of the mother's death was included. What must it have been like for the mother to give so much that she never took time to nourish herself? To have failed to set limits and say, "You have had enough. Stop." To have failed to care for her own needs and renew herself? Weingarten wonders whether we downplay our parts in stories also.[3] Do we deny our experiences of life? Do we discount our own feelings of what it means to be exhausted from giving? Do we trivialize our responses to life? These feelings and responses can help us stop and renew ourselves. I sometimes suggest to clients who are feeling burned out that they take and rewrite *The Giving Tree*. Some clips from the rewritings follow:

- I became very bare when you took all of my leaves. I wondered why this boy felt entitled to be a king at my expense. Does the boy know that more than 70 percent of the world's 1.3 billion people who live in poverty are women?
- I needed my branches to grow and be regal too. With branches I can enjoy the wind moving my limbs back and forth. Was it right for me to tell the boy to take all the branches? I think he could have taken a few, but it was unjust for him to have taken all my branches.
- I don't mind sharing a few apples with you, but don't exploit me by taking all the apples. I need some to fertilize the ground for next year's crop too.
- I am a stump now, without hope and sap running through my limbs. Son, learn to be more careful of others' feelings. I am angry that I am in this state of depletion.
- I feel so depressed being a stump for others to sit on. I will not let this happen again. No one will cut me down in the future.
- I had a hysterectomy when I was twenty-five years old. Like the branches, I feel cut down. I now question the physician's decision. I feel taken from without justification.
- I had no help from the father of my children after the divorce. Child support became more difficult to get. I lost a lot through the divorce. I can identify with the stump.
- I see that the tree was not cared for. I wonder what would have happened if the tree was treated well, fertilized, watered by the boy weekly, and gazed upon with pride versus his entitlement to take everything and destroy the tree in the end.

In the past twenty years, research has shown that women have often undergone unnecessary surgery. Some surgeons remove the uterus as a treatment for fibroids. Women often regret these decisions later. Before embarking on a course of treatment a woman should allow herself time to gather necessary information and weigh all the options; getting a second opinion is a good idea.[4]

Other cultures can teach us much about achieving balance in women's lives. Sherman Alexie, a Native American writer, includes many wonderful stories in his book *The Lone Ranger and Tonto Fist-fight in Heaven,* and this one contains wisdom for all women, and all people:

> "I remember your mother when she was the best traditional dancer in the world," my father said. "Everyone wanted to call her sweetheart. But she only danced for me. That is how it was. She told me that every other step was just for me."
>
> "But that is only half of the dance," I said.
>
> "Yeah," my father said. "She was keeping the rest for herself. Nobody can give everything away. It ain't healthy."[5]

A brave woman was interviewed on National Public Radio's *Fresh Air.* Rana Hassani is a female Jordanian crime reporter. She has written about a common practice, "honor killings," and has exposed the injustice of the system regarding women in Jordan. Hassani covered a story in 1998 about a woman whose home was broken into by a strange man. The woman's brother killed her, assuming falsely that she had seduced this intruder. The brother felt justified in killing her to save the family honor, never pausing to suspect his sister's innocence and victimization.[6]

SECRETS

This growing inability of women to be silent in the face of injustice is important. As a marriage and family therapist, I often see the toxic power of family secrets. The dynamics are well illustrated by Frederick Buechner in his *Telling Secrets: A Memoir.* The author's daughter had an eating disorder and was the scapegoat for a family secret that had occurred in the previous generation. Her grandfather, the author's father, had committed suicide. Silence was the means of coping with this tragic death. Frederick Buechner writes:

> We didn't talk about my father with each other, and we didn't talk about him outside the family either, partly at least because the suicide was looked on as something a little shabby and shameful in those days.

And then when I married and had children, there were all the secrets of that new family which my wife and I had created, secrets rooted deep, of course, in the secrets of the two families that had created the two of us. What, for one, was the secret that was too dark or dangerous or private or complicated to tell in any other language which our daughter could bring herself to talk about only in the symbolic language of anorexia?[7]

As Buechner develops the story of his family's dynamics after he is married and has children, he sees how his daughter's eating disorder is related to the family pattern of not being able to talk about things that really matter. He also focused on himself and the healing work he needed to do.

Secrets are defined as information concealed from those whose lives are directly affected by it. One can observe the atmosphere of guardedness and the loss of spontaneity within a family system when family secrets are being protected. An unnamed sense of shame and anxiety is present. Once the family addresses the secret, healing can occur. In the case of Frederick Buechner, the previous generation had not grieved the loss of Buechner's father nor dealt with the feelings of guilt, shame, and anger involved with the suicide of a loved one. Keeping silent only intensifies these feelings. Tremendous fear that this could happen again—that someone else in the family might despair and act to take his or her life—is present. Once Buechner's daughter got help for her eating disorder, the family history came tumbling out and healing could begin. Eating disorders can be seen as a gradual suicide if no intervention occurs.

Many women have been brought up not to question the men in their family system. This submissiveness leads to vast injustices. Part of the problem with any attempt to change is that the rule makers are often male. In the country of Jordan, the parliament is made up of males only. In the family system, it is often the male who communicates that the unspeakable ought to remain that way to preserve loyalty in the family. Women and girls need to develop better skills in questioning family norms and culture.

Even though I have focused on women, I cannot stress enough that examining what we teach girls is important. We must get back to looking at what families truly value. If we do not, says Mary Pipher, author of *Reviving Ophelia,* when she was interviewed by Richard Simon, editor of the *The Family Therapy Networker:*

It has become clearer and clearer to me that if families just let the culture happen to them, they end up fat, addicted, broke, with a house full of junk and no time.[8]

Teaching young women to be active and positive agents of change is important. Affairs and infidelity are another common secret with which families struggle. Emily Brown, an expert on treatment of affairs, estimates that 70 percent of marriages will be affected by infidelity. A common cause of affairs is conflict avoidance.[9] (For more details on skills for resolving conflict see Chapter 17.)

The challenge is to speak up and to conquer the fears involved. Perhaps a bigger challenge is to make oneself heard. John Gottman, who has done numerous studies on couple dynamics, says he often sees stonewalling or "tuning out" of the female by the male.[10] Breaking the silence does not necessarily mean being heard. The famous case of Anita Hill versus Clarence Thomas reflects an incident of stonewalling. As Senator Edward Kennedy remarked to Anita Hill, "These gentlemen cannot hear you because they do not wish to hear you."[11] (For more on secrets in families see Chapter 12.)

Recognizing negative messages and rewriting these messages to be life affirming rather than death dealing is essential for positive growth to occur. The following questions assist in this reauthoring process.

REFLECTION QUESTIONS

1. Did you grow up with any messages focusing on women being silent? Were you encouraged to question decisions? Do you recall any book or other source that encouraged silence?
2. Write a modern proverb for your daughter or your niece. What beliefs about women do you want passed on?
3. Did you ever protest a decision and take a stand? Describe the experience.
4. Are you aware of any self-destructive behaviors in yourself?
5. Are you aware of any secrets in your family history? What was the meaning given to these secrets?
6. Name three values you want to be a part of your life. What values do you communicate to others, especially to the young?

7. If one of the secrets was an affair in your family, how was it re-solved? Name the feelings you have regarding this secret.
8. Have you had an unnecessary surgery? Do you know women who have? What are your thoughts and feelings about these surgeries?
9. Were you encouraged to live a balanced life (giving and re-ceiving in harmony)?
10. List ten luxuries you would enjoy. Over the next six months try to implement one or some of them.
11. Using the metaphor of dance, describe which steps you do for others and which steps you do for yourself.
12. Have you ever experienced "stonewalling"? Describe your experience. Rewrite it to end in a positive way for you.

PART III:
SEEING THROUGH DEMEANING
CULTURAL MESSAGES

Chapter 8

You Are Nobody

To bear a girl is to bear a problem.

Ethiopian proverb
Source of Evil: African Proverbs and Sayings on Women

If a woman ignores these wrongs, then may women as a sex continue to suffer them; there is no help for any of us—let us be dumb and die.

Elizabeth Barrett Browning
Letters of Elizabeth Barrett Browning

Woman is an unfinished man, left standing on a lower step in the scale of development.

Aristotle

GIRLS ARE NOT VALUED

Christiane Northrup, an obstetrician, writes in her book about how sad it is when a baby girl is born and the parents are disappointed that the baby is not a boy.[1] She notes, "I have been in the delivery room countless times when a female baby is born and the woman who has just given birth looks up at her husband and says, 'Honey, I'm sorry'—apologizing because the baby is not a son!" From birth, negative messages are encoded in the cells and the self of this helpless infant.

This is a type of emotional abuse. Our culture conveys negative messages to females very early on in their lives, including the traumatizing notion that they must apologize for who they are. Stories of abuse of female children all over the world are abundant. The Ethiopian proverb that to bear a girl is to bear a problem gets to the heart of misogyny. Millions of female babies in China are up for adoption because they are not valued as a male infant would be. In India, sonograms are taken to identify the sex of the fetus; girls are often aborted. Five areas of abuse I focus on are (1) infanticide, (2) foot binding, historical practice, (3) genital mutilation, (4) dowry deaths, and (5) family violence. Whether contemporary concerns or historical examples, they point out important negative messages to and about women and girls.

INFANTICIDE

Female infanticide has a long history. The Koran calls for a correction of the pagan practice of burying female children alive. The Koran refers to infanticide as a sign that the end of time is near:

> When the female (infant),
> Buried alive, is questioned—
> For what crime
> She was killed;
>
> (Koran 81: 8-9)

The Koran was written in the early seventh century; even at this early time its passages condemn female infanticide and contempt of girls:

> When news is brought
> To one of them, of a female,
> His face darkens, and he is filled with inward grief!
> With shame does he hide
> Himself from his people,
> Because of the bad news
> He has had!
> Shall he retain it
> On contempt,
> Or bury it in the dust?
> Ah! What an evil
> They decide on?
>
> (Koran 16: 58-59)

This historic practice of burying female children alive is difficult to write and read about. To see and name clearly these sins against women is important. Awareness is always the first step in constructive change.

Joan Johnson, a health care administrator, visited India as a guest of the Medical Mission Sisters. She told me a heartrending story about a three-month-old girl that she found lying in a hut with a floor of cow dung (see Figure 8.1). The baby had been abandoned and left to die. As Joan entered the hut, the baby, sensing human presence, threw her arms up and smiled. Joan saw hope; she wanted to take the baby to safety but was told she could not defy local custom and laws. The little girl had no value to the village. Joan says she still has nightmares of the infant girl's face and the flies that covered her body.

FOOT BINDING

The foot-binding ritual is a traditional practice that no longer takes place in Asian societies. This practice numbed and denied identity to

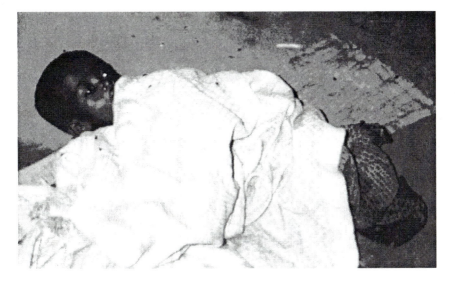

FIGURE 8.1. Photo of an infant left to die because she was a girl. Note the flies surrounding her. Beneath her is cow dung. Taken by Joan Johnson while in the Bihar state of India.

parts of a woman's body. The brutal Chinese rite caught on rapidly; it began in the period between the T'ang (618-907) and Sung (960-1279) dynasties, and spread throughout China and into Korea. By the twelfth century, it was a widely accepted practice. In the Orient, one man described his sister's ordeal when, as a child, she was forced to walk with bound feet:

> Auntie dragged her hobbling along, to keep the blood circulating, sister wept throughout but mother and auntie didn't pity her in the slightest, saying that if one loved a daughter, one could not love her feet.[2]

One interpretation of this destructive ritual is that by crippling a young girl's feet, it was a way to keep her "pure"; she could not "run around" on her master. In this ritual, bones in the feet were broken and deformed. The maimed feet resembled hooks because the large toe was pointed upward, and the others were crushed and bent under the plantar.

Beverly Jackson writes, in *Splendid Slippers,* that the practice of foot binding was an erotic turn-on for Asian men. When the feet were reduced in size to three or three and a half inches, it caused women to walk with a sway in their hips that was considered sexual. A tightness of the thigh muscles would also occur, which perpetuated the "virgin" experience for the male during intercourse. In addition, a cleft was formed from the binding in the arch of the foot that was two and half inches deep. This was considered a "second vagina."[3] Foot binding is no longer practiced, but there are still one million women in China that live with the painful effects of this practice, which ended in 1949.

Women who experienced foot binding often embroidered slippers for their deformed feet. Beverly Jackson collects these embroidered slippers for their artistic qualities. She possesses 174 pairs of slippers. Her collection began her research into the thousand-year-old practice of foot binding.

This ritual was difficult to stop. After seeing the horrible pain it caused young girls, missionaries to China attempted to end it. Scholars also attempted to call for an end to foot binding. However, it was communism that stopped the practice in 1949. The power of the Communist Party to spy on and have control of the rituals of the people brought an end to this cruel practice.

This thousand-year-old ritual no longer exists, but attitudes toward women's bodies remain the same. "Small in women is better," is a message that pervades even our culture today. In addition, the idea that women need "makeovers" communicates that women are not acceptable as they are.

Foot binding and genital mutilation are demeaning because they are performed on powerless young girls who have no choice and often no knowledge of what will happen to their bodies. They are both forms of abuse.

GENITAL MUTILATION

Genital mutilation of millions of young women in Africa is practiced routinely today. Mary Daly writes about this atrocity in *Gyn/Ecology: The Metaethics of Radical Feminism.* "Indeed this profound silencing of the mind's imaginative and critical powers is one basic function of the sado-ritual, which teaches women never to forget to murder their own divinity," writes Daly. Those who survive these atrocities live their entire lifetimes preoccupied with pain.[4] There are three distinct practices of genital mutilation:

1. Sunna circumcision is a removal of the prepuce (the fold of skin that covers the clitoris) and/or tip of the clitoris. This is the mildest type of mutilation and occurs in only a small portion of the millions of women concerned.
2. Excision of the entire clitoris as well as the labia minora. In some cases, the labia majora are removed but with no stitches sewn after removal.
3. Excision and infibulation involves more severe disfiguration. This means excision of the entire clitoris, labia minora, and parts of the labia majora. The vaginal opening is all but closed. A small opening is left so urine and menstrual blood can pass. Girls who have infibulation have difficulty with intercourse and birthing. Recutting and resewing may need to occur throughout her reproductive life. The girl is immobilized for up to forty days to permit the formation of scar tissue. Her legs are tied together.

Research is lacking on the psychological aspects of these practices, but many personal accounts contain repeated references to anxiety prior to the operation, terror at the moment of being seized by an aunt or village matron, unbearable pain during the procedure, and the subsequent sense of humiliation and being betrayed by parents, especially the mother. Efua Dorkenoo recounts the story of a seventeen-year-old adolescent in her book, *Cutting the Rose: Female Genital Mutilation.*

> At the age of 17, after she had completed her high school education, she was invited by her parental aunt to spend her holidays with her cousin. According to Miami those were the worst holidays she had spent. One week after her holiday began, she was informed that she and her cousins were to attend a ceremony for mature girls . . . No sooner did Miami enter the house when all the women grabbed her and stripped her. At first she thought she was going to be slaughtered like a sheep as she was thrown to the ground and her hands and legs were tied up.[5]

Alice Walker and Pratibha Parmar write about the complexities of change. Efua Dorkenoo is the director of FORWARD International (Foundation for Women's Health, Research, and Development), an activist and educational organization that works to eradicate female genital mutilation (FGM). Alice Walker interviewed Efua Dorkenoo, who said:

> In any society, once you start raising issues of gender, there's going to be resistance. In terms of our national struggle, we're trying to break free from the wider oppression of racism. But our women are often confused because we are told that the most important issue to focus on is the national struggle and that once we free ourselves from colonial domination, everything will be OK, and then we can address the women's question . . . it's not just the cutting of women's genitals; it's also the symbolic power of it: it has implications for her psychology and character development. And therefore male-dominated society sees any attempt to change it as a threat.[6]

The first conference in the West on female genital mutilation took place in 1991. The conference brought together community workers and professionals in health care and social work from France, Germany, Italy, the Netherlands, Sweden, the United Kingdom, the United States, and Gambia. Some of the recommendations made by the conference follow:

1. Any form of genital mutilation of, or genital injury to, the girl child was a violation of her basic human rights and must be abolished.
2. Combating genital mutilation of the girl child within each country is the primary responsibility of the government.
3. Legal frameworks for action were urged.[7]

Efua Dorkenoo hopes to build up a grassroots international women's human rights organization similar to Amnesty International, which addresses general human rights abuse.

African women are beginning to speak out against genital mutilation. Sometimes accidents occur during the operation: the bladder or rectum may be pierced; sometimes the child, in a spasm of agony, may bite off part of her tongue. Infections are common. Death statistics are not available to date.

Although this problem is usually identified as occurring in Africa, some sources report that the practice continues in Muslim communities in over thirty countries, including Indonesia, Malaysia, India, Pakistan, Oman, South Yemen, and the United Arab Emirates, and in immigrant communities in the Philippines, Europe, and North America, in addition to countries in North and Central Africa. The World Health Organization estimates that over 130 million women have been subjected to female genital mutilation (FGM). Bioethicist Loretta Kopelman reports that each year an additional 4 to 5 million girls undergo this procedure in which all or parts of their genitals are surgically removed, often without anesthesia.[8]

The Centers for Disease Control and Prevention estimate that over 168,000 girls in the United States are at risk for the procedure due to their ethnic origin. In 1996, Congress enacted a law prohibiting FGM of females under the age of eighteen in this country, and a directive was adopted to take action to eradicate the practice outside the United States.

Two Somalian models who grew up in the same tribe were interviewed by *Vogue*. Iman was forty-two years of age at the time she was interviewed. She grew up with parents who were progressive-thinking urban professionals. The family was exiled during a coup. Iman's mother rejected the practice of FGM. In addition, her mother sold her jewels to see that Iman got an education. Waris Dirie was not so lucky. She is not sure of her age. Her parents were nomads, wandering the countryside seeking food and shelter. When Dirie was five years old, her mother led her into the dark desert night, told her not to struggle, and let a traveling gypsy woman slice off her daughter's external genitalia—just as her own mother had done to her. Afterward, Dirie's vagina was stitched up with thorns. In Africa, 130 million girls and women have undergone FGM. It helps to hear Iman's story, one woman allowed to escape this tradition through her mother's power.[9]

In addition to individual women pressing for change, understanding male sexuality is essential in changing the practice of FGM. It is, indeed, a systemic problem. A family's decision whether or not to circumcise a daughter bears directly on whether the daughter will fulfill marriage requirements set by her future husband or bear the stigma of social deviance.

The myths surrounding what FGM can do for women and by extension men are seemingly infinite: FGM is said to curb sexual desire so that women are chaste prior to marriage and do not place too many demands on the husband during marriage. FGM is also supposed to make female genitalia appear more feminine (the clitoris is believed to grow over time to resemble a penis) and to improve hygiene, among other beliefs.

The reasons given to support FGM in some current research include providing "greater pleasure of the husband"; it is perceived as a good tradition (58.3 percent); and it is part of religious practice (30.8 percent).[10] Although Alice Walker points out in her interviews that the Koran never condones the practice, FGM has been given religious meaning through the years. Most scholars try to justify FGM by explaining that when the prophet Muhammad migrated from Mecca to Medina, he happened to find a woman called Um'Apiah who carried out the female circumcision operation. The prophet told Um'Apiah to be very careful. Then Muhammad explained how to do it, and that if the procedure were too extreme it could cause harm.[11]

DOWRY DEATHS

Within the Hindu tradition, women generally are accorded a low status in the Hindu texts of the Vedas and scripture. Scholars point out that women are not protected by law and ethics. Dowry deaths occur when newly married women are burned to death because they did not bring enough money as a dowry from their natal homes. Vasudha Narayanan points out that feminists have their work cut out for them in her country: "This is not the luxury of seeking ordination as a minister or contemplating the sex of God, but in saving human lives from the tyranny of Hindu culture."[12]

VIOLENCE AGAINST WOMEN

Closer to home, the final area to examine is violence toward women in the United States. The following are some data from current research:

- An estimated 3 to 4 million women in the United States are battered each year by their husbands or partners.[13]
- Violence will occur at least once in two-thirds of all marriages.
- Ninety percent of the victims of domestic violence are women.
- Forty percent of wife assaults begin during the time of the wife's first pregnancy.[14]
- Two million elderly suffer physical abuse or neglect each year.
- Sixty-seven percent of young women reporting rape were violated on a date.[15]

Traditionally, some churches have responded to violence in the family with silence, which is an indication of complicity in perpetuating the patterns of chronic abuse of women. Violence and abuse within the family strike at the very core of individual and family life and can be much more devastating than violence between strangers. The place where one expects to find nurturing, care, safety, and intimacy is instead, for many, a place of fear and violence—a place where trust is betrayed. Abuses of power thrive in silence and shame.

As a marriage and family therapist, I hear women's stories of disempowerment caused by internalization of negative cultural messages. Women tell of marital decisions made only by the man, of the woman's opinion being discounted as too emotional, and of women who suffer depression as they lose themselves, forgetting that they, as well as other family members, have needs. To empower women, Thelma Jean Goodrich, editor of *Woman and Power,* writes that we also need to engage in social activism.[16]

Some women disempower themselves and do not take the time to nourish themselves. When was the last time that you cared for yourself? When was the last time that you took the time to do something that you really enjoy?

REFLECTION QUESTIONS

1. Has anyone has made you feel that you are not valuable? Who?
2. What practices do you experience that discredit women?
3. Have you ever witnessed abuse of women?
4. What ways can you take better care of yourself?
5. How have you refuted the negative cultural message that "you are nobody"?
6. Name three things you really enjoy. Try to do one this week.
7. Learn the name of a woman you meet this week. How do you feel about your name?
8. Describe the person you want to become. How can you best help yourself become that person?

Chapter 9

You Are Helpless

It is forbidden to beat your wife after 10:00 p.m.

> Early American noise ordinance
> *A Woman's Place*

The man who is not master of his wife is not worthy of being born.

> Eighteenth-century French saying
> *A Woman's Place*

You must do the thing you think you cannot do.

> Eleanor Roosevelt
> *You Learn by Living*

Women struggle to have a "sense of mastery," research on depression in women by E. McGrath and colleagues has shown in *Women and Depression: Risk Factors and Treatment Issues*.[1] The American Psychological Association states that one in every four women and one in every eight men will suffer from serious clinical depression. One of the primary risk factors identified for women was that action and mastery skills were not encouraged. Women have been conditioned to be passive and dependent.

Cultural messages from the past make it clear that it is acceptable to beat your wife, and that the man needs to be master of his woman. The deep-seated and long-standing resistance to the Equal Rights Amendment in the United States is evidence that women are not perceived as equal. Women and children have been perceived as the property of men—objects that can be discarded. Only a generation ago, in 1970, banks in the United States changed the rules so married women could have private bank accounts in their own names.

HARASSMENT

Read the newspaper; listen to the news; talk to a friend: you will be faced with the costly effects surrounding the harassment of women in the workplace. In 1995, sexual harassment cases in the United States numbered 15,549.[2] Catherine MacKinnon pioneered sexual harassment law. *Time* reported on the Mitsubishi Motors Corporation case involving a record payment settlement to women on the assembly line of $34 million.[3] This was the most costly harassment case to date.

Following are some descriptions of harassment:

1. Unwelcome or unwanted advances, including sexual advances.
2. Requests or demands for favors, including sexual favors, such as a date accompanied by an implied or stated promise for preferential treatment, or negative consequence for refusal.
3. Verbal abuse or joking that is oriented toward a prohibited form of harassment, including that which is sexually directed and considered unacceptable by another individual. This includes comments about the body or appearance going beyond mere courtesy and the telling of dirty jokes or stories that are unwanted and offend others.
4. Sexually oriented conduct or other forms of harassment interfering with another's work performance. An example would be displaying suggestive pictures on lockers or in open places where anyone can see them.
5. Creating an environment that is intimidating, hostile, abusive, or offensive because of unwelcome or unwanted conversations, suggestions, requests, demands, physical contacts, or attentions.
6. Treating women in a demeaning manner, even without sexual overtones, is also sexual harassment.[4]

I once saw a nurse in therapy who worked as an occupational health care worker. The physician she worked with made inappropriate comments to her, including discussing the size of her breasts. She was able to confront him and let him know that if he continued to be inappropriate she would take action and report him to the department of human resources for harassment. His harassing comments stopped.

Sexual harassment is an abuse of perceived power by one person over another. It is learned behavior. Preventive education needs to begin as early as possible and should be revisited often as a reminder.

Silencing is a part of the harassment. (For more on women and secrets see Chapter 12.) Cases of sexual harassment are often covered in the media. There seems to be a cloud over Washington, DC, regarding political figures and issues of sexual harassment. First, during the Anita Hill and Clarence Thomas hearings, which many of us watched on television, Anita Hill presented her story with much credibility, but she was never "officially" validated for courageously exposing the wrongdoing before the nation. Second, Oregon Senator Robert Packwood was accused of sexually harassing his workers. He was not reelected. Third, there was the controversy regarding former President Bill Clinton. Kenneth Starr, attempting to demonstrate a pattern of sexual harassment, did influence the impeachment of the president on these grounds. These much-discussed controversies are good opportunities for families to confront these issues and learn from them.

Other problems in our culture are abuse and violence. I addressed these issues in Chapter 8, describing the extent of the problem. The next section will examine resolution.

BLACK-AND-BLUE NARRATIVES

We need to understand abuse in the context of the oppression of a class of people. One of the most moving descriptions of domestic violence was written by Anna Quindlen in her best-selling novel, *Black and Blue*. In this novel, Bobby Benedetto, a man who identifies himself as religious, beats his wife, Fran. Fran takes their son and leaves him, but Bobby manages to retain control over her, and he eventually finds her in another state, beats her, and takes their son away to live with him.

One reason abuse is so prevalent in our society is that it is one way to control the thoughts and actions of women. The media is also a powerful tool of communication for many families. Many R-rated movies show only nudity, yet PG-rated movies show violence and degrading images of women. This contradiction teaches children that sexuality is obscene, while degradation, objectification, and violence are acceptable.[5]

There is a great need to educate families about alternatives to violence, such as:

1. *Assertion, speaking the truth.* To see and hear the truth is not easy. Sometimes we think: if I were to acknowledge the truth of all this violence and the pervasive oppression against women, it would be too terrible. Change will never happen until we let ourselves see the reality of violence. (See Chapter 14 for more on assertion.)
2. *Appropriate anger management:* For example, carry a package of pencils in a briefcase or bag. The next time you are angry enough that you feel like destroying something, take the pencils out and break each one. (See Chapter 11 for more on healthy expressions of anger.)

I was working with a family in therapy in 1988. The husband had been hospitalized for depression following a stroke. I was asked to work with this couple to help resolve their marital distress. I had no idea spousal abuse was going on until I made a home visit. When I called to say I was on my way, the wife thought I was her daughter-in-law. She said, "He is doing it again." She sounded very frightened. I left immediately for the home, stopping at the police station first to request assistance. It was obvious upon arrival that the husband had hit his wife: she was black and blue. He stopped when she was no longer silent about it. She had broken the cycle, if only temporarily. It was sad that the police officer said to me, "I can't do a thing except lecture him." Since that time the laws have changed and the police have the authority to arrest the offending husband. Spousal abuse has finally been declared a crime.

In this case, the victim needed to speak out and address what was going on. Information regarding shelters available to the wife were provided. A referral to RAVEN (Rape and Violence End Now) was made; this Saint Louis organization deals with men who struggle with abusive behavior. Most local organizations are loosely affiliated with the National Coalition Against Domestic Violence. Group therapy is often the best therapy as members confront and challenge each other regarding their destructive behavior. As part of the cycle of abuse the husband will want to reconcile but will have no intention to change his behavior. The cycle often includes a period in which the abuser apologizes, the spouse lets down her guard, and the abuse continues.

This example is not meant to negate the reality that women also are perpetrators of violence. Presently, this situation occurs in about 1 percent of the spousal abuse cases reported.

The highest percentage of men who batter and abuse are in the police force, military, and clerical ministry. These professions often stress control. They also stand for protection, which is ironic because it is in these vocations that abuse most often occurs. Violence in families crosses all the socioeconomic categories.[6]

According to Ted Meltzer, an expert in spousal/relational abuse, abusive men typically

1. have low self-esteem;
2. blame others for their actions;
3. believe in male supremacy;
4. have severe stress reactions, which they might try to escape through drinking and wife beating;
5. do not believe their violent behavior should have negative consequences;
6. have an explosive temper and an external locus of control;
7. have a family history of domestic violence;
8. accept violence as a viable method of problem solving and maintaining an intact family;
9. show a high degree of job dissatisfaction;
10. maintain close contact with their family; and
11. have power and control issues.

Battered and abused women typically

1. have low self-esteem;
2. believe in family unity and the prescribed stereotype of the female sex role;
3. are willing to accept responsibility for the batterers' actions;

4. suffer from guilt while denying the anger and fear they feel;
5. have a passive personality (programs such as ALIVE [Alternatives to Living in Violent Environments] help women draw on their inner emotional strength to see they have options which can prevent further abuse, violence, and their death. ALIVE gives shelter to women and children in abusive relationships);
6. have severe stress with psychophysical complaints;
7. are martyrlike and believe that no one can help them escape their predicament;
8. are emotionally and economically dependent on their husbands;
9. give into their husbands' demands to protect their children and pets;
10. were abused in their family of origin or witnessed violence;
11. are often employed but not allowed to control finances; and
12. lose contact with their own family due to their embarrassment or forced isolation.[7]

Abuse and violence toward women are major problems. Half of the women who read this book will be hit by a partner. The idea that women are helpless in the face of abuse must be reversed. Society must examine the cause for these abuses.

Dutton has researched the causes of abuse and discovered three components:

1. The origin of the aggression needs to be examined. Dutton notes that television can predispose one to violent behavior through the acquisition of cognitive scripts. Studies show that men who had witnessed violence increased their chances of becoming a perpetrator.
2. Instigators of aggression have to be understood. An example of a triggering event might be a barroom fight that begins when someone at the bar makes fun of another person.
3. The conscience becomes neutralized. Often there is a mental construction of the abuse, such as, "My wife deserves everything I dish out." Dehumanizing the victim occurs. Often minimization happens: "I get mad at her only when I drink; it's no big deal."[8]

Violence in the family is disturbing, as is public violence. Kindlon and Thompson write that family violence began with Cain and Abel. The most powerful expression of anger is violence.[9] We need specific education regarding emotions in our culture. Perhaps more emotional education would have meant a different outcome for the two Jonesboro, Arkansas, youths, ages ten and eleven, who ambushed their classmates with guns in the schoolyard. I experienced a tragedy of public violence, described in the next section. Violence has touched people in every community and in most families.

KILLINGS—A PERSONAL STORY

My favorite aunt was shot and killed in Killeen, Texas, in a massacre. Her murderer was George Hennard, who had seen a movie, *The Fisher King,* which has scenes of violence and which some say triggered his shooting rampage. Hennard had a history of substance abuse and hatred for women. It was the women he targeted in Luby's Cafeteria. My cousin Judy and her husband Steve were also shot and wounded, but they recovered from their physical wounds. My uncle, Aunt Vee's husband, was untouched by bullets yet his life changed dramatically.

My Aunt Vee was a good woman. She was known by many for her sewing and needlework. For my wedding, she cross-stitched these words on some towels: "When loves moves in, you have a home." Her words stand in contrast to the actions of her killer. As a family, we have the comfort of knowing that she died in the loving arms of her daughter, Judy.

Our good-byes to her were stifled. Due to the bullet wounds to her neck and her bruised face, the casket was closed.

At the burial mass, Father Byrne referred to her as a martyr. She gave her life in the face of evil and violence. She was a valiant woman. Her hands were always doing things for others, and she was a gem of great value to all who knew her.

Family celebrations have traditionally been occasions of safety and comfort. This has drastically changed as violence has become more acceptable in our culture. In the case of my aunt, she was visiting her daughter for a family wedding the following weekend. Generalized anxiety in our society is on the rise due to the decrease in safe connections we experience.

Edward Hallowell challenges us to examine and deepen our positive connections.[10] Hallowell, a psychiatrist, believes many depressed people feel unconnected to others. Too much technology can lead to breaks in face-to-face encounters that are so necessary for emotional nurturance.

RAPE

Rape is another form of abuse; it can affect the victim for a lifetime, doing emotional and psychological damage. Some startling facts about rape are:

1. Ninety-eight percent of rape victims will not see their attackers apprehended, convicted, or incarcerated.
2. Over half of all rape prosecutions result in either a dismissal or an acquittal.
3. Adding together the convicted rapists sentenced to probation and those sentenced to local jails, almost half of all convicted rapists are sentenced to less than one year behind bars.[11]

Rape is usually an act perpetrated by men to maintain their dominance over women through the use of force. *State of Florida v. William Smith* involved allegations of rape brought against a member of the Kennedy family. The victim alleged that William Kennedy Smith had picked her up and took her to a beach house where he raped her. Smith, a medical student, was acquitted on all charges.

If you have experienced any form of violence discussed in this chapter and need help to heal from the past and to live a more productive life now and in the future, refer to the Appendix for names of supporting organizations to contact. Following are some questions to increase your awareness of any experiences of helplessness you may have faced.

REFLECTION QUESTIONS

1. Have you ever experienced sexual harassment in the workplace? Do you know someone who has?
2. How do you manage angry feelings?
3. Has abuse or violence happened to a family member or a friend? Describe the situation.
4. How are women aided in your faith community? Have there been any continuing education programs on domestic violence?
5. Name three resources that assist abused women and families.
6. What training and education is happening in your community regarding domestic violence?
7. Name three media programs that you feel overemphasize violence.
8. Do you protect yourself against violence? How? (Some universities now provide escort services to students taking evening courses.)
9. How should persons who inflict harm or injury be held accountable?

Chapter 10

You Should Feel Shame
and Inhibition

If you really want to know why this child is a mess, just look at
its mother!

Informal assessments by psychologists
In *Don't Blame Mother*

Advertisers exploit adolescents' social anxiety and need for
approval and independence to sell them crap, some of it addictive . . .

Mary Pipher,
In Kilbourne's *Deadly Persuasion*

I have set my face like flint, knowing that I shall not be put to
shame.

Isaiah 50:7

In this section, I have examined how women are kept oppressed by
cultural messages. Foot binding kept women feeling ashamed of their
feet. Female genital mutilation keeps women sexually inhibited. Violence toward women attempts to control mind, body, and spirit. This
chapter examines advertisements and how they contain destructive
and negative cultural messages to girls and women.

ADVERTISING

Jean Kilbourne writes that the average American is exposed to
3,000 ads a day. Seventy percent of newspapers are advertising, and

fifty percent of our mail is ad related. The Internet greets us with pop-up and banner ads at every click of the mouse. Television programs are full of advertising. Radio ads often bombard us. Billboards replace the natural beauty of trees and shrubs.

We are influenced by advertising, mostly on a subconscious level. In a consumer society we are not seen as people but as products, objects to be manipulated into a profit for the company. Advertisers try to shame us into buying and consuming. Companies manipulate our need for intimacy and love to sell us their products. Some of us feel guilty that we cannot spend more time with our children and family. Advertisers play on this guilt. Jean Kilbourne demonstrates this well as she writes about an ad:

> A stunning example of this kind of confusion between products and people occurs in an ad featuring a girl running into the open arms of a woman, presumably her mother. The copy says, "Open your eyes. What's important is right in front of you." One hopes, expects, that what is important to this woman is her child. But no, it turns out the ad is referring to her shoes.[1]

Another exploitative aspect of advertising is how the consumer becomes a walking advertisement for these companies. It is as if Nike, New Balance, or Ralph Lauren is entitled to use us to sell their product. We become an extension of the company. Boundaries between advertising and personal identity are blurred. I would like to challenge a shoe company to make a sport shoe without the company logo on the outside of the shoe, thus showing respect for the individual wearing the product. Products such as purses and sportswear have the names of their manufacturers on them also. Today I was aware that Speedo is on my swimsuit, goggles, and cap. My shoes have Saucony on the heel for others to see. Cars also become traveling ads; bumper stickers have the name of the dealership on them, or the dealer's name is on a license plate holder.

Advertising creates a make-believe world and takes meaning away from significant relationships. As Kilbourne points out, Mazda advertises, "It's not a family car. It's family." Nissan's president says, "When I am in this car, I'm in command of my future."[2] Could it be that life is more complex than that? The creators of these ads play on the vulnerability of the public. Some people are worried about the future, and have issues regarding power and control. Ads for sport utility vehicles (SUVs) play on the American people's perception that unless they drive an enormous vehicle, they are in grave danger. The facts do not always support the perception. Sport utility vehicles are dangerous, but mostly to people driving smaller cars. SUVs block visibility, and "are three times more likely to roll over during crashes than are passenger cars," states Jean Kilbourne.[3]

It is important to ask: Why do we buy certain items? For some, the status of wearing a certain brand name of clothing is important. Some are worried that they will not fit in if they do not follow fashion trends. This may lead to a deeper question: Am I struggling with my identity, my human needs, and/or my anxiety?

Although I realize that businesses need to advertise to stay competitive, I take issue with the negative messages and false information communicated.

Advertising can contribute to an unhealthy lifestyle. We need to ask what the consequences are that soft drinks have replaced milk in the nutritional intake of our youth. Kilbourne states, "Twenty years ago, teens drank almost twice as much milk as soda. Today they drink twice as much soda as milk. Some data suggest this contributes to broken bones. . . ."[4] The main drink and food ads on television are for (1) fast foods, (2) sugar-coated cereals, (3) soft drinks and alcohol, and (4) candy. The messages we are bombarded with are not for fruits and vegetables, whose properties now have been shown to help prevent cancer and heart disease. Again, we need to be aware of the effects of these ads on the choices we make. Often these ads play on compulsive and addictive tendencies. Many food ads are geared toward women, and increasingly automobile ads are targeting women with the promise of safety and security.

Alcohol ads teach that drinking leads to good times, great sex, athletic prowess, and general success without causing any negative consequences. Bacardi Rum ads suggest to women that they can be fulfilled through the bottle; the message: "Alcohol can liberate you." A young woman is featured smoking a cigar and laughing uproariously, with the tag line, "Politically correct by day. Bacardi by night." Advertising such as this trivializes the consequences of both smoking and drinking by describing the opposition as mere political correctness. It also normalizes personality change due to drinking, one of the symptoms of alcoholism.

Food ads normalize and glamorize harmful attitudes toward food and eating. An ice cream ad says:

> I pride myself on my levelheaded approach to life. . . . But all it takes is one smooth taste of . . . ice cream and I find myself letting go. . . . I must do something about this . . . maybe I could organize it, structure it, or control it . . . tomorrow!

This ad promotes binge behavior. If a woman feels too controlled, or has too few avenues for nurturance, she may turn to food as an unhealthy way to relax. Food cannot provide love as the ad suggests.

The comic strip character Cathy, by Cathy Guisewhite, is often obsessed with eating. Guilt and shame about eating and then the need to exercise off excess weight is communicated with humor.

Eighty million Americans are clinically obese. Eight million suffer from an eating disorder, and as many as 10 percent of all college women are bulimic. Advertising plays to these struggles. Ads for dieting products and candy are often in the same magazine, and these products need each other to keep us buying and spending, encouraging us to eat lots of fat and then to try to lose weight. See the Appendix for organizations that can assist you or loved ones who suffer from an eating disorder or other addictions.

Jane, twenty-five years of age, came to me for an evaluation. She was depressed, had an eating disorder, and was using laxatives routinely after she binged on sweets. As we progressed in therapy, she told me she did not have healthy self-esteem. She blamed herself for the death of her father, who died when she was five years old. We talked about how children often do this, and she began to let go of the feelings of shame. Jane had a job she hated, but it was connected to working through the shame she felt about her father's death. She began looking for another job and did not realize how happy she could be at work. Talking about the culture we live in also took some of the pressure off her. We externalized the problem so she understood that she was not the problem. As she began to experience the problem as being outside of her, it helped her cope with her feelings. Women are under tremendous pressure in our culture to look like Calista Flockhart's Ally McBeal and other very thin television characters.

Smoking is rising among teenage girls. If a girl begins smoking, she usually begins between the ages of ten and sixteen. There have been massive efforts by the government to get the word out about the health hazards of smoking,[5] but advertising has done its job and influenced youth and adults to buy dangerous products. One-third of high school adolescents in the United States smoke regularly.

All addictions for women are rooted in trauma. Sharon Wilsnach found that sexual abuse in childhood is the strongest predictor of alcoholism in women.[6] Of the 4 million female alcoholics in the United States, she estimates that half were sexually abused. Becky Thompson (1999), cited in Kilbourne, estimates that half the women with eating disorders have been sexually abused.[7] In the movie, *Girl, Interrupted* (1999), it becomes clear that the main character's smoking addiction is related to her sexual abuse by a "friend of the family" and her professor.

SHAME

Being ashamed can lead to hiding or covering up painful feelings of guilt or incompetence. Advertising can build on shame. Ads can create a set of standards, such as you are not cool unless you buy and wear Nike shoes to middle school. Teens may use this standard to shame their parents into buying these expensive shoes.

Shame affects women because women have been objectified for ages. We do not know Marilyn Monroe, the person, but we are familiar with Marilyn Monroe, the sex symbol, whose portrait was painted by Andy Warhol. Objectification is shaming to humans no matter one's gender.

Joan Borysenko points out that shame creates a state of diminishment regardless of what we do or do not do.[8] It is a painful state in which we feel defective, phony, flawed, or unworthy, and it is the core emotion that healthy and unhealthy guilt comes from. Healthy guilt is about developing a conscience. If I cheat on a test, I feel guilty, and I learn not to repeat that behavior. An example of unhealthy guilt is the blame people put on themselves for things that are not their fault, their responsibility, or even their business. Borysenko refers to the twenty-one expressions of unhealthy guilt:

1. I am overcommitted.
2. I really know how to worry.
3. I am a compulsive helper.
4. I am always apologizing for myself.

5. I often wake up feeling anxious.
6. I am always blaming myself.
7. I worry about what other people think of me.
8. I hate it when other people are angry with me.
9. I am not as good as other people think I am.
10. I am a doormat.
11. I never have any time for myself.
12. I worry that other people are better than I am.
13. I think *must* and *should* are my favorite words.
14. I cannot stand criticism.
15. I am a perfectionist.
16. I worry about being selfish in an unhealthy way.
17. I hate to take any assistance or ask for help.
18. I cannot take compliments.
19. Sometimes I worry that I am being punished for my sins.
20. I worry about my body a lot.
21. I cannot say no.

Pessimistic thinking is a hallmark of unhealthy guilt and reinforces the helplessness that is so central to shame as an identity.

Donald Nathanson elaborates on the many faces of shame. He points out that when shame is present, eyes are averted and downcast, and neck and shoulders begin to slump. When shaming occurs, mental confusion is present. In a moment of embarrassment, there is "cognitive shock," during which the higher thinking centers are affected.[9] Results of shaming might be the loss of confidence and the diminished ability to form judgments.

Our culture places on women a feeling of shame and complete responsibility for how their children turn out. Caplan writes that in our culture it is acceptable to blame the mother.[10] Rather than deal with our idealized images of our mothers and see them instead as humans with many other responsibilities and problems to grapple with, we expect them to be perfect. The less a group is valued and respected, the easier it is to target its members as scapegoats. Language often reflects this reality. Expressions such as "mama's boy" and the parallel, "daddy's girl" are not equivalent. "Mama's boy" brings up negative associations of overprotectiveness and smothering behavior on the part of the mother. However, "daddy's girl" relates an endearing description of a close-knit parent-child relationship.

THE NEED TO RECOGNIZE
OUTSTANDING WOMEN

My husband and I had been invited to a gathering of twenty-four people—teachers, physicians, and social workers. The purpose of the meeting was to name outstanding people of the twentieth century in various categories such as politics, athletics, inventions, creative artistry, and war heroics. Few women were mentioned, and when it came time to vote on the person who was considered number one by all, no woman made it to the ballot. Names were mentioned such as Freud, Einstein, Patton, Gandhi, Mother Teresa, Susan B. Anthony, Golda Meir, and Jackie Joyner-Kersee. I felt a certain shame that evening for naming so many women. Afterward I wondered why. I was going against the traditional way of thinking, and women remaining second-class citizens was part of the group dynamic that night.

FEARS OF FAILURE

Research by Carol Dweck and Carol Licht found that girls were less successful in responding to failure initially and less resilient in recovering from it after the fact. Girls appeared to carry over the negative effects of failure into new situations. Their confidence was fragile and easily dissipated.[11] How can we help girls know that it is acceptable to fall down, pull yourself together, and get up and go on? It has been my experience that sports can help in this area, as can music.

One of the best theories about failure was one I learned from my hammered dulcimer teacher, Rick Thumb, who told me he wanted me to make mistakes because those were teachable moments. If I stumbled over a chord, he would show me an easier way to play the chord using different strings on the instrument. (For more on the use of music, see Chapter 24.) Music is a source of healing, as are twelve-step programs in the recovery from addictions.

SPIRITUALITY AND ADDICTION

When an addict enters recovery, major changes take place. Something happens to thinking, feeling, and acting in the addict's world.

Alterations to one's lifestyle and life perspective occur. Those in recovery become more honest, more engaged in relationships, and more grateful. Spirituality heals the mistaken shame identity at its deepest level. That is why Alcoholics Anonymous (AA) works. It brings about self-awareness, behavior changes, and a reconnection with the spirit. When the mind calms down, we become aware of the life force, which is love. (See "Spiritual Practices for Women," Chapter 24.) We then know loving kindness toward ourselves and others. Spiritual connection is the opposite of feeling unhealthy shame and guilt.

REFLECTION QUESTIONS

1. Did you observe an ad today that you found demeaning either to you or to your relationships?
2. Name any ads that shame you, lie, or cover up the truth. List the names of companies that use you to advertise their products.
3. Are there any changes you would like to make in advertising?
4. What are some of the reasons you make purchases?
5. Do you know anyone with an eating disorder?
6. How do you handle failure?
7. Does shame play a role in your life? Are there any areas where you feel flawed?
8. How does shame get played out in your body?
9. Name any unhealthy guilt you struggle with.
10. Name women that you feel are outstanding in the twentieth and twenty-first century.
11. Select a piece of music that calms and centers you. Play that piece, feel the rhythm, and hear the melody filling you. Let it flow past feelings of shame.
12. Does spirituality assist you in keeping a perspective? Explain.

Chapter 11

You Are Not Allowed
to Express Anger

Soul is something creative, something active. Soul is honesty . . .
feelings take courage.

Aretha Franklin

No one should have to dance backwards all their life.

Jill Ruckleshaus

Recognize anger's challenge to keep on growing up into the
range of emotion, into the fullness of justice anger.

Carroll Saussy
The Gift of Anger

In Chapter 3, I discussed the use of the genogram in examining
gender issues in families. The genogram can also be used to reflect on
other patterns and behaviors learned early in life. Parents model and
teach different messages about feelings and expression or repression
of feelings. Anger can be a difficult emotion for women to express.
Some women are taught to be quiet and sweet but may not be taught
how to be aware of and express their negative emotions. Lerner writes
that patriarchy trains women to pretend as a way of life and then
trivializes its destructive effect on both women and men.[1] Expression
of anger and its many facets are discussed in this chapter.

HEALTHY EXPRESSIONS OF ANGER

David Viscott encourages women to express their anger indirectly in the beginning as they are experimenting with normal negative feelings. Some of the techniques he uses include:

1. *Angry letters.* List your complaints and get them outside yourself. Write them in red if it helps. Place the complaints in an envelope and dispose of it in some meaningful way.
2. *Taking angry steps.* Write what you are upset about on the bottom of your shoe and walk it out.[2]
3. *Psychodrama.* Pretend the person you are angry with is sitting in an empty chair that is in your view. Speak freely to the person and then sit in the empty chair and respond as you believe the person might respond. Keep switching back and forth until you are satisfied with the results.

Repressed anger can grow out of proportion. I use the metaphor with my clients of putting a stone into a bag. The stone represents an angry feeling about a situation or a person. When another situation makes you angry, another stone goes into the bag. As the stones collect, the feelings grow with unexpression. A final, minor incident may occur and all this feeling may come tumbling out, like a huge bag full of stones ripping open and crashing to the floor.

Know your feelings. Do not be afraid of trying to figure out what is bothering you. Ignoring feelings does not make them go away, as the stone metaphor illustrates. Facing your feelings honestly prevents them from exercising control over you. Often women are afraid of anger; they may worry about being called a "bitch," and thus end up depressed and/or withdrawn. Feelings do not have to be blurted out, but they should be acknowledged. You may choose to talk to someone about those feelings or to reflect on them, understanding what it is that was triggered in you by this person or situation.

Anger may mean that something is wrong in the relationship or with the situation. Anger is a warning. Justifiable outrage can lead to building a just world. Change happens when people are paying attention to their feelings and choose to express themselves in healthy ways, such as through peaceful demonstrations. In 1916, St. Louis was chosen as the site of the Democratic National Convention. F. Shinkle with the *St. Louis Post-Dispatch* wrote that members of the St. Louis Equal Suffrage League organized a protest. The delegates to the convention had to walk through the "golden parade" where 7,000 women dressed in white with yellow parasols lined Locust Street between the Hotel Jefferson and the Coliseum. It was at this convention that the Democratic Party included a plank for women's suffrage, the first time a national political body had declared itself for the cause.[3]

Grievances often help bring about change, as Harriet Woods writes:

> The original purpose of the National Women's Political Caucus . . . was to establish the representation of women at all levels of government, in both elective and appointive office, in numbers proportionate to, our percentage in population.

This establishment moved the idea from the talking stage to implementing a just system of government.

> Women could still get excused from jury duty just by saying they were women: they were still denied the most basic property rights and were still paid less than men for doing the same work. The grievances were building up that would push women to become political players. They were beginning to realize that they were indeed, dancing backwards. . . . In 1961, President Kennedy kept his word, creating the Commission on the Status of Women.[4]

GRIEF AND LOSS

Anger can also be related to grief. When we lose someone we love there is often a feeling of abandonment. When my mother died, I felt both relief and anger: relief because it was difficult to watch her suffer; anger because I knew she would no longer be there for me to talk with, to share important happenings (I was forced to grow up and stand on my own two feet). Attending a grief group helped me to feel all the feelings that occur with a death of a parent. The members of the group encouraged one another to share the complex feelings that were present in each unique loss. Grief is a major part of life.

In the Old Testament, Job (1:8) is called "blameless and upright." Yet he suffers a series of devastating losses, including his children, his animals, and finally his health. He has done nothing to deserve such treatment. Job is an example of taking anger and turning it into positive energy. Job complains to God about his losses. God accepts his persistent complaints and restores Job's fortune.[5]

OPTIMAL FAMILY HEALTH

W. Robert Beavers, who was director of the Southwest Family Institute in Dallas, did research on what makes healthy, competent families. His research is refreshing because it focuses on what works in families; he does not focus on pathology and processes of destruction. In a five-year study, he found five developmental levels in families ranging from "optimal" to "severely disturbed":

1. The bottom of the scale includes murky uncertainty pervading the system and a lack of leadership from parents. This uncertainty creates apprehension, fears, and a sense of danger in the members of the family. No rules or few rules exist.
2. In the next emotional universe there is neither much gray area nor space to negotiate individual differences. Black-and-white rules are made. They are set in a rigid fashion. You are either in control or out of control, good or bad, right or wrong. Intimidation by a tyrant rules the system.
3. In the middle level control is no longer external but is seen as coming from within each individual member of the group. Midrange families use the tremendous power and influence inherent in close relationships to keep the people within the family in line. In this system people can be confused about whether they are thinking or acting in certain ways because they want to or because it is expected of them.
4. Families at the healthier end of the clinical ladder are found to be comfortable with both loving feelings as well as with feelings of annoyance and frustration. Parents form an adequate coalition and work well as a team.

5. Members in the best level take responsibility for their ambivalent thoughts and feelings, which reduces the tendency to blame another or project onto a scapegoat. They are goal oriented and express themselves with clarity. Rules are not seen as edicts but as guidelines that can be questioned and undergo change. A feeling exists that conflicts can be resolved and that "we can work things out." A real sense of pleasure happens in the company of these family members.[6]

CLINICAL APPLICATIONS

The graduate students I teach work with a genogram. This semester we discussed all the emotional cutoffs in the families we studied. Relatives did not talk to each other. Sometimes anger can show the face of silence, with the angry person pretending that the other person does not exist. Distancing occurs.

Bea came to me because she was frustrated with her mother, Lil, who had just been diagnosed with Alzheimer's disease. Bea talked about how Lil would put meat in the bread box and bread in the freezer. Bea needed to talk about her frustration because she had gained twenty pounds and was feeling depressed.

Lil loved to play the piano, which was a very therapeutic activity for both Bea and Lil. We talked about how our range of feelings was like the keys on a piano. You need the black keys and the white keys to give the instrument a capacity to express the notes, chords, and scales to make good music. This metaphor helped Bea accept her range of feelings and the importance of expressing them.

I encourage the clients I work with to journey from emotional slavery to emotional liberation. Some people have the false notion that they are responsible for the feelings of others. This can lead to seeing the people close to us as burdens. Contrarily, when we take responsibility for our own feelings and respond to the needs of others out of compassion, not out of guilt or shame, we are freer in our relationships.[7]

Another couple, Joe and Jean, would get bogged down in their relationship with how to handle their angry feelings. Joe grew up in a family where angry feelings were suppressed, and Jean's family would "get out of control" to express anger. They were eventually able to find a middle ground where they could talk through these feelings with new compassion and each could appreciate where the other was coming from.

REFLECTION QUESTIONS

1. How was anger dealt with in the family you grew up in? What were some acceptable ways of expressing anger?
2. How did you feel when your parents got angry? With each other? With you?
3. How were "angry situations" cleared up? What practices do you carry into the present that you learned then?
4. Are there any changes you want to make in expressing anger?
5. List five people with whom you are angry. Prioritize the names. Write a letter to the first person on your list, expressing your hurt and your desire to let go of resentments. Ask yourself if you can forgive this person with the knowledge that you will be freer and less controlled by him or her if you can. These letters are not meant to be sent; they are meant to allow you to express your feelings.
6. Think of a recent situation when you felt anger. Break the situation down into parts:
   a. Were you aware of your feelings at the time?
   b. Was there hurt under the anger?
   c. How did you deal with your feelings?
7. Are there any causes that you use to express your anger and outrage (for instance, a march you participate in or a walk to fight against a disease)? Name and describe.
8. Is there a connection for you between loss and anger? Explain.
9. How are you with ambivalence? Explain.
10. What faces does anger take in your life? Are there any emotional cutoffs in your family?
11. Play a musical instrument without any self-judgment.
12. Do you feel responsible for the feelings of others? How does this weigh on you?

Chapter 12

You Are a Keeper of Secrets

In the truth itself, there is healing.

Ellen Bass
I Never Told Anyone

I have a lot of things to prove to myself. One is that I can live my life fearlessly.

Oprah Winfrey

Any large family secret, or mystification of what is real, can ultimately lead to a more generalized prohibition against knowing, seeing, talking, feeling and asking.

Harriet Goldhor Lerner
The Dance of Deception

Our culture asks a lot of questions about secrets, privacy, and families. Oprah Winfrey revealed her once-secret abuse. Madeleine Albright discovered that she is both Jewish and Catholic. Monica Lewinsky told all to Barbara Walters about her affair with then President Bill Clinton.

Secrets and privacy are commonly defined, respectively, as (1) information concealed from those whose lives are directly affected by it and (2) information that belongs to a particular person. There are many kinds of secrets. Paradoxically, the very same action used to create secrets that engender pain can be used to create joy. One of my favorite Christmas songs is all about secrets. It is estimated to have been written circa the year 1000 A.D.:

Jolly old Saint Nicholas,
Lean your ear this way!
Don't you tell a single soul
What I'm going to say;
Christmas Eve is coming soon;
Now, you dear old man,
Whisper what you'll bring to me.
Tell me, if you can.

Enforced silence, selective telling, covert talking, and whispered confidences—all can be used to plan something as wonderful as Christmas or as awful as protecting a father who sexually abuses his daughter. Secrets can cause pain for families, and especially for women.

EFFECTS OF SECRET KEEPING
ON FAMILIES

The Secret Life of Families by Evan Imber-Black gives us a number of insights into understanding the effects secrets have upon family life.[1]

1. One can observe the development of the atmosphere of guardedness and the loss of spontaneity within the family. Family members give messages such as, "Be careful about what you say to outsiders." This leads to a lack of trust; it encourages a reticence to seek outside resource support. A good example of this is shown in a recent movie, *A Family Thing* (1996). Robert Duvall plays a son who receives a letter from his dying mother, which reveals a family secret. As the mother dies, her husband is standing in the doorway across the room from her.[2] The movie illustrates how distance develops between members of a secretive family. As I watched this movie, I felt the pain of this dying woman who was isolated even in death by family secrets. The dying "mother" had written a letter to her son telling him who his real mother was. The letter was meant to be read after she died—the coward's way out. In healthy families, the person could talk face to face with the individual learning the secret information.

2. Secretiveness causes shame and anxiety in the family system. Later on, I elaborate more on addictions and secrets. For the moment, it should be noted that shame is evident in family members when a person admits to a drinking problem. Elements of an addictive disease are denial and then shame, which occurs when family members begin to address the addiction problem. This can be the beginning of a healing process. Anxiety is often observed in a family that has had a long-standing "no talk" rule and then begins to deal honestly with the issues.

3. A sense of burden exists in the family. It takes a lot of energy to repress truth. This is illustrated in the movie *Secrets and Lies* (1996). Brenda Blethyn, as the mother who gave up her first daughter for adoption, conveys to us the burden that weighs upon her and that is relieved only when she reconnects with her first child, portrayed as an adult by Marianne Jean-Baptiste. This movie also illustrates the racial tensions for a white mother and a black daughter who are reunited.[3]

Secrets can grow like weeds through the generations, sending unexpected tendrils into the corners of family life. I think of Cathy, who came for therapy because she was having an affair, only to find out through the course of therapy that her husband was also having an affair. To complicate things further, Cathy's adolescent years had been overshadowed by a never-discussed affair by her mother.

Infertility is a painful secret for some couples. The movie *Kadosh* shows how the woman in a family can become the target for blame.[4] Shame has been attached to infertility throughout time, and the ordeal associated with infertility needs to be acknowledged before and after the long-wished-for baby comes home, if adoption should take place.

Technology brings another challenge to secrets and children. There is the famous case of Dr. Cecil Jacobson in 1992, who told lies to his patients, giving these women "anonymous" sperm for donor insemination when, in fact, it was his own sperm. He was convicted of fifty-two counts of fraud.

WHAT TO CONSIDER IN OPENING A SECRET

Spirituality can be a positive force in this process, the movement from darkness to light being at the heart of many spiritual practices. A practice I like to recommend to families is the use of morning pages (see Chapter 24 for more details). This is a way to reclaim one's own thoughts and feelings, and to practice honesty. Julia Cameron recommends, in *The Vein of Gold,* using morning pages. She refers to them as a Western form of meditation. This exercise involves a stream of consciousness of writing when you first awaken in the morning. She insists on writing at least three pages, for the purpose of clearing and focusing the mind. It also allows prioritizing and examining alternative solutions to problems. Morning pages allows you to stand back and look at your thoughts and feelings.[5] Sometimes we have secrets from ourselves—what our needs are, or what we desire and dream about.

Openness and direct communication is important. A young woman from a blended family asked a question, "Who is the father of my stepsister?" This had previously been a family secret not discussed openly with the family. I asked the stepmother how she felt about the question being asked and what it was like for the young woman to ask it. The young woman said, "I like to know things." We began to see the family as a place, similar to school, to learn and know. That approach took some of the defensiveness out of the question for the young women.

In order to avoid the reckless telling of secrets, the following is an exercise to help you prepare for the telling of a secret:

- Think about the effects of opening the secret on each person in your family. For example, a dangerous family secret that is kept from an adolescent is the secret most likely to be reenacted in an adolescent's life. A woman gets pregnant before marriage, and the couple has never worked through this secret. Their teenage daughter, Esther, is sexually active. Esther is at risk of repeating the family pattern and dealing with an unwanted pregnancy.
- Think about the effects of opening your secret for each relationship in your significant circle of friends and family (for example, you and your mother; you and your father; your mother and your father; you and a close friend, and so on).
- Think about the advantages and disadvantages of opening your secret for your whole family. Today on talk shows, an individual may open a secret in a public forum, not being responsible for the consequences of their actions on his or her larger family.

The following exercise places you in an imagined future in your network of relationships. It allows you to anticipate catastrophes that we imagine, as well as the good possibilities. The following are some motivations for opening a secret; keep in mind these are often complex issues:

1. Anger
2. Revenge
3. Desire to split loyalties
4. Alleviation of guilt
5. Wish to shift a burden from self to others
6. Hope to heal relationships
7. Need to regain balance, integrity, and identity
8. Name a villain and a victim
9. Need for clarity regarding inheritance

The following are some questions to assist in deciding whether to reveal secrets to children.

1. Are you protecting your children from more than they can handle?
2. Are you protecting yourself from their penetrating and uncomfortable questions?
3. Are you opening a secret so your child can take care of you? Children often think the content of toxic secrets is their responsibility to fix. Children need to be reassured that the topic is not their fault, nor is it their job to fix.
4. Is opening a particular secret more about your need to tell than it is about your children's need to hear?
5. Will opening a secret outside your family put your family in jeopardy?
6. Are the issues strictly adult matters? If so, resolve your distress by discussing it with another adult. Our children watch us carefully. When they see us taking care of our business, they return to their own lives.

CLINICAL CASES

Addictions

I use alcohol addiction to talk about secrets. You can apply this to other areas, such as, gambling, sex, or work. During the drinking stage, the alcoholic, spouse, and family adjust to alcoholism as the central organizing principle for the family. It permeates the thoughts, feelings, perceptions, and behavior of everyone involved, who must also deny its existence. This double bind leads to a range of different experiences but most often to chaos, confusion, mistrust, loneliness, and isolation from self and others for all members. The alcoholic engages in alcoholic thinking, which attributes problems to outside circumstances—"the boss" or "the spouse." There is often chronic trauma: a state of unpredictability, terror, arguments, and/or psychological and physical abandonment. Abuse is the norm.

Roles often substitute for the healthy self in the alcoholic family. False identities and beliefs are necessary to maintain the drinking system. For example, a child may play the role of the family clown, and the laughter and humor may distract from the alcoholic facing his or her problem.

Rituals become an excuse for heavy drinking, such as birthdays and Christmas. Often the alcoholic becomes a child, as can be seen in the movie *Deconstructing Harry*.[6] Woody Allen remains childish throughout the movie, never committing to a relationship, and never parenting his son in a responsible way.

A family I was seeing often spoke in code. Dad's drunken state was called "the situation." His wife, Doris, stated what a relief it was to begin talking about the drinking in an open way. Doris became aware of how much tension her body carried. She talked about her jaws feeling so tight that her dentist thought she might need surgery. The children in recovery spoke about a "voice" inside that wanted to speak about the worry they felt when their father would drive after drinking excessively. Part of the therapy was to attend to a "false sense of self" that family members had developed. If you or your family struggles with addictions, see the Appendix for names of organizations that can be of assistance.

Abuse and Violence

Donald Dutton writes that we have avoided talking about abuse and violence. Perhaps the mental health professionals have been secretive as well. From 1939 through 1969 there is no reference in the *Journal of Marriage and Family* to violence. Words such as "conflicted" were used to describe marital unrest.[7]

Theresa, a client, came in for therapy, yet she would hardly speak. Gradually, Theresa began feeling safe enough to talk about herself. As an artist Theresa used drawing as an outlet when she could not find words for her feelings. She was beaten by her husband during her first pregnancy. It is common that violence in the family often starts during the first trimester of pregnancy.

I would encourage you to read *Black and Blue* by Anna Quindlen to expand your understanding of battering. (See Chapter 9 for more details.)

Adoption

Adoption touches the lives of many Americans. There are an estimated 6 million adoptees, according to the American Adoption Congress. In working with these families the following are important points to keep in mind.

1. For a long time, adoption was based on the view of biological parenting and fostered a rejection of difference. Little information was given about the child's background. Often there is a stigma attached to unmarried parents who bring a child into the world, and some of the secrecy is to protect the child from the "shameful" circumstances of his or her birth. Mothers who give up their children were often told to forget and move on. They became invisible. The mothers I have seen in therapy never forget the children they gave up, and often the child has a desire to meet his or her birth parent.
2. The adoptee often feels a void and a vacuum in his or her life. Often there is a difference in race and heritage between the adoptee and the adoptive parents. One adoptee writes, "Because I was adopted, I grew up with a part of me missing. In place of ancestors, I had a void." Right now I am seeing a little girl from

Korea who has a fear that things will be taken from her. She needs more reassurance regarding object constancy issues. On the positive side, it is important that she can be a daughter with two parents. If the adoption had not occurred, she would still be in an orphanage and perhaps never know what it means to be a daughter.

3. Now "open" adoption is encouraged in many states where full exchange of information is provided.

4. Adoptees need to feel confident that they have the ability to handle their own lives and important relationships with sensitivity and good judgment.

5. Birth fathers often have unresolved pain and loss. One client told me, "I hurt every day. I can't go any place without wondering if every six-year-old girl I see is my daughter."

6. Therapy can often help adoptees make sense of their life stories in which both adoption stories and search stories can be discussed. Self-definition occurs through this telling. A narrative approach can be most helpful.

7. A systems approach helps the therapist and family see how complete cutoffs often intensify with the absent persons. The presence of secrets hurt the heart of family life; anxiety is increased. Trust becomes an issue, as does loyalty. It helps when the adopted parents can give their blessing to the search for the birth parents.[8]

8. A good history ought to include the question, "Were any family members adopted?"

Illness and Death

Death can come suddenly, unexpectedly, or after long anticipation. It is difficult to talk about, often a taboo subject. Secrets can also come up as a way of dealing with unfinished business.

Grief can be buried, causing family problems. I once worked with a Hispanic couple who lost a child in a fire and it became a subject never to be talked about. This couple eventually separated because of the years of resentment that had built up.

Lorraine Wright and Jane Nagy explore the impact of constraining beliefs and the importance of the meaning of death and illness to the family. They write about the relationship between change and a shift in the constraining belief.[9] For instance, a constraining belief might be that a family member cannot handle the idea of death, and that it will be far too burdensome to talk about it. However, the knowledge that death is pending may in reality help the family be more honest with one another, and even facilitate dying well. Appropriate good-byes can be said, and letting go can make for an easier dying process.

Gender

Women's lives have been one of the best kept secrets. Women's voices are still not heard. *Time* has been featuring stories of the twentieth century's greatest minds. Few women have been mentioned and featured. Out of the 100 persons mentioned as most influential, only fourteen women were named.[10]

Women were not officially allowed to run in the Boston marathon until 1972. Kathrine Switzer ran in 1967 and an official tried to rip off her race number.

EFFECTS OF REVEALING SECRETS AND INSTITUTIONAL SECRET KEEPING

Secrets within institutions and institutional arrogance are areas that need to be examined. For example, adoption agencies today often maintain sealed records, although the laws are changing in this area. How does this impact the family?

The following are toxic elements in institutions as listed by Evan Imber-Black:

1. A rigid hierarchy of relationships exists within the institution and between the institution and those who are served by the organization.
2. All power is located at the top of the organization.
3. Tight boundaries manage information entering or existing in the institution. This point and others were well illustrated in the movie *Erin Brockovich* (2000). Julia Roberts stars as the title character who manages to get information regarding water contamination in a scandal involving a giant utility company.
4. Arrogance is a dominant trait of those in power.

5. Silencing strategies are maintained by those in power.
6. Avoid scandal, regardless of the cost to the individuals involved.
7. Require obedience and deference to those who have power by those who do not.
8. Loyalty to the institution should be unquestioned.
9. There is a lack of accountability by the institution to those it purports to serve.[11]

I hope this chapter has encouraged you to explore family secrets or institutional secrets in a way that fosters healing. Please take the time to reflect on the following questions.

REFLECTION QUESTIONS

1. How did your family of origin make its own rules about what was secret and what was private?
2. Did you know how much money your parents earned? If not, what effect did that lack of knowledge have on you?
3. Were there differences in what information men and women could keep private?
4. How do you define privacy and secrecy in your adult life?
5. If there were secrets in your family, was a person burdened with the secret ? Who was excluded?
6. What impact do you think this burden is having on various relationships in your family?
7. Does the presence of secrets affect closeness and distance in your family relationships?
8. Have secrets had an impact on the rituals in your family life?
9. How have secrets affected the development of individuals and relationships in your family?
10. Are you living a double life, e.g., professing religious beliefs while secretly violating them? What effect does this have on your sense of self and your capacity to relate authentically to others?
11. Have there been social class shifts up or down in your family that have led to silence and secrets?
12. What has been your experience as a woman or man with secrets that spring from gender?

PART IV:
NEW NARRATIVES

Chapter 13

I Am Knowing

I myself have never been able to find out precisely what feminism is: I only know that people call me a feminist whenever I express sentiments that differentiate me from a doormat.

Rebecca West
The Clarion (1913)

Within reason little girls need the freedom to explore, to exult, to climb trees, and to become themselves . . . perhaps the greatest danger overall is the failure to nurture courage and initiative in our daughters.

Joan Borysenko
A Woman's Book of Life

Creative minds have always been known to survive any kind of bad training.

Anna Freud
1968

Countless women have challenged the cultural stereotype that women are less knowledgeable than men. Enheduanna, the first known poet; Pat Schroeder, U.S. Congresswoman for twenty-four years; Carol Gilligan, author and researcher; Nancy Goldberger, Jill Tarule, Blythe Clinchy, and Mary Belenky, co-editors of *Knowledge, Difference, and Power* and co-authors of *Women's Ways of Knowing,* all challenge the notion that women are limited. Goldberger, Tarule, Clinchy, and Belenky developed a theory of women's psychology, development, and ways of knowing that has been applied to the fields of social sciences, women's studies, the humanities, education, law, and psychology. Maureen Holohan writes hopeful stories for and about young women. Katherine Graham and Edith Hendry inspire us with their narratives.

FIRST POET

It has long been taught that primary ancient documents written by women were very hard to come by; it was also thought that women did not read or write. But Tikva Frymer-Kensky discovered that the earliest great poems of Sumer were written by a woman named Enheduanna (2285-2250 B.C.E.).[1] She was a priestess who wrote hymns of praise. She lived in what is currently Iraq, during the Akkadian period (2300 to 2100 B.C.E.), and she was the Shakespeare of ancient Sumerian literature. People recited and studied her beautiful compositions for more than 500 years after her death. The hymns of Enheduanna are in part narrative poems. In the Ninmesarra hymn, Enheduanna relates the rebellion that deposed her and speaks of the goddess Inanna's aid in restoring her to office. Inanna is the goddess of play who brings happiness to children and the spirit of dance to the people. She represents bodily based female power. The first part of the Hymn to Inanna by Enheduanna reads:

> Lady of all powers,
> In whom light appears,
> Radiant one
> Beloved of Heaven and Earth,
> Tiara-crowned
> Priestess of the Highest God,
> My Lady, you are the guardian
> Of all greatness.
> Your hand holds the seven powers;
> You lift the powers of being,
> You have hung them over your fingers,
> You have gathered the many powers,
> You have clasped them now
> Like the necklaces onto your breast.[2]

Cultural arts grew out of the household role of women. Women often were called upon to explain the world to their children and to interpret their dreams (Gilgamesh's mother serves in this role). Mothers sang lullabies to their children. The art of healing also grew out of this household role; the wise woman often had knowledge of plants and medicinal practices of the time. She would be responsible to care for dependent members of the household. It should therefore be no surprise that the first composer of poetry was a woman. However, it is inspiring that a woman was the first poet.[3]

Many cultures have venerated the knowledge of women. This respect is manifested in poetry and art. In the Taoist tradition, a respect for female knowledge is demonstrated in *Immortal Sisters: Secret Teachings of Taoist Women,* translated and edited by Thomas Cleary.[4] In the Navajo tradition the Corn Mother is important; she is remembered with respect today whenever the Navajo eat corn.[5] The Corn Mother inspires sand paintings and other forms of Indian art.

U.S. CONGRESSWOMAN

An intelligent woman of our times, Pat Schroeder, U.S. Congresswoman for twenty-four years, in an interview with Terry Gross on National Public Radio's *Fresh Air,* talked about her experience of serving on the Armed Services Committee. The chair of this committee treated her as half of a person, appointing a man to share her job. Besides being a pilot and aviator[6] Schroeder was one of the most qualified U.S. Congress members to serve on the Armed Services Committee. Pat Schroeder is living proof that smart women can succeed and gain the public's confidence.

MODERN ROLE MODELS

Carol Gilligan challenged the views of her mentor, Lawrence Kohlberg, regarding moral developmental theory. Kohlberg had undertaken a study using only young men as subjects, yet generalizing his findings to both genders. Gilligan writes, "Kohlberg derives his theory as if females did not exist."[7] Gilligan, on the other hand, includes some powerful stories of women in her book, *In a Different Voice.* The following passage is one such story of a middle-aged woman:

> As a woman, I feel I never understood that I was a person, that I could make decisions and I had a right to make decisions. I always felt that that belonged to my father or my husband in some way, or church, which was always represented by a male clergyman, and they had much more to say about what I should and shouldn't do. . . . It only lately has occurred to me that I never rebelled against it, and . . . I still let things happen to me rather than make them happen.[8]

Gilligan, with colleagues Rogers and Tolman, has also conducted studies on developmental issues in adolescent girls. When girls in the studies were asked a variety of questions, the researchers recorded how many times the interviewee answered, "I don't know." The results showed that girls' sense of knowing decreased during high school instead of increased.[9] Perhaps women and girls "know" in ways that the education system does not support. For example, intuition is important to feminine knowledge and being in responsive mentoring relationships.

Nancy Rule Goldberger, Jill Mattuck Tarule, Blythe McVicker Clinchy, and Mary Field Belenky have wonderfully articulated the ways that women are "knowing." Two important concepts they stress are voice and connection.[10] Voice relates to a woman's capacity to formulate and express her thoughts, along with the belief that she has something worthwhile to say and that she feels she is understood. "Connected knowing" is the ability to enter into the perspective of the other, to reason with the other, and to achieve understanding. Its opposite is "separate knowing," which entails challenging the other's reasoning. Connected knowing is more common to women; separate knowing tends to be used more in institutions of learning.

Having access to stories of courageous women is vital to progress. Women can begin to feel connection, empathy, and identification. Women should not underestimate themselves as a source of knowing. Day-to-day living experiences provide important knowledge and wisdom.

WOMEN HAVE STRENGTH

Maureen Holohan writes a wonderful series of books for young women called the *Broadway Ballplayers*. In her second book in the series, she develops the theme of strength in young women through her character Rosie Jonzie, the only girl baseball player on the all-star team.[11] Holohan has a gift for showing the development of her characters' intellectual abilities, as well as their athletic talents. Rosie's healthy aggression expressed in her ballplaying is balanced with her intellectual curiosity. She enjoys spending time in the library. She reveals her athletic skill when she pitches to the coach, who had previously overlooked her during many practice sessions and not given her the opportunity to play. Rosie's reaction to the comment made by the coach's son that "girls don't belong on the field" causes the coach to blame Rosie for the escalating conflict between Rosie and the coach's son. When her brilliant pitches strike out the coach, Rosie achieves immense vindication: the team, recognizing her talents, demands that the coach put her in the game.

Edith Hendry, a strong athlete that I had the pleasure of meeting, is ninety years old. She recently swam in the Senior Olympics, winning a number of gold medals. Watching her easily swim the 200-yard Individual Medley, I knew that this woman had great determination. During the social event that followed the swimming competition, I sat next to her niece, who told me about the significant obstacles Edith had overcome. Three years ago, colon cancer struck, and last year she broke a hip, but Edith was determined in each situation to swim again. She was back in full swing this year, swimming all twelve events.

Another strong woman who has dealt with family illness and career shifts is Katherine Graham. Her autobiography, *Personal History,* is a national best-seller filled with stories of courage.[12] Katherine Graham piloted *The Washington Post* through the crises of Watergate. She discovered her strength after her husband's suicide, as she dealt with her grief and filled her husband's position at the helm of the *Post*. She writes with honesty about her husband's affair and how she dealt with the hurt and rejection of this part of her life.

Rosie, the all-star ballplayer; Edith Hendry, the ninety-year-old competitive swimmer; Katherine Graham, owner of the Washington Post Company until her death in 2001—all three of these women exhibit strength and courage in their own way. Do not discredit your strength!

REFLECTION QUESTIONS

1. Do you enjoy poetry? What is your favorite poem?
2. Describe times you felt circumstances were unfavorable to your contributions. For example, you have a talent for playing the guitar, but you do not play your song due to a perception that you are not welcome by the group sponsoring the event.
3. List the people who give you hope and encouragement in using your talents.
4. Write down your accomplishments and post them where you can see them daily.
5. Name three courageous women and how they influence or have affected your life.
6. Describe your experience of knowing. How is voice and connection important for you? For example, do you learn more in relationship, in talking with another person about a subject? Is articulating what you know important?
7. Name three strengths you possess. When was the last time you used one of these strengths? Describe the event.
8. Consider three times you felt intimidated and write about how you dealt with the intimidating person or situation.
9. Describe three obstacles to using the strengths you described in question number 7. For example, I may find it hard to find people who will listen to me. I may need to change my relationships to include fewer overbearing persons who may do much talking and little listening.

Chapter 14

I Have a Voice

When we got out of school, all the mothers would ask their children what they had learned that day. My mother would inquire instead, "what did you ask in class?"

Rabbi Nilton Bonder
Yiddishe Kop: Creative Problem Solving
in Jewish Learning, Lore, and Humor

If you set out to be successful, then you already are.

Katherine Dunham

Poverty, racial and ethnic separation, limited training, poor health, and heavy family responsibilities all played out differently for women, yet most couldn't conceive of speaking out, or becoming leaders, because it took all their energies just to survive. It was our job to help them find their voices.

Harriett Woods
Stepping Up to Power

There is an appointed time for everything . . . a time to be silent and a time to speak.

Ecclesiastes 3:1-7

OPPRESSION

As women deal with their oppression individually and collectively, their contributions will start to be taken seriously. As women reflect on their history, they are often outraged at the injustice they find. When I visited the National Women's Hall of Fame in Seneca Falls, New York, I wondered why such an important part of history came as a revelation this late in life. Why had I not studied about the women's movement in school? Something new to me was the *Women's Bible,* edited by the suffragist Elizabeth Cady Stanton. I now realize how many chapters could have been written about the courage of the women who fought for the right to vote and for the other rights that were associated with the movement, such as the right to an education. Women were jailed for protesting their treatment as possessions and extensions of their husbands, rather than as persons with a voice and a right to vote. Why was it missing from the history I studied? Could it be that women's contributions are often passed over?

The Bible is a powerful book, functioning as a force for life, for hope, and for liberation. Poor women, accustomed to feeding their families with a handful of flour and a little oil (1 Kings 17:12), find in the Bible confidence to carry on with life. At the same time women have found themselves on unfamiliar ground while men seem to have a clear place in the Bible. Rarely do women in the Bible speak for themselves. They are often portrayed from the perspective of male authors and in the context of religious communities where authority was vested in men and where men's experience was the norm. As women today write commentaries on the Bible they move from being objects to subjects. Agency happens for women as well as men. Women have a voice and connection.

Some interesting facts are now coming to light about the literature used in schools. Stories about men and their contributions are more plentiful than stories about women. In one study, 134 elementary school readers from sixteen different publishers were examined, and it was found that boy-centered stories outnumbered girl-centered stories five to two. Stories about women tended to stress the rewards of passivity rather than assertiveness.[1] The American Association of University Women conducted a study whose results showed that boys are called on more often than are girls. When teachers posed questions to the class, sometimes girls were ignored when they raised their hands to respond to questions.[2] The educational experience of many women does not build confidence or encourage a sense of inner authority. No wonder many women struggle to find the answers within themselves.

Our culture creates oppressive expectations about beauty, regarding it as an exterior characteristic. Another study by the American Association of University Women found that 60 percent of elementary school girls were happy with themselves, and by high school the numbers dropped to 30 percent.[3]

Lack of self-esteem arises from other problems as well. Reports of boys sexually harassing girls in school are increasing at an alarming rate, according to a recent study on girls and education by the American Association of University Women.[4] When sexual harassment is treated casually, a damaging message is sent to both boys and girls: Girls are not worthy of respect; appropriate behavior for boys includes exerting power over girls.

LEADERSHIP

Harriett Woods is an example of a strong leader. She is the former president of the National Women's Political Caucus and former lieutenant governor of Missouri, the first woman elected to a statewide office in Missouri. She teaches courses on women in public service at the University of Missouri. I first met her in the St. Louis County municipality of Kinloch at a parish clinic fund-raiser. This neighborhood was one of the most disadvantaged in the St. Louis area. Harriett Woods uses her leadership to assist such needy communities and to support other women. She tells the story of Congresswoman Bella Abzug who went against a long tradition in Orthodox Judaism when, at the death of her father, she recited kaddish for him along with the male relatives. When no one tried to stop her, Woods said she "came to understand that one way to change outmoded traditions was to challenge them."[5] Woods writes about how women work harder at both being heard and speaking up. She shares her own struggles in asking people in the community for money for her political campaign. However, with practice she could request a thousand dollars or more with ease. She affirms that women have experienced a lifetime of being told that asking for money for oneself was unseemly.

Geraldine Ferraro was the first woman nominated for vice president. Woods notes that, unfortunately, the press did not write about Ferraro's ideas but about her short-sleeved dresses. Pat Schroeder said, "It is stupid. All this focus on her haircut, hemlines, manners and how many pearls she has trivializes Gerry's candidacy. It's an affront to all women."[6] Her husband became the main focus because he failed to make public his tax returns. His finances became more important than her ideas about leadership. In spite of all this, Ferraro broke a seemingly impenetrable glass ceiling.

NARRATIVES

Diane Rehm, acclaimed public radio host, shares her struggles with developing her courage to speak out in her book *Finding My Voice*.[7] She writes honestly about the dynamics in her family and the struggle she experienced with her mother's silences toward her. She discusses openly the physical and emotional abuse she experienced. After reading her book, I found myself appreciating the struggle many women have to find their voice. Diane Rehm gives impetus to all women to grow in the area of assertiveness.

Mary Pipher's *Reviving Ophelia* explores her work with adolescent girls and the struggle of young women in our culture to have a voice. She focuses on the enculturation of women to be pleasing to others rather than to be true to themselves. Pipher validates young women who challenge negative comments made to them and encourages the reality that many women want to be valued for more than their appearance.[8]

A challenge for both men and women is how to give voice to issues that really matter in our lives. Relationships, especially in marriage, are endangered by a lack of truthfulness. Frank Pittman challenges couples to examine the honesty in their communications.[9]

Women can lose their ability to identify their own wants and needs in a relationship. Ralph Earle, marriage and family therapist in Scottsdale, Arizona, coined the term *enlightened selfishness* as a tool to assist his women clients to gain awareness of their needs and wants during decision-making times. Women by nature are caretakers. Enlightened selfishness means taking care of others but not at the expense of self. In other words, do not give the self away as this may cause depression and anxiety. Scripture instructs us to live a balanced and self-reverential life when we are told to love God, neighbor, and self.[10]

In a healthy marriage, spouses promote and encourage each other's growth as well as their own. In *all about love: new visions,* hooks challenges her readers to confront lovelessness as a part of the healing and growth process. It is important in an intimate relationship both to give and to receive love.[11]

REFLECTION QUESTIONS

1. Write down any goals you have, any dreams you may have not expressed. Can you give yourself permission to move toward those goals and dreams? What would the first step be?
2. What strong and expressive women stand out in your mind?
3. Name some issues you have spoken out about recently.
4. What gender stories did you hear when you were growing up? What beliefs were communicated about men speaking up and women having a voice?
5. What happens when you do not express yourself? Do you experience physical repercussions? Some women get headaches or backaches, or experience increased stress.
6. How do you feel about asking for help?
7. Did any family messages interfere with you having a voice and/or speaking out? Is your communication direct? Straightforward?
8. How do feel about challenging negative comments made to you?
9. Write a litany of self-acceptance. For example, I accept the sound of my voice, my mouth, and the neck I have been created with that holds my vocal cords.
10. How honest are you in your relationships? What keeps you from being honest? Do you struggle with the need to please other people?
11. Elaborate on your current needs and wants. How do these areas of your life impact your decision-making process? How do you feel about the concept of enlightened selfishness?

Chapter 15

I Have a Divine Herstory

I truly believe that I should be here and I can't even tell you why
. . . . God's palpable presence has never been more real ever
since we came to Salvador.

Ita Ford
In *Ita Ford: Missionary Martyr*

I like living. I sometimes have been wildly, despairingly, acutely
miserable, racked with sorrow, but through it all I still know
quite certainly that just to be alive is a grand thing.

Agatha Christie
"An Autobiography" (1977)

Where were the saints to try and change the social order, not just
to minister to the slaves, but to do away with slavery?

Dorothy Day
Dorothy Day: Selected Writings

In the spring of 1998, I taught a graduate course titled Community
Health Spirituality which enlightened me and the students to the reality of the great women on whose shoulders we stand. We studied Etty
Hillesum, Jewish mystic of the Holocaust; Käthe Kollwitz, socialist
and pacifist artist; Caroline Stephen, Quaker mystic and author;
Julian of Norwich, Catholic mystic of the fourteenth century; Teresa
of Avila, sixteenth-century doctor of the church; and Ita Ford, modern activist and martyr. All six of these women used their talents of

self-expression to build up community and to create hope in times of darkness, giving witness to the power of the integration of the human and the divine.

JEWISH MYSTIC OF THE HOLOCAUST

In 1914, Etty (her given name was Esther) Hillesum was born into a privileged Dutch Jewish family in Amsterdam. Her mother, Rebecca Bernstein, was Russian by birth; however, she left Russia because of the massacre of the Jews in her home country. Etty's father, Dr. L. Hillesum, taught classical languages. Etty and her siblings were very talented. Her brother, Mischa, was one of the most promising pianists in Europe, and Jaap became a physician.

Etty went to the University of Amsterdam where she received her first degree in law. She was studying psychology when World War II broke out. Her diary is a journey through her inner world, and in a remarkable way her inner world is not governed by the war. In 1940, the Germans first began to isolate the Jews. Her diary begins on March 9, 1941. The first big roundup of Jews took place in July 1942. Etty volunteered to go with the captured Jews to Westerbork. Her father called her the "little abbess." Etty was a beacon of light to her companions after they were placed in a concentration camp. She longed to share some of the richness she found inside herself. She wrote in July 1942:

> And don't we live an entire life each one of our days?. . . I am in Poland everyday, on the battlefields . . . I often see poisonous green smoke; I am with the hungry, with the ill-treated and the dying, everyday, but I am also with the jasmine and with that piece of sky beyond my window; there is room for everything in a single life. For belief in God and a miserable end.[1]

On September 15, 1943, two farmers found a postcard on the ground outside Westerbork and mailed it. Etty wrote to her friend Christine from the train heading to Auschwitz: "We left the camp singing."[2] These are her last recorded words—found on a postcard thrown from a train.

Etty wrote eight exercise (journal) books. The first entry was dated November 10, 1941: "Mortal fear in every fibre. Complete collapse. Lack of self confidence. Aversion." She wrote on July 3, 1942:

> Very well then, this new certainty, that they are after our total destruction, I accept it. I know it now and I shall not burden others with my fears. I shall not be bitter if others fail to grasp what is happening to the Jews. I work and continue to live with the same conviction and I find life meaningful.[3]

Carol Ochs and Kerry Olitzky write that each of us needs to find our own spiritual map. We need to know that God speaks to us. In Hebrew, a female spiritual guide is called a *morei derekh*.[4] Etty Hillesum grows between those two entries to insights that are beyond human understanding. The spirit of God is so alive in her words. Etty is a light of hope shining brightly in the midst of the evils of genocide.

GERMAN ARTIST DEPICTING THE EVILS OF WAR

Käthe Kollwitz shone through her expression of art. She used only black and white in her prints and drawings because she believed in the power of line and gesture. She, like Etty, wanted to speak directly and boldly. Both were dedicated to God, although they belonged to different faith traditions. Käthe made a vow to herself and her son to honor God with direct, unembellished work.

Born in 1867, Käthe Kollwitz was the first woman elected to the Berlin Academy of Art. Renowned for her prints, drawings, and sculpture, Käthe had the gift of combining her personal values with political influence. Her son, Peter, died in World War I. War memorials were sculpted by her out of this experience of grief. One of her famous sayings was: "At such moments, when I know I am working with an international society opposed to war, I am filled with a warm sense of contentment."[5]

She developed three themes in her art: (1) revolutionary energy, (2) a mother's love for her children, and (3) death. Kollwitz was censured by the Nazis when they came to power in the 1920s. The theme of social protest in her work caused her to be banned from public exhibition, and it cost her husband his medical practice. She was able to transform those losses and defeats into more evocative prints, drawings, and sculptures.[6]

One of my favorite works of Käthe Kollwitz is called *"Brot"* (Bread). This lithograph demonstrates how Kollwitz brought the long-standing subject of mother and child into the unidealized, realistic context of German life between the two wars. Kollwitz portrayed a mother unable to sufficiently feed her two children. Conflict is so evident in the figures she draws. Does she feed one and not the other? The figure of the mother bent in despair with the two young children clutching her from either side is powerful in its emotional content (see Figure 15.1).[7]

In addition to her focus on motherhood, Kollwitz concentrated on the working class. Her husband was a physician, and she would draw the sick and the infirm as they awaited treatment. She saw blue-collar workers, in contrast to the middle class, as the true embodiment of strength and beauty; and she drew for political education.

QUAKER MYSTIC AND AUTHOR

Caroline Stephen, similar to Käthe, was an educator. Both recognized the inwardness of the light of truth. Stephen, born in 1834, belonged to a distinguished British family. Her father was a professor of history at Cambridge and her niece was Virginia Woolf.

In her book, *Quaker Strongholds,* she blesses the Quakers with a highly articulate account of what she thought to be an authentic witness of Quaker values. This Quaker classic appeared in 1890 and has gone through several printings. She wrote:

> A true mystic believes that all men have, . . . an inward life, into which as into a secret chamber, he can retreat at will. In this inner chamber, he finds refuge from the ever-changing aspects of outward existence; from the multitude of cares and pleasures and agitations which belong to the life of the senses; from human judgments; from all change, and chance, and turmoil, and distraction. He finds there, first repose, then awful guidance; a light which burns and purifies; a voice which subdues; he finds himself in the presence of his God.[8]

FIGURE 15.1. This German lithograph by Käthe Kollwitz (1924) shows the maternal conflict over which child to feed, a common wartime dilemma. Her art was a form of social protest. She and her husband were pacifists. Note the child's face. Saint Louis Art Museum, gift of Mr. and Mrs. William Schield. © 2002 Artists Rights Society (ARS), New York/VG Bild-Kunst, Bonn.

Caroline Stephen used the language of her time, which was not gender inclusive. Julian of Norwich, on the other hand, five centuries earlier, made use of language to express a feminine side of God.

CATHOLIC LAY MYSTIC EXPRESSING FEMININE SPIRITUALITY

Julian of Norwich, at the age of thirty, entered her anchorhold at the Church of Saint Julian in Conisford at Norwich. Many came to her anchorhold to seek spiritual counsel, including Margery Kempe of Lynne, who wrote of a unique way to follow Christ through contemplation, active works, and pilgrimage. Margery had recourse to Julian as one known to be an expert in spiritual guidance.

Julian of Norwich wrote sixteen "showings" or revelations of God's love and made a significant contribution to Catholic spirituality. She wrote: "As truly as God is our father, so truly is God our mother."[9]

Julian of Norwich was born in 1342, a time when new forms of religious expression were springing up throughout Europe. Much of the new spirituality emerged as laypeople aspired to lives of holiness outside conventional religious orders. Writing about the central problems of the spiritual life, Julian represented the feminine teacher and feminine insight that are rare in Christian traditions. Of all the doctrinal issues that she addressed, the most timely was her insistence on referring to God as a mother. She had great facility for reconciling the human and the divine, psychology and theology. In Chapter 60 she wrote, "To the property of motherhood belong nature, love, wisdom, and knowledge, and this is God."[10]

MYSTIC AND DOCTOR OF THE CHURCH

Teresa was born in 1515 in Avila, Spain, and is a towering figure in Christian history at a time when a woman's voice was given little attention. She was the first woman, in 1970, to be named doctor of the church. There are thirty men who have been given this title, but Teresa is one of only three women to have been given it. She founded seventeen convents, authored four books, and was a spiritual guide. Teresa's grandfather was a *converso,* one of the many Spanish Jews who converted to Christianity under the threat of exile. At the age of thirty-nine Teresa had a conversion experience in the Carmelite convent. She viewed the image of Christ suffering on the cross and became aware of the mediocrity of her spiritual life, deciding to establish a reformed Carmelite house.

Saint Teresa was a teacher of mystical doctrine and a poet. Robert Ellsberg summarizes Teresa's life as a woman and a reformer who based her authority on private visions. Teresa's activities entailed considerable risk. She underwent a formal investigation by the dreaded Spanish Inquisition. One of my favorite quotes of hers follows:

> Let nothing disturb you, nothing dismay you. All things are passing, God never changes. Patient endurance attains all things. . . . God alone suffices.[11]

SOLIDARITY AND MARTYRDOM WITH THE OPPRESSED

Ita Ford was born in Brooklyn, New York, in 1940 and died forty years later in El Salvador. She was a Maryknoll missionary who spent her missionary years in Chile and Central America. I had the privilege of meeting her in Santiago, Chile, while visiting my brother who was also stationed there as a Maryknoll priest. Ita Ford and her companions invited me for dinner one night. I can still see her sparkling eyes dance as she talked about her work with the people in the barrios. Hunger was a problem, but some nutrition centers had been set up to provide needed food for the community. Her ability to care for people is manifested in a letter she sent to her niece the year she was killed (From the Same Fate As the Poor collection; Ita Ford Letters; Maryknoll Sisters Archives; Maryknoll Mission Archives, Maryknoll, NY. Reprinted with permission.):

August 16, 1980

Dear Jennifer,

The odds that this note will arrive for your birthday are poor— but know I'm with you in spirit as you celebrate 16 big ones. . . . I love you & care about you. I'm sure you know that. And that holds if you are an angel or a goof-off, a genius or a jerk. A lot of that is up to you and what you decide to do with your life.

What I want to say—some of it isn't too jolly birthday talk, but it's real. Yesterday I stood looking down at a 16 year old who had been killed a few hours earlier. I know a lot of kids even younger that are dead. This is a terrible time—El Salvador for youth. A lot of idealism and commitment is getting snuffed out here now. . . .

All I know is that I want to say to you—don't waste the gifts & opportunities you have to make yourself and other people happy. . . .

A very happy birthday to you & much, much love.

Ita[12]

In December of that same year, Ita was shot at close range in the back of the head and quite probably raped by one or more of the five guardsmen from the airport detachment of the El Salvador National Guard who crowded into the vehicle carrying her and her three companions.

Many lessons can be learned from these great women: trust in your experience as a woman; have courage to express your beliefs; maintaining hope is possible in darkness and desolation; self-knowledge gives the courage to be yourself; love is eternal; and have confidence in your abilities to make unique contributions to your community.

REFLECTION QUESTIONS

1. Name any spiritual guides you have or have had.
2. Are there any artists who speak to you and your experience? List them.
3. Which women role models come to mind as you reflect on people you admire?
4. How does your spirituality get you through the rough times in life?

5. Is there room in your experience of God for the feminine? What do you think about the motherhood of God? What other metaphors come to mind?
6. How would you describe your experience of prayer?
7. Are you aware of the oppressed in your community? How could you reach out more?
8. When was the last time you wrote a letter to give encouragement to a young person?

Chapter 16

I Can Take Credit

The woman who fears the Lord is to be praised. Give her a reward of her labors, and let her works praise her at the city gates.

Proverbs 31:30-31

Despite the encouraging and wonderful gains and the changes for women which have occurred in my lifetime, there is still room to advance and promote correction of the remaining deficiencies and imbalances.

Sandra Day O'Connor
First woman Supreme Court justice of the United States
Conference speech, *The New York Times* (1989)

Like the sun rising in the Lord's heavens, the beauty of a virtuous wife is the radiance of her home.

Sirach 26:16

PERSONAL NARRATIVE

My mother's influence is great in our family. The kitchen, her "domain," was my favorite place to sit and leisurely tell stories. Mom decided in 1954 to take a Dale Carnegie course. For a homework assignment she had to prepare a talk about a family event. She chose to talk about a basketball game in which I had scored the most points in an eighth-grade regional tournament. She noted how surprised my brother was that I was such a good athlete. All those basketball games he and I had played together paid off. My favorite basketball variation was a game called horse. One player would take a position on the court and shoot from that place, then all the players had to try to make a basket from that spot. If you missed, you got an H, then an O, and so on. As I reflect on the story, my mother was encouraging me to take credit for my skills. I have had to overcome a lot of false humility through the years. I eventually learned that it is good to "let your light shine."

CLINICAL NARRATIVE

Sylvia came to see me after she had given birth to a beautiful daughter that she and her husband had named Kathleen. She worried that she might repeat the pattern of forming distant relationships that she had experienced in her family of origin. The connection and bond she had formed with her baby became evident in the hour we spent together. She gazed lovingly at Kathleen and nursed her openly during the session. I encouraged her to take credit for the growth she had accomplished in therapy. Sylvia was able to face some of the painful feelings of isolation and hurt she experienced with her mother, and to deal with her father's ultimately fatal addiction to alcohol. Now she was freer to make choices about relationships in her nuclear family. Awareness is the first step in making positive change.

As we talked, Sylvia's tense demeanor relaxed. Relief became evident in her face. Sylvia taught me the power of taking credit for personal growth. In addition, she gave proof of the positive energy of encouragement and optimism.

A number of ways can assist in the growth of our ability to take credit: (1) imaging, (2) building self-confidence through assertiveness, (3) looking to women role models who break barriers, (4) acknowledging our blessings and composing blessings, and (5) openness to mentoring.

IMAGING

Jack Lesyk writes in *Developing Sport Psychology Within Your Clinical Practice*:

> Successful, elite athletes are able to imagine themselves performing specific behaviors at a high level of excellence clearly and vividly, using multiple sensory modalities: mentally rehearsing situations and performances in advance and dealing

with errors and poor performances through mental imagery correction, rather than reliving the mistake mentally.[1] (See Chapter 24 for an example of an imaging practice.)

Our culture can be tough on women, as we examined in Part III on negative messages (Chapters 8 through 12). Women can believe themselves defective—always needing makeovers, never being the proper weight, not having the needed talent to advance in the workplace. Irene Stiver writes:

> It is noteworthy how often women express enormous doubt about their abilities and their competence. Repeatedly I am struck by the degree to which women still minimize and negate signs of their effectiveness.[2]

Imaging can assist in self-acceptance and fulfillment. It can be a way to release the perfectionist attitude that some women have.

SELF-CONFIDENCE

David Olson at the University of Minnesota is doing extensive research on couple dynamics. He found assertiveness in partners increased the self-confidence of both people in the relationship and created a positive constructive cycle in their communication. On the other hand, when assertiveness is lacking, avoidance of each other occurs, creating a destructive cycle in which one person feels dominated by the other.[3]

Another aspect of self-confidence is the ability to take charge and have the "illusion of control." Susan Vaughan writes about how women who take charge of their treatment for cancer and as a result have less pain, live longer, and enjoy themselves more compared to demoralized cancer patients who feel the cancer is beyond their control. The illusion of control can be a self-fulfilling prophecy.[4]

WOMEN WHO BREAK BARRIERS

Artist Marie Louise Elisabeth Vigée-Lebrun (1755-1842) became famous for her talent in portraiture (see Figure 16.1). She lost her

FIGURE 16.1. *The Artist's Brother,* oil painting by Marie Louise Elisabeth Vigée-Lebrun. Later in life her brother turned his back on her; she left the country during the French Revolution due to political connections. The Saint Louis Art Museum, Purchase.

father when she was twelve. He was also her teacher, as was often the case for female artists; they were barred from attending the Royal Academy. She was a court painter, charming and self-confident with the ability to present her portrait sitters in their best light. She kept her professional reputation during a period of political upheaval. By the age of fifteen she was earning enough money from her art to support herself, her widowed mother, and her younger brother. In Figure 16.1, she portrayed him as a young scholar. Her brother later betrayed her as France became politically divided. Vigée-Lebrun did portraits of Marie Antoinette, with whom she had developed a close relationship. This closeness made it impossible for her to remain in France once the revolution broke out, and thus began twelve years of exile in Italy, Austria, and Russia where she continued to charm the nobility. She amassed a considerable fortune from her portraits, living in comfort the rest of her eighty-seven years.[5]

In 1849, Elizabeth Blackwell became the first female physician in modern history. She was rejected by seventeen medical schools before she was finally admitted for her course of studies.

Another female physician, Gao Yaojie, was awarded the Jonathan Mann Award for Health and Human Rights in 2001 for her efforts to help poor farmers in the Henan province of China suffering from AIDS. Her government would not allow her to accept it.

In 1967, Kathrine Switzer decided to run the Boston marathon. Many years later, she appeared on the Oprah Winfrey show to tell her story and received a standing ovation; a marked contrast to the hostile reception she received at the time she ran the marathon.[6] One of her goals in running in an all-male event was to open up sports opportunities for women. On the run she was accosted by the race director, Jock Semple, who tried to remove her physically from "his" race. Switzer finished the race "unofficially." She says, "It is what you do with life's bumps that makes you the person you are." In *Running and Walking for Women Over 40: The Road to Sanity and Vanity,* Switzer encourages all women to exercise.[7] She says, "You do not run and stay mad!"[8]

Tori McClure became the first woman to row solo across the Atlantic Ocean. She accomplished this in eighty-five days with eighteen capsizes. She encourages all women to step up to all their potential. For her, rowing is a challenge. She brings heart and determination to finish what she begins in spite of the obstacles along the journey.

A number of women have used sports to deepen their spirituality and/or to push the boundaries for women. Many athletes pray before they play. Sports involves collaborating with teammates, making important decisions, overcoming obstacles, and the discipline of practicing and conditioning. The first Olympic games in Greece were seen as a spiritual event. Thomas Ryan says it well: Jesus invited people to come as free human beings and to believe that, with God's grace, their feelings of fragility, vulnerability, timidity, deep-seated fear, and insecurity could be confronted and healed.[9] More women who have pushed boundaries are those who have been a part of space missions.

Sally Ride became the first American woman to explore space. She talks about the joy she feels in being a role model for women. Ride earned a PhD in physics from Stanford in 1977. Her first flight into space was made from June 18 to 24, 1983, aboard the shuttle *Challenger*. As a flight engineer she took part in launching two communications satellites and in launching and retrieving a test satellite. The first woman in space was Valentina Tereshkova, Soviet cosmonaut, in 1963.

In 1999, Eileen Collins became the first woman shuttle commander of a space mission. Collins has said the highlights of her experience in space were (1) the experience of weightlessness and the feeling of a whole new world it creates for the person, and (2) the ability to look at the Earth seeing its fragility, and how motivated we need to be to take good care of Mother Earth. She hopes in the future many citizens can travel into space.

At the end of the twentieth century, 25 percent of NASA's astronauts were women. Nearly one-third of the agency's workforce are women and 16 percent of the scientists and engineers are women. Of course, many other women have broken barriers in traditionally male disciplines.

BLESSING

Marcia Falk

A professor of religious studies, Marcia Falk encourages us to examine the enormous power of "God-talk" to educate and shape our lives. She states, "With *n'varekh,* we reclaim our voices, take back the power of naming, addressing divinity in our own voices, using language that reflects our own experiences."[10] Encouraging women to affirm themselves into a place where they have been erased is Marcia Falk's challenge. For instance, one of the twelve blessings recited at morning prayer by a male Orthodox Jew is, "Blessed are You, HASHEM, our God, King of the universe, for not having made me a woman."[11] Blessings are powerful tools for expressing spirituality. Rabbi Meir believes that to utter 100 blessings a day is a good practice. As women write blessings, they are more likely to use gender-inclusive language. Blessings enhance life and mark both ordinary and the extraordinary events. Another example of a blessing is "Blessed are You, our God, who brings forth bread." A good exercise with this blessing is to see all the connections going into the making of bread—the hands of people kneading it, the farmer who sows the grains of wheat, and the people packaging and selling the bread. This assists us to appreciate our interdependence.

The following are some starting points for seeing blessings in our lives:

1. Life itself is holy. Seeing a rainbow or meeting a wise person can inspire blessings.
2. The sacred dimension of life is not confined to the sanctuary. From a feminist perspective, we find blessings in unexpected spaces, such as a living room or an entryway, in addition to standard spaces, such as in stained glass images and the pulpit.
3. The movement of the Holy Spirit brings about blessings. The sudden emergence of insight, laughter, or tears is not viewed as disruptive but as grace.[12]

MENTORING

For women, the role of mentoring is an ancient one. Athena, goddess of wisdom, assisted the Greeks in their quest for answers. Mentors often model behavior, traditions, characteristics, and skills we need to learn.[13]

I am a part of a parish nurse research project that demonstrates the value of mentoring. The first year, the new parish nurse is mentored by an experienced senior nurse. The foundation supporting these nurses gives credit to the experienced, talented nurses. Taking credit empowers the whole organization and creates stability for all served.

REFLECTION QUESTIONS

1. List five accomplishments. Is it easy for you to take credit, or do you possess false humility by not claiming your own accomplishments?
2. Name any work inhibitions you struggle with or negative perceptions you have regarding your abilities and talents.
3. How do you let your light shine?
4. How optimistic are you? Is the glass half full or half empty?
5. Name three areas in which imaging could assist you.
6. Name five occasions in the past three weeks when you were assertive.
7. Do you find you are able to take charge? Is the "illusion of control" at work in your life? How?
8. Name some women who have broken the barrier for the stereotype of women.
9. What are some blessings in your life this week? Try writing a blessing.
10. Name some mentors in your life. Name some men or women you have mentored. Describe these experiences.

Chapter 17

I Can Resolve Conflict

Don't compromise yourself, you are all you've got.

Betty Ford

Character contributes to beauty. It fortifies a woman as her youth fades. A mode of conduct, a standard of courage, discipline, fortitude and integrity can do a great deal to make a woman beautiful.

Jacqueline Bisset
Los Angeles Times (1974)

I am not easily frightened. Not because I am brave but because I know that I am dealing with human beings, and that I must try as hard as I can to understand everything that anyone ever does.

Elly Hillesum
In *Nonviolent Communication*

Out beyond ideas of wrong doing and right doing, there is a field. I'll meet you there.

Rumi
The Divan-i Shams

Conflict resolution skills serve women well. Character and standing up for one's beliefs as well as being open to learning from life are important aspects of conflict resolution. Five aspects of conflict resolution skills include: (1) untangling the past from the present, (2) honest expression of your thoughts and feelings, and clarification, (3) Rosenberg's model of nonviolent communication, (4) boundaries, and (5) developing an action plan.

UNTANGLING THE PAST
FROM THE PRESENT

It is well known that the rules, beliefs, and scripts that children learn in their family of origin tend to be a factor when adults are in conflicted situations. For instance, contrary to Betty Ford's philosophy, some of us have learned that we do have to compromise. We may have been taught that pleasing other people is more important than fulfilling our own needs and desires.

There is a wonderful story about a woman named Martha who went shopping for a suit. She tried on a suit of the color and style she liked, but she said to herself, "This does not fit me in the shoulders." The salesperson said, "Just drop your shoulders forward, and it will fit fine." So she slumped a bit, obediently following the suggestion of the salesperson. Then Martha said, "The pant legs are a bit long." The salesperson said, "There is a simple solution. Just bend your knees and the length of the pants will be corrected." As she walked out of the store wearing her new suit with her shoulders slumped forward and her knees bent, two other women, Jackie and Judy, were entering the shop. Judy said to Jackie, "Look at that poor deformed woman." Jackie replied, "But she is wearing a smart looking suit."

Women often are not in touch with what fits for them emotionally and spiritually. We might be content to wear ill-fitting suits of old beliefs and rules about life and ourselves,[1] such as "I have no rights"; "I am helpless"; "I am bad if I have a different opinion"; rather than "I can speak up"; "I can do something to change the situation"; and "I have a right to my thoughts and feelings."

HONEST EXPRESSION OF YOUR THOUGHTS
AND FEELINGS AND THEIR CLARIFICATION

A program called interactive focusing has a useful view of the process of conflict resolution. Janet Klein and Mary McGuire discuss the importance of being both a storyteller and a teacher of our own experiences. We can all go deep inside of ourselves and say what is there, and what does and does not fit for us. Our bodies often tell us with what we are or are not comfortable.[2]

Once you know what works for you, do more of it. This is a principle of narrative therapy. On the other hand, if something does not work, do not do it again. Try something different. Narrative therapy can assist in setting a positive tone in resolving conflict. Valuing many perspectives of reality, validating everyone's voice, and being especially sensitive to the minority voice and the oppressed parties involved in the conflict are useful tools. Hearing the language and the individual and social discourses used are important aspects as well. The therapist tries to connect to the clients with a hopeful attitude. Therapists run the risk of getting too focused on problem-saturated stories. A hope-filled therapist relates differently to clients. Sometimes a therapist needs to have hope for the client, as in cases of extreme depression.

Yapko suggests that we could all use better skills in communicating both our feelings and our thoughts. He encourages us to look at what attributions might be happening with a conflict.[3] In other words, what we think another person might be trying to communicate is often not the case. Analyzing anything we may be projecting is helpful to be aware of. We run the risk of attributing a false meaning and therefore need to check with the person more thoroughly before we draw our conclusions. People may feel depressed when they think someone is upset with them, which may cause them to withdraw from the relationship. When talking with someone you may discover that he or she is not really upset but preoccupied with another situation or problem.

MODEL FOR COMMUNICATION

Rosenberg challenges his reader to replace old patterns of defending, withdrawing, or attacking in the face of criticism with the skills of focus and understanding.[4] Focusing allows one to clarify what is being observed, felt, and needed rather than making a judgment about the other person. Rosenberg encourages deep listening to ourselves and others. He provides four elements in his nonviolent communication model:

1. We observe what others are saying and doing, noting what is or is not enriching our lives.
2. We state our feelings. Are we hurt, angry, joyful, amused?
3. We state which of our needs are connected to our feelings. For example, we might say, "I feel irritated when you take towels out of the dryer and create piles of them around the house. I have a need for some order."
4. A specific request follows, such as, "I need to have order in the house, and your folding the towels helps create the feeling that things have a place." Requests help us get what we need to help to make life more enjoyable or pleasant.

BOUNDARIES

We have the right to defend our boundaries. We are not born to be victims. Even babies can communicate discomfort, and small children, when frightened, draw back and say "no." "No" is an honest defense when there is harm. When you protect yourself from harm, you empower yourself.

A client, Jane, was sharing with me the pain she experienced as a young adolescent. She felt that she had neither protection nor monitoring when she was dating. Her mother was a heavy drinker and her father had abandoned the family, leaving Jane to fend for herself. Jane bore two children out of wedlock before she married. She wanted something different for her own daughter, Holly. After Jane married, she and her husband set a family rule that they would meet their daughter's friends and get to know them. Jane felt she was giving her daughter the protection she had never experienced. She also wanted Holly to know that she could say "no" to a pursuer.

With healthy boundaries, one has a sense of where one begins and one ends. I have my thoughts and feelings and you have yours, and they may be very different perceptions of the same reality. I do not have to feel the same way that you do, and I may think quite differently. Healthy relationships affirm differences rather than become threatened by them. Boundaries too permeable leads to enmeshment (becoming overbonded). If a mother cannot let her daughter individuate, the mother will perceive the daughter's experiences as happening to her. Individuation is the process of developing a sense of self separate from another yet staying connected to each other.

Once I worked with a family in which the mother listened to the same music as her sixteen-year-old daughter and wore similar clothes. Both the daughter and the mother were struggling to gain a sense of self. The mother had to take responsibility for her own issues. She had not had a chance to "be a teenager" and have fun, but she could not live vicariously through her daughter. It was not fair to the daughter to impose the mother's issues on her. A sign of enmeshment is speaking for the other person and responding to events as the other person would. Healthy boundaries protect without isolating, contain without imprisoning, and preserve identity while connecting with others.[5]

ACTION PLAN

The process of conflict resolution best ends with a prevention plan upon which all parties can agree. For example, a couple I have been working with has struggled with extramarital affairs in their married life together. Cathy and Tom identified several factors that played a key role in their history of having affairs. One factor was that they tended to avoid talking about anything controversial. It was difficult for them to have strong different opinions and be satisfied with their decision to disagree. Another factor was that they had never seen their parents resolving differences so they had no role models upon which to base their own resolution of conflicts. Their plan of action was:

1. To keep current with each other; taking the risk to be honest with each other became important, as did having a process to resolve problems.
2. They decided never to lie to each other; they knew firsthand the damage lying had done to their relationship.
3. They decided to let each other grieve the loss of the relationship they had once wished for and to forgive each other for their failings.
4. They decided to let go of idealized expectations of each other and replace them with realistic ones.

5. They decided that they would not stop too soon when conversing with each other. In the past they would stop when things felt heated, rather than work things through by talking and continuing to reveal where each was coming from.

REFLECTION QUESTIONS

1. As you reflect on the emotional and spiritual "suit" you received from your family of origin, ask if there are any rules or beliefs about conflict that you want to examine.
2. Can you think of a recent conflict? When you pay attention to your thoughts and feelings about it, where in your body do you experience the conflict? Is there head, back, or neck tension? Is there any wisdom that your body wants to give you about the conflict?
3. What feelings are invoked for you when there is a conflict? Can you allow yourself time to look at different plans?
4. Can you think of an attribution you assigned to a person only to find out later that you had projected your ideas onto them and that they were coming from another place entirely?
5. Can you think of a situation where you could apply Rosenberg's model of nonviolent communication? Spell out observations, feelings, needs, and requests.
6. How do you feel about making requests?
7. Can you say no? Do you think you have healthy boundaries?
8. Is there any action that you need to plan for in resolving conflict?

PART V:
WILD WOMEN STORIES

Chapter 18

Women Who Soar

Courage is the price that Life exacts for granting peace.

Amelia Earhart (1898-1937)
Courage

And the trouble is, if you don't risk anything, you risk even more.

Erica Jong (b. 1942)
How to Save Your Own Life

If you have made mistakes . . . there is always another chance for you . . . you may have a fresh start any moment you choose, for this thing we call "failure" is not the falling down, but the staying down.

Mary Pickford (1892-1979)

Soaring is what life is about. There are many inspiring women in science, sports, and in everyday life. These fourteen women who soar are profiled in this chapter: Marie Curie, Virginia Woolf, Wilma Rudolph, Sarah Chang, Artemisia Gentileschi, Margaret Thatcher, Jenny Thompson, Sheryl Swoopes, Jackie Joyner-Kersee, Gail Devers, Martha Pituch, Caryl Simon, Lillian Weger, and Jacqueline Cochran. Some of these women are famous and well known. Some are women I have known and some are known to a small circle of people, but these are all extraordinary women.

MARIE CURIE

In 1903, Marie Curie (1867-1934) shared the Nobel prize for physics with Henri Becquerel and her husband Pierre Curie for their discovery of radioactivity. In 1911, she won a second Nobel prize for chemistry for isolating the radioactive element radium. Marie Curie was the first woman to be honored with the Nobel prize.

Curie was born in 1867 in Warsaw, Poland. As a young woman she studied mathematics, chemistry, and physics in Paris. She studied at the Sorbonne in 1891, and she was the first woman to teach there. In 1914, she founded the Radium Institute in Paris and became its first director. When World War I broke out, Marie Curie thought X rays would help locate the bullet wounds and facilitate surgery. She designed portable X-ray machines to bring to the wounded so they would not have to be moved, and she trained 150 female attendants to assist the wounded. Her visits to the hospitals of the Red Cross convinced her of the need for trained staff. Women from a variety of backgrounds—army nurses, Red Cross nurses, and young women with a solid education—were trained by her for six weeks and then sent to radiology posts around the country to work as X-ray technicians.[1]

VIRGINIA WOOLF

A brilliant British essayist, novelist, and critic, Virginia Woolf (1882-1941) was an artistic genius of the twentieth century. As is characteristic of many celebrated artistic people, she struggled with depression.

Woolf's writing explores themes of time, memory, and people's inner consciousness. *Mrs. Dalloway* (1925) is a good example of the consciousness of several people during the course of a day with the emphasis on exploring both the external and internal sense of time. It is remarkable in its humanity and depth of perception. She emphasizes patterns of consciousness rather than sequences of events. Woolf used the stream of consciousness technique. Her plots are generated by the inner lives of her characters. Her writing is rich in the use of symbolism, imagery, and metaphor.

Woolf saw women as intuitive, close to the core of things, and liberating the masculine intellect from enslavement to abstract concepts.

In 1917 the Woolfs founded Hogarth Press, which published early works of T. S. Eliot and Sigmund Freud. In addition, most of Virginia's works were published by Hogarth.[2]

From the time of her mother's death in 1895, Virginia Woolf suffered from bipolar disorder. Her life ended tragically with suicide; she drowned herself in a river. One interpretation of her suicide is that she was overcome by the horrors of World War II. She may never have known how great a contribution she made to the world and to women in particular.

WILMA RUDOLPH

Wilma Rudolph (1940-1994) was the twentieth of twenty-two children in the segregated South. Partially paralyzed by polio, her strong will and determination helped her to walk and then run to win three Olympic gold medals in track and field. She was also a fine basketball player and set a state record in Tennessee by scoring 803 points in twenty-five games.

Her life and athletic career were documented in *Wilma,* a 1977 television movie. In 1980 Rudolph was named to the Black Sports Hall of Fame, and she was given the honor of lighting the torch to open the 1987 Pan American Games.

She is remembered as one of America's greatest female athletes and is highlighted in one volume of the ten-volume video set *American Women of Achievement.*[3]

SARAH CHANG

Violinist Sarah Chang (b. 1981) is recognized as one of the world's most captivating and gifted artists. In 1999, she received the Avery Fisher Career Grant, one of the most prestigious awards given to instrumentalists. Her notable recital engagements include her Carnegie Hall debut in November 1997 and performances at the Kennedy Center in Washington, DC, Orchestra Hall in Chicago, Symphony Hall in Boston, the Barbican Centre in London, the Philharmonie in Berlin, and the Concertgebouw in Amsterdam.

Born in Philadelphia, Sarah Chang began her violin studies when she was four years old. By the time she was five, she had already performed with several orchestras. She graduated from the precollege program at the Juillard School. She communicates confidence with her body and remarkable rhythm and beauty in her violin playing.

ARTEMISIA GENTILESCHI

Artemisia Gentileschi (1593-1652) was the quintessential female painter of the Baroque era. Artists of this period often used religious and mythological themes, featuring a strong contrast between lightness and darkness.[4] The heroine Danaë (see Figure 18.1) is visited by the god Zeus, who has transformed himself into a shower of golden

FIGURE 18.1. "Danaë," oil painting by Artemisia Gentileschi in 1612. Saint Louis Art Museum, Museum Funds, by exchange, gift of Edward Mallinckrodt, Sydney M. Shoenberg Sr., Horace Morison, Mrs. Florence E. Bing, Morton D. May in honor of Perry T. Rathbone, James Lee Johnson, Oscar Johnson, Fredonia J. Moss, Mrs. Arthur Drefs, Mrs. W. Welles Hoyt, Mr. J. Lionberger Davis, Jacob M. Heimann, Virginia Linn Bullock in memory of her husband George Benbow Bullock, C. Wickham Moore, Mrs. Lyda D'Oench Turley and Miss Elizabeth F. D'Oench and J. Harold Pettus, by exchange; and bequests of Mr. Alfred Keller and Cora E. Ludwig, by exchange.

coins in the painting by Gentileschi. The artist interprets the narrative in a bold and dramatic way—Danaë does not await her visitor; the contact between earthly princess and divine lover has already occurred.

Only since the twentieth century have we seen women's art decorating the walls of art museums.

MARGARET THATCHER

In 1979, Margaret Thatcher became England's first female prime minister. A champion of free minds, she led with courage and hope. In an interview for a women's leadership project, she said that being a woman was an asset. She was used to getting a lot done in one day; she brought organization and decisiveness to the position. Being sensitive, she said, is out of the question because it will diminish your power to lead. She had a practice of never reading articles in the paper criticizing her. She believes the important aspects of leadership are acting on principles and making up one's own mind and not following the crowd, but rather getting the crowd to follow you through your ability to get your point across. Her leadership style embraces the belief that she must do the right thing.[5]

Born in 1925 as Margaret Hilda Roberts, she worked her way to Oxford and received degrees in chemistry and law. Her fascination with politics led her into parliament at the age of thirty-four. Her quick mind and tongue served her well.

In 1992, she was awarded the title of Baroness Thatcher of Kesteven and now holds a seat in the House of Lords.

JENNY THOMPSON

The story of Jenny Thompson, five-time swimming Olympic gold medalist, is an amazing one. Although she can now say, "Swimming to me is like brushing my teeth," she also knows about overcoming adversity.[6] She broke her arm in 1994 before the Olympics and had surgery, but she still swam in the Olympics, she says, "for the fun of it." She knew her chances to medal would be nearly zero because of the recent surgery. She understands the importance of enjoying the sport, not just the act of competing. Jenny has a balanced attitude toward swimming; she knows her priorities—it is not just about winning. She has said that she resents society's attitude that strong athletic women are not acceptable. She had a boyfriend who liked her but not her strong arms. She was able to affirm herself through statements such as "My arms are what make me swim fast and they are an important part of who I am." She keeps a rigorous training schedule for competitions and is managing to complete her dream of finishing medical school.

SHERYL SWOOPES

Sheryl Swoopes, Olympic gold medalist in basketball, says she learned determination from her mother, who worked three jobs in order to raise her children. Sheryl's two older brothers did not like the fact that she played basketball. When they told her it was a boys' game, it made her even more determined to play and to believe in her own ability to do so. To this day she says it bothers her to hear fathers tell their daughters that they should not play basketball—that they should be cheerleaders or piano players instead. She believes you can play basketball and maintain your femininity.

JACKIE JOYNER-KERSEE

Christina Lessa wrote that Jackie Joyner-Kersee, world and Olympic record holder for the heptathlon, is unique because her husband Bob Kersee is her coach.[7] They respect each other and when they are on the field they laugh and have fun. Joyner-Kersee overcame her biggest physical hurdle, asthma. She said, "I am allergic to grass and pollen. . . . I started to think of my asthma as part of my training . . . " She began to see herself as controlling the asthma rather than letting the asthma control her.

GAIL DEVERS

Gail Devers, two-time Olympic gold medalist and holder of eleven 100-meter championship titles, is a source of support to Jackie Joyner-

Kersee; they offer each other encouragement through their ups and downs. Gail and Jackie try to stay as fit as possible without endangering their health. In 1988, Gail experienced changes in her health: weight fluctuations, fainting spells, and increased menstrual bleeding. Graves' disease (a rare form of hyperthyroidism) interfered with her running career and forced her to stop. To treat the disease she was battling, she went through radiation treatments and more of her thyroid was treated than was necessary. Her feet began to swell and ooze; her skin cracked and bled. She had to be carried to the bathroom. Her radiation therapy was changed and in a month she was able to walk again. However, her resourcefulness won out. Two months later she was hurdling, and three months later she won the silver medal in the 1991 World Championships in Tokyo. She has a rare spiritual strength. She said, "If I keep the faith, nothing bad can happen." And before every race she recites Luke 11:9, "Ask and you will receive; Seek and you shall find; Knock and it shall be opened to you."[8]

MARTHA PITUCH

When I was a graduate student at the University of Michigan in 1969, Martha Pituch was my advisor. She was a wonderful mentor to me. She told me that public health nursing was about the "laying on of the heart." She not only spoke the words but lived this philosophy. She assisted me in organizing a group for single pregnant teenagers and guided me to accompany these young teens rather than impose a "program" on them. She also supervised my practicum with the Pittsburgh Health Department the summer before I graduated. She was a lot of fun. I still remember taking the cable car with her and another student. Martha was afraid of heights, but she took the car ride up Mount Washington anyway. We had a great view of the city as we had dinner and shared our new ideas about preventive health care. After she left the University of Michigan, she worked with the homeless population in Toledo, Ohio. We have kept in touch for thirty-one years. She recently retired from teaching at the university level and is involved in her second career as an artist.

Through my experience with Martha, I realize how important the mentoring relationship is. I recently received a card from one of my students, and I attribute my success with students to Martha. The card said:

> I want to extend my gratitude to you for your sitting on my Comprehensives Committee. In addition, I would like to say thanks for your teaching and supervision. You have contributed greatly to my formation!

CARYL SIMON

Caryl Simon is a sixty-four-year-old Saint Louis swimmer and coach who competes at the National Senior Olympic Games. She is an inspiration to me. When I asked her how long she thinks she will continue to compete in the Senior Olympics, she said, "Right now the highest age category is ninety to ninety-five years old, and I think I ought to create a new one, ninety-five to one hundred years old." She playfully said, "Don't you think so too?"[9]

Caryl sees the pool as a safe place. When she coaches, she says, "No injuries in the pool." She focuses on good technique and relates to her trainees with nurturance and interest. One woman in the swim club said, "Where was she when God was handing out mothers? I wish I had her as my mom."

Caryl shared with me her enthusiasm for being a grandmother. She said:

> My daughter and her husband went away for a weekend and I was fortunate to babysit little Jason for the weekend. I loved everything about the experience, the crib, the baby food, the high chair, and the love Jason brings to me, it was such a joy for me.[10]

LILLIAN WEGER

Lillian Weger (1934-1999) was my teacher when I was working on my doctorate. Her knowledge of therapy was rich, and I loved it when she taught from her clinical experience. I treasure the time I had with her more informally at my home with other colleagues, and at breakfast meetings just to "shoot the breeze." We talked about travel and family gatherings that were a part of our lives. Lillian died at the age of sixty-five. During the last year of her life she was diagnosed with stomach cancer. Working until her death, she continued to supervise therapists, and teach and see clients. She amazed all who knew her. She modeled a sense of female authority. Perhaps this trait was best described by Dale Kuhn at her memorial service. Although he was in fact her boss, he felt that Lillian had no boss. A source of nurturance and wisdom to many, she was nicknamed "Earth Mother." She had a poetic side; one of her many creative expressions was a Christmas reflection she penned in 1995, three and a half years before her death. This excerpt describes a holy experience she shared with other travelers to the coast of Spain, as they watched a giant green sea turtle lay its eggs. A full text of the reflection was passed out at her memorial service to all who attended.

> With singular purpose she confidently found a compatible place, burrowed into the bush, and began to scoop out her cradle. We were permitted to form an arc behind her vigorous hind feet. Our hope and intention infused her labor. After almost an hour she was ready and the exquisitely shaped inflated hosts began to fill her cup. There was enough for our entire congregation. When she had honored her contract with God, she provided her promise kept with a generous cover. We gratefully waited until her work was complete.[11]

JACQUELINE COCHRAN

Jacqueline Cochran literally did soar. Cochran was a pilot in World War II. She was the visionary behind WASP (Women Air Force Service Pilots). She had been the winner of seventeen world flying records and persuaded Hap Arnold, chief of the Army Air Force, to start the program. Between 1942 and 1944, 1,000 women served to ferry planes and cargo to free men for combat. They trained in Sweetwater, Texas, the only all-female base in U.S. history. These women expanded their roles in aviation to be test pilots and flight instructors. Some of the Air Force's male pilots saw no role for female pilots, but Jacqueline Cochran was a good political leader, using her influence to demonstrate the value of female pilots. She had an office in the Pentagon and was named director of women pilots on August 5, 1943.[12]

Cochran grew up in poverty in Florida. Her birth name was Bessie Mae Pittman. One day she decided to pick a new name out of the phone book and thus began a fresh journey. She says, "I may have been born in a hovel, but I was determined to travel with the wind and the stars."[13] Enid Shomer wrote *Stars at Noon: Poems from the Life of Jacqueline Cochran.* Shomer's poems reflect the woman pilot's life and describe her as "Outspoken and ambitious, Cochran remained active in aviation until she was sixty, ran for Congress, and generally placed herself in the path of history in a life she described as a 'passage from sawdust to stardust.' She was a devout Catholic."[14]

Heroines inspire growth. Several women have been presented in this chapter to encourage and inspire readers to reflect on themselves and on other women who are sources of hope and courage.

REFLECTION QUESTIONS

1. Name three talents you have.
2. Describe how you excel in using your talents.
3. How do you express creativity and intuition?
4. Name three obstacles you have come across in exercising your talents.
5. Describe how you overcame these obstacles.
6. Name three mentors you have had on your journey.
7. Are you mentoring others now? Describe.
8. Name three women who inspire you and why.
9. Visit an art museum and take note of the works of women artists. Describe your findings.
10. Are there any new roles in which you would like to see women soar (for example, president of the United States, stronger leadership roles in churches, synagogues, and mosques)?

Chapter 19

Be True to Yourself

Most mothers are instinctive philosophers.

Harriet Beecher Stowe

Protocol is not there to dictate to you. It's there to help you. You have to have the courage and security to do it your way.

Barbara Bush

It is not fair to ask others what you are not willing to do yourself.

Eleanor Roosevelt

CHINA'S MYTH: MULAN

I believe it is important to find one's authentic self, which is a search that happens from deep within. Walt Disney's *Mulan* illustrates this point.[1] The character Mulan goes through the painful process of disappointing her family because their expectations for her do not fit where she wants to be in her life. To be attractive to her potential husband, Mulan visits a matchmaker who wants her to have a tiny waist and be the silent type. Mulan, on the other hand, does not enjoy having a white-painted face and keeping quiet. The heroine finds her mission in life by taking her father's place in the military and eventually becomes a savior figure for her country. Along the way, she disgraces her family by leaving behind the traditional female role of being a wife and chooses instead the role of warrior. Her identity is hidden until she is wounded.

When the troops discover she is a woman, they abandon her even though she previously saved their lives. Mulan undergoes a transformation from a shy, sweet girl to a warrior and a heroine. This story communicates a new gender awareness that has been missing from past animated films, such as *Beauty and the Beast* (1991) and *Aladdin* (1992), in which the mother figures are missing. Chinese history suggests that Mulan's character has a basis in fact.

Just as Mulan's journey and struggles helped her find her true self, so do our own struggles and experiences. Examining the lives of women who have gone before us can also help us on our journey.

HERSTORY

Today women have opportunities afforded them that were rarely available to women in the past. Going to medical school was not an option for my grandmother, but it is an option for female college students today. Alice Gertrude Bryant (1862-1942) became one of the first two women admitted to the American College of Surgeons in 1914. Bryant graduated from Vassar College in 1885 and from the Women's Medical College of the New York Infirmary in 1890. She invented the tongue depressor and the tonsil separator (a device used by surgeons to separate the tonsils from the tonsil bed). Harriot Kezia Hunt (1805-1875) was the first woman to practice medicine in the United States (1835). She taught school from 1827 to 1833, then in 1833 studied anatomy and physiology with a physician. In 1835 she and her sister set up a medical practice that was mainly for women and children. Hunt applied repeatedly to Harvard Medical School. In 1850 she was accepted, the same year black students were admitted for the first time. Male students rioted in protest; Hunt was forced to withdraw.[2] She organized the Ladies' Physiology Society in 1843 and gave lectures. In 1853 she was awarded an honorary degree from the Female Medical College of Pennsylvania.

Alice Hamilton, MD (1869-1970):
Industrial Toxicology Pioneer

A pioneer in industrial toxicology, Alice Hamilton studied poisonous substances in the workplace. A social activist, she lived at the Hull House, a settlement house that gave assistance to the poor in Chicago. She was encouraged by Jane Addams and other reformers to apply her knowledge to current social problems. Alice Hamilton supported social causes such as the enactment of work compensation laws and the withdrawal of troops during the Vietnam War.

In 1919 Hamilton became the first female faculty member of Harvard University. Her books include *Industrial Poisons in the United States* (1925) and *Industrial Toxicology* (1934).[3] Although she was treated shabbily, and excluded from the faculty club and the commencement procession, her research helped promote safety in the workplace. Her work with the poisons she studied had beneficial consequences on the health of workers in many different industries—munitions and lead and copper mining, to name a few.

CURRENT NARRATIVES

Wilma Mankiller: First Woman Tribal Chief

In a historic tribal election in July 1987, Wilma Mankiller became the first female tribal leader of the Cherokee Indians of Oklahoma. The Cherokee Indians represent the second largest tribe in the United States, second only to the Navajo. At first, people were skeptical and hostile about a woman being their leader. Her tires were slashed and she received death threats. Not only did she gradually win acceptance, but she was so successful in her first term that she was elected for two additional terms.

Proud Deer interviewed Wilma Mankiller for the *Saint Louis Times*. He reports:

> Overcoming stereotypical views about her gender has been just a small part of Wilma Mankiller's campaign. Perhaps more significant is the battle to overcome antiquated views of who Native American people are. "The big-time media used to call" when she first became chief, she explained, "and they would say, 'Will you dress in your traditional outfit?' And I really felt like saying, 'When you call up the President, do you ask him to dress like a pilgrim?'"[4]

Her job as chief was similar to being head of state. She governed 140,000 people and had an annual budget of $75 million with 1,200 employees. In 1991, she won the election for chief by an 80 percent majority and was reelected for four more years (her third term).

In 1995, Wilma Mankiller chose not to run for a fourth term as principal chief. That same year, she received a Chubb Fellowship from Yale University. Currently she is writing her autobiography and compiling a collection of interviews with Native American women.[5] She writes about her Cherokee name in her memoir:

> As I matured, I learned that *Mankiller* could be spelled different ways and was a coveted war name. One version is the literal *Asgaya,* meaning "man" combined with the personal name suffix *dihi,* or killer. Another is *Outacity*—an honorary title which also means "Man-killer."

> There were times . . . when I had to put up with a lot of teasing . . . The name Mankiller carries with it a lot of history. It is a strong name. I am proud of my name—very proud. And I am proud of the long line of men and women who have been called Mankiller. I hope to honor my ancestors by keeping the name alive.[6]

Mankiller has been able to trace the name back four generations and says it is similar to calling someone captain or major. Wilma Mankiller researched her identity; she grew in understanding her roots. She is an example of a minority woman leader who communicates her story and herself with authenticity.

Mary Robinson: First Female Leader of Ireland (1990)

Mary Robinson used her gifts as a woman. An old pattern of thinking among the Irish included a resentment that many had left Ireland to live in other countries; she was able to use this pattern to promote a sense of networking. The Clinton-appointed U.S. ambassador to Ireland, Jean Kennedy Smith, quoted President Robinson's 1995 address to the United Nations and referred to Robinson's inspiration for the 70 million Irish abroad: "Irishness is not simply territorial . . . 'the men and women of our diaspora represent not simply a series of departures and losses' but 'a precious reflection of our growth and change.'"[7] She saw that Ireland had allies around the world; many people who had Irish roots could connect with the desire of many to help the economy in Ireland.[8] For instance, there is a trend for universities to start Irish studies programs, influenced by Mary Robinson's networking approach. This affords the opportunity to bring speakers from Ireland to educate and influence students and faculty.

Mary Robinson believed that women needed to trust their experience, to be true to themselves. Because women are minorities themselves they often understand those who are outcasts or underdogs. This compassion can be used in public service and in many vocational choices. She often implored the nations of the world to stand up to their duty to all humankind, to act on the reality that we are one human family. This truth became ritualized by keeping a light shining in the window of one's home—the famous low-watt bulb for the diaspora. Light comes out of darkness.

CLINICAL NARRATIVE

Misty came with her husband, Bill, for marriage therapy. Misty talked about some of her fears: "It seems so stupid to feel fear when Bill is out of town." When she would hear noises in the basement, she would call him and say, "I need to check the basement. Stay on the phone with me. I need to go and make sure no one is down there." I tried to reassure Misty that her fears were not stupid, that they were real for her; it was important to talk further about the fears so we could understand them together. Bill also told her to trust her experience.

In addition to owning her fears, Misty was wondering what she wanted to do with her career. She was working in the communications field but was not happy. She decided to become a consultant. Once she had the courage to make the change, she found she was happier. As Misty got in touch with her dreams, her life changed for the better. Communication improved between Misty and Bill as they stopped avoiding what they were not satisfied with and instead could be themselves with each other.

In my experience, discounting feelings and experiences is a common theme with women. Such messages as, "Don't cry; be a big girl or boy!" and "You should not feel scared" remain with people until they realize those messages no longer work for them and perhaps never did. Our feelings need affirmation. Always, I try to encourage truthfulness in the session.

Another client, Sue, is in therapy for an eating disorder. We worked together on her feeling she needed to look a certain way. She saw herself as fat even though she was skeletal in appearance when she began therapy. As she claimed more of her true self, she became less obsessed about her weight.

Looking at the icons that are held up for women and girls to emulate in our culture throws light on the tension women feel. Models are very thin; they weigh 23 percent less than the average woman. Digital imaging can create icons or images of women whose faces and bodies are flawless. (For further discussion see Chapter 10.)

REFLECTION QUESTIONS

1. How would you describe your mission in life?
2. List ten things you would love to do or are now doing that you enjoy.
3. What are some obstacles you have experienced along the way to being true to yourself?
4. Have you ever been criticized for being a woman? Describe.
5. Name three women you admire for their ability to be true to themselves.
6. Do you accept your feelings and experiences?
7. What are your roots? How has your personal history influenced you?
8. Make a collage of images of women from magazines. Write a commentary on the ideal of beauty that is created and the real beauty that is present in the women you know. What are the differences you notice between the ideal and the real?
9. What pressures are created for women from the use of such icons?
10. Rent a Disney movie and trace the role of women and girls. Do the stories inspire you or negate you? Analyze the messages conveyed to girls throughout the story.

Chapter 20

Surviving to Thriving

One's philosophy is not best expressed in words, it is expressed in the choices one makes. . . . In the long run we shape our lives and we shape ourselves. . . . And the choices we make are ultimately our responsibility.

Eleanor Roosevelt

Composing a life involves a continual reimaging of the future and reinterpretation of the past to give meaning to the present.

Mary Catherine Bateson
Composing a Life

The Lord speaks of peace to the people.

Psalm 85:8

Good health is not the elimination of disease, but falling in love with the poignancy of being alive.

Joan Iten Sutherland

In spite of significant social advances in balancing gender roles, women and girls continue to labor under the burden of constricting messages. Eleanor Roosevelt challenges us to make wise choices as she did. She chose to stand for civil rights, resigning from the board of the American Daughters of the Revolution when Marian Anderson was banned from singing in Washington, DC, because of the color of her skin. Wise choices bring meaning, peace, and vitality.

The reflective process of narrative therapy (see Preface) can assist in ameliorating the destructive messages aimed at women. Narrative approaches involve identifying restrictive processes and replacing those messages with constructive ones. This movement can be accelerated by examining some constricting messages (such as, "I am helpless," "I have no voice," "I am nobody") and constructive messages (such as, "I have a voice," "I can take credit," "I can resolve conflict," and "I have a divine herstory"). In addition to understanding narrative approaches, this chapter looks at resiliency, a search for meaning, the role of play for both children and adults, and faith.

NARRATIVE APPROACHES TO THRIVING

Narrative therapy influences thinking regarding growth and inspires positive change. The therapeutic course takes into account the effect of discourse practices that constitute the self. Therapy then becomes the practice of externalizing these stories in favor of other alternative and/or preferred self stories, such as changing, "I am deficient" to "I have strengths I can use today." These narratives may have been in existence already, but have been subordinated to the dominant story. This approach to therapy does not view the person as the problem but rather the internalization of certain ideas about the self that circulate in a given culture.

Progress toward facilitating messages involves being aware of the constricting messages. This book has been about the growing awareness of these scripts and therefore the movement from surviving life events to thriving each day. Thriving means that we need to strengthen our use of resiliency skills.

RESILIENCE

Walsh gives a model for resiliency in families:

1. *The shared construction of crisis experience.* Walsh points out the importance of meaning given to a crisis. Difficult things become easier to bear when there is clarity regarding the meaning. For example, if a family going through a divorce talks about their situation openly, a difficult reality becomes easier to bear. When the divorcing couple is able to say, "This is our joint story, and this is the meaning we give to the crisis," the transition can be smoother.

2. *A sense of coherence.* One assumes the stress-producing nature of the human environment, our "normal" state, is disorder and chaos rather than stability and homeostasis. A sense of coherence includes the ability to clarify the nature of problems so that they seem ordered, predictable, and explicable. Demands are believed to be manageable by mobilizing useful resources that include relational resources. In other words, to normalize a crisis can be useful for a distressed family.

3. *The ability to seek help when necessary.* Studies of highly resilient people have found that this population possesses the ability to reach out for help when it is needed. Turning to kin, to social and religious support systems, and to professionals is an important aspect of recovery from the crisis.

4. *Causal and explanatory beliefs.* In many cultures, people turn to respected shamans or faith healers to confirm beliefs they are not at fault for their problems. Problems often arise from many variables rather than one cause.

5. *Future expectations and fears.* In healthy families there is an acceptance of human limitation and understanding that no one is completely helpless or omnipotent in any situation. Three self-defeating attitudes are
   a. minimizing or underestimating strengths,
   b. magnifying or exaggerating the seriousness of each mistake, and
   c. "catastrophizing" or expecting total disaster.[1]

SEARCH FOR MEANING

Lelwica believes the root cause of eating disorders for women is unmet spiritual longings.[2] She demonstrates that the meaning given to women in the Garden of Eden, "Eve's story," holds false messages. In the story, sin is unleashed on earth by the act of a woman eating. This story in Genesis has been used for centuries to justify women's subordination to men, their guilt about eating, and their constricted roles of cleaning, cooking, and bearing children. Some say Eve must give up a sense of agency and a feeling of peace about her own body. This view of female sin obscures another interpretation of "salvation." The Latin word *salve* means "good health." There is no garden to return to, but we are all on a journey in search of healing in our lives.

Two women poets come to mind who found meaning in the midst of tragedy. Poetry seems to be a source of healing for them. One is Mary Dorcey, professor at Trinity College in Dublin, Ireland. The other is Elizabeth Bishop who was the first woman and American to receive the Neustadt prize for literature. Dorcey's poems stem from her experience of watching her mother suffer from Alzheimer's disease. Poems such as "Frost" and "Grist to the Mill" become opportunities for her as a writer to express the belief that a writer can use everything for inspiration—from the aging of parents to wiping an elderly mother's chin with a napkin at the nursing home. Both poets use loss as inspiration.[3] Bishop lost her parents at an early age and was raised by extended family, first by her maternal grandparents in Nova Scotia and then by her father's family in Boston. She was very happy living with her maternal grandparents and felt great loss when she had to leave them. Her poems "Moose" and "One Art" speak of moving on to new places, saying good-bye, and the spiritual experiences that sustain us through losses.[4]

PLAY

The importance of play is evident for children but it also contributes to a sense of thriving when we are adults. Sometimes I will ask my students who are studying play as a part of family therapy to reflect on their feelings regarding play when they were children. What was communicated when you were told as a child to "Go out and play?" Did it mean "Go and enjoy yourself"? Or was it "Get lost; I am tired. Stop bothering me"?

Many couples I work with do better if they can make a "date" with each other. They have become too serious and need to have some fun together. Life is more enjoyable when we can plan time to go to a play or attend a couples cooking class—do something that we have been wanting to do but never find the time to accomplish.

I am often amazed at cancer survivors who have built play and/or athletics into their lives and who inspire all who watch their competitive events. Lance Armstrong, who recently won the Tour de France again, overcame testicular cancer. While participating in a winter walk called the "Snowball Series," I met a woman who had walked several marathons as a way to cope with breast cancer and get her mind off the chemotherapy and radiation treatments.

Play is a way that we can find and better understand ourselves. Poet e. e. cummings expresses the heart of play:

> maggie and milly and molly and may
> went down to the beach(to play one day)
> For whatever we lose(like a you or a me)
> it's always ourselves we find in the sea

It is play in the sea that gives each girl the opportunity to discover something about herself.[5]

FAITH

While working with clients and we reach a block in our progress, I might ask, "What do you think God would tell you about this dilemma?" I find bringing God into the conversation can be a helpful intervention when I am working with people who are faithful. Faith can help motivate families to change. I find this to be especially true in working with couples for whom forgiveness and making repairs in the relationship is a continuous process.

Anne Grizzle writes how faith is a rich resource to offer hope in dark hours and how support from a faith community in the process of change and transition is valuable.[6]

Jim Wallis writes, "To change the world, our community, we first have to understand it. . . . We have to cross the barriers that divide people."[7] He encourages the simple act of getting out of the house. This is the beginning of a spiritual journey: facing the challenges this stepping out brings and finding the resources available to you.

REFLECTION QUESTIONS

1. What choices have you made in the last month that you were proud of?
2. List constricting messages operating in your life. List facilitating beliefs that are operating.

3. How have you experienced resiliency in the past three months?
4. What role does healing play in your life? Describe an area that needs healing, such as a relationship.
5. Write a poem or a song from an experience that is meaningful to you.
6. What comes to mind when you were a child and you were told to go out and play?
7. If you are married, do you continue to have dates with your partner?
8. Do you plan creativity dates? (See Chapter 24.)
9. List five things that would increase your sense of play and do one this week.
10. How is faith a resource to you in times of struggle?
11. Name some ways you could get out of the house more and increase your understanding of people different from yourself.

Chapter 21

Mind-Body Connection

My face is a mask I order to say nothing
About the fragile feelings hiding in my soul.

Mohawk poem
In *The Body Speaks*

When you neglect the basics of life, such as eating a good meal, taking a brisk walk, getting touched enough, or spending time in meaningful conversation, your brain chemistry suffers.

Joan Borysenko
Inner Peace for Busy People

An unholy relationship is based on differences, where each one thinks the other has what she has not. . . . A holy relationship starts from a different premise. Each one has looked within and seen no lack.

A Course in Miracles

Holistic approaches are making progress and being accepted by health care professionals and patients. The previous quotes illustrate the power of masked emotions, an unfocused mind, and the treasure of finding one's center and being at home there.

In Chapter 20 we saw the importance of the role of resiliency and play as we strive to thrive in life. This chapter examines the following mind-body topics:

1. The placebo effect
2. The body as friend—giving us messages daily
3. Discovering the meaning of our experience

4. Risking doing something new
5. Reflection questions and exercises to assist in mind-body awareness—focusing and meditation

The body is the physical structure and the material organism of an individual, animal, or plant. Sometimes it is used to describe substance, such as "the wine has body." There are over forty meanings listed in the dictionary for the word *mind*. It is the element that reasons, thinks, feels, wills, perceives, and judges. In my profession, we refer to the mind as the totality of conscious and unconscious mental processes. Other definitions are attention, assurance, or noticing. One of the goals of this chapter is to know what your own thoughts and feelings are and how they affect your body. Let us rewrite the Mohawk poem quoted in the opening of the chapter: "My face is unmasked and I allow my feelings to come out of hiding."

PLACEBO EFFECT

At Harvard, I heard a series of lectures titled, "Spirituality and Healing." It brought home to me the power of our internal belief system. In a study, one group of patients was placed on some medication to treat cancer, and the other group of patients was given a sugar pill (placebo). A patient taking the sugar pill (who did not know which he was on) began to feel better. He had been bedridden, but after taking the pill he began to walk around again. His family was surprised by this miracle drug. After the completion of the study, however, the man was told he was receiving only a placebo. He died the following day.[1]

A recent study published in the *Journal of the American Medical Association* discusses both the effectiveness of a drug called Venlafine Extended-Release (XR) capsules and the placebo effect. In the study, 69 percent or more of the patients treated with Venlafine XR (Effexor XR) showed improvement in symptoms of general anxiety disorder for up to six months compared to 42 percent to 46 percent given a placebo.[2] Up to 46 percent of the population improving with just the placebo illustrates the power a person's belief system can have upon the outcome of the treatment.

Consider your own beliefs about the body and healing. Later in this chapter I will provide some exercises in this area. I strongly recommend you complete the questions about your experience.

BODY AS FRIEND

Our bodies are indeed good friends to us. As a therapist I understand the importance of this concept. I see people rejecting their bodies. "If only this headache would go away," a client said to me recently. In many ways, the headache is the body speaking. As the client and I talked about this symptom we determined together what the body was saying: "You are trying to do too much. It makes sense to say no and set some limits." Poor physical health can be the result of poor emotional health.

I often hear stories of health care staff failing to listen to patients. A friend of mine often dropped her hair brush and experienced blurred vision—symptoms that she was having a stroke. However, when she went to the emergency room, the stroke was not diagnosed and she was sent home with medication for a headache. Her health worsened and she was finally admitted to the hospital for the treatment she needed. She was listening to her body, but the staff attending her were not; had they listened, her rehabilitation time could have been cut in half.

I once found a lump in my breast that turned out to be an infection. At the time, I was caring for my elderly mother with little support from other family members. I saw a relationship between this infection and a lack of emotional and physical support. However, my physician was extremely supportive, and I believe my body was telling me to find additional support. Hiring home health aides and finding a physician who would see my mom at home was a blessing and a support.

Cultural messages and alternatives regarding women's bodies are impoverished. Laura Fraser discusses how dieting has become a religion. She writes of diet gurus who become father confessors; of bathroom scales that become shrines the faithful turn to daily for affirming their self-worth. In place of the idea of the body as a friend, an adversarial relationship is suggested. Controlling weight is an obsession in our culture, especially for women. Fraser discusses how she was placed on a diet at age five. Are we bound by inner corsets in our thinking about our bodies?[3] In addition to respect for the body, physical movement should be appreciated.

Movement can help free the body and the mind. Studies now show that exercise can alleviate anxiety and depression.[4] Phil Jackson discusses the connection between awareness and movement. Basketball assisted him in becoming more aware. If your mind wanders momentarily on the court, opportunities to score may be lost, which adds to the possibility of the team losing the game.[5]

One of the best theologies of the body was written by Toni Morrison in her novel *Beloved:*

> Love your hands! Love them. Raise them up and kiss them. Touch others with them, pat them together, stroke them on your face 'cause they don't love that either. *You* got to love it, *you!* And no they ain't in love with your mouth.[6]

DISCOVER MEANING IN LIFE

Discovering meaning in life is energizing. Julia Cameron writes of Martin Ritt's philosophy of film directing in *The Vein of Gold: A Journey to Your Creative Heart:*

> All actors have a certain territory, a certain range, they were born to play. I call that range their "vein of gold." If you cast that actor within that vein, he will always give you a brilliant performance.[7]

I think of Susan Sarandon as having been born to act in *Dead Man Walking* (1995) and *Lorenzo's Oil* (1993). She has a gift for portraying dedication to and passion about a cause. Each of us has a vein of gold, and gifts only we as individuals can share. When we find those gifts and use them, we often experience joy.

Joan Borysenko, in *The Power of the Mind to Heal,* discusses the role joy plays in keeping the immune system healthy and how endorphins are released into the body. She also points out that anxiety and stress can cause tension in our bodies.[8]

RISK DOING SOMETHING NEW

Gabrielle Roth said in *Maps to Ecstasy,* "Healing is a journey. It involves stepping out of our habitual roles, our conventional scripts, and improvising a dancing path."[9] Ingerman writes about the common elements of shamanism which include induction into the shamanic state of consciousness through drumming, entry into nonordinary reality through an opening in the earth, work with power animals and spirit helpers, exploration of nonordinary worlds, and practices for bringing back healing information for oneself and one's community.[10]

Many art museums hold public lecture series. In St. Louis, for instance, lectures are held twice a week; they are wonderful.

Our imagination is often opened by art, making room in our psyche for something new. Trying something new may be as simple as breaking a routine.

- Find a new way to work/school
- Make more time for yourself
- Take a class
- Read a good book
- Volunteer for a cause you support
- Attend a concert or visit the zoo
- Meet new people who challenge you
- Set aside time to meditate or reflect
- Dance
- Play music

These are a few suggestions that can stretch our daily perceptions and make mind-body awareness come alive.

REFLECTION QUESTIONS

1. List five of your favorite movies. Ask yourself what is it that you like about them. Are there common themes? For example, I love the movie *Little Women;* the loving and tender relationships among the girls is heartwarming to me.

2. Write morning pages (see Chapter 24) about your feelings and thoughts. This is an important step toward finding your inner guidance. Often we respond to others' expectations of us and are not conscious of what we want and desire for ourselves. When women accommodate, then they become angry about and resentful of their powerless position. We can negotiate when we are in touch with what we think, feel, and need and when we know which requests would be helpful to make.

3. List five of your favorite pieces of music. Play them and let the music enter your mind and body. Music can be healing. "Ashgrove" (an ancient Welsh tune) and "Snow Blind" (composed by Walt Michaels) are two of my favorite pieces to play on the hammered dulcimer.

4. How is movement and exercise a part of your life? Do you notice mental changes when you exercise? Describe them.

5. Schedule some creativity dates for yourself to nourish your imagination. For example, I went to a costume store that I would not ordinarily visit and ended up finding a Halloween outfit for a party I was invited to. Initially, my reaction had been that I did not have time for parties and finding costumes, but then I thought, "Life is too short not to have some fun!" (See Chapter 24.)

6. Name five occasions in the past two weeks when you have experienced joy. Do you have plans for the next two weeks that might lead to joyful experiences?

7. Writing out twenty manifestations from your morning pages is one way to focus on what is important to you. For instance, this year I hope that the love between my husband and myself will deepen. I want to run a 10K race. I want to write and publish. I desire to get to know my family better. I want to make a new friend. Make a litany of these when you walk or do other exercise.

8. Take some time to meditate this week. (See Chapter 24.)

9. Reread the opening epigraph from *A Course in Miracles* (provides a way to find your "Internal Teacher") and write what treasures you discover when you look within.

PART VI:
WISE WOMEN

Chapter 22

Portraits of Wise Women

Our deepest fear is not that we are inadequate. Our deepest fear is that we are powerful beyond measure. It is our light, not our darkness, that most frightens us. We ask ourselves, who am I to be brilliant, gorgeous, talented, and fabulous? Actually, who are you not to be? You are a child of God. Your playing small doesn't serve the world. There is nothing enlightened about shrinking so that other people will not feel insecure around you. . . . As we are liberated from our own fear, our presence automatically liberates others.

Marianne Williamson
A Return to Love

The Mapuche (Indigenous Chileans) have a pantheon of gods who work for the good of the people. These gods are both male and female, as well as being both young and old, so they give rise to four characters—the Old Man, the Old Woman, the Youth, and the Young Girl.

Nick Caistor
The Rain Stick Pack

WOMEN ATHLETES

Strong Minds, Strong Bodies is a research project that explores what motivates women over sixty years of age to exercise.[1] A colleague at Saint Louis University and physical therapist, Peg Herning and I interviewed twenty women over sixty years of age who participated in the Saint Louis Senior Olympics swimming and track events in 1998 or 1999. We were trying to understand what motivates these women to exercise. Six women stand out as individuals who transformed me through the interview process: Carolyn Wilson, Polly Bailey-McCarthy, Sister Madonna Buder, Loretta Hopgood, June Jordan, and Maurine Lia. Their answers inspired me to alter my own health habits. Peg Herning called after she began her interviews and said, "I would be willing to do more interviews. I get such a high after talking to these women."

Carolyn Wilson

Carolyn Wilson, a sixty-year-old retired teacher, is very involved with her grandsons, playing basketball with them often two to three hours a week. The drive and endurance she exhibits is impressive. She won a gold medal in the 1,500-meter run with the time of 6:42.0, the best time in all the age groups at the Saint Louis Senior Olympics in 1999. In addition, she organized and plays on a bronze-medal-winning women's basketball team, "The Hoop Dreamers."

Carolyn emanates vitality. She and her husband, both runners, purchased a home adjacent to a high school to take advantage of the track. Carolyn and her husband are vegetarians. She believes that they "have chosen a healthy lifestyle."

Polly Bailey-McCarthy

"Age cannot wither her, nor custom stale her infinite variety"—this Shakespearean quote from *Antony and Cleopatra,* Act II, Scene II, can also be applied to Polly. In the 100-yard butterfly event in the age category seventy-five to seventy-nine years of age, Polly won a gold medal. Being able to swim this event is amazing, especially considering that she does this after a full morning of track, including some events such as the 50-meter dash, the 800-meter run, javelin, discus, and shot put.

She met her new husband at a marathon. Both had previously lost a spouse to cancer. Their meeting resulted from a foot problem: Polly usually stops and rubs her feet in the middle of a run to stimulate her circulation. Her future husband saw her rubbing her feet and asked, "Could I do that for you?" It was love.

Polly, never troubled with depression, believes exercise is a preventive measure. Her daughter from her first marriage does struggle with depression. Polly believes that her daughter's stress level would decrease with more exercise.

Sister Madonna Buder

Sister Madonna Buder, a tall, lean, confident woman, loves the outdoors. Faith is important to her and she exercises it by using her God-given talents. An excellent athlete, she competed in the age category of sixty-five to sixty-nine, and won a gold medal in the 1,500-meter run with the excellent time of 7:16:77. Madonna also won medals in swimming and cycling. She talks about participating in triathlons with a great love of athletics and competition.

Loretta Hopgood

Loretta Hopgood competes in the age category sixty to sixty-four in basketball, shot put, and javelin. She takes good care of herself and she has a trainer who assists her with preparing for events. She said she loves to visit local health food stores. She is a retired public health nurse and talked about common stresses today and how exercise is a good reliever of stress. She organized the first senior women's basketball team in the St. Louis area. In July 1999, her team competed at the National Senior Olympic event in Orlando, Florida. She speaks of her team's charisma and about how sad she is when these events, which she so much enjoys, are over.

June Jordan

June Jordan, a competitive swimmer, age category sixty-five to sixty-nine, is very vivacious and communicates a love of swimming, an activity she does six days a week. She had a stroke at age fifty-three and recovered through medication and exercise. Pointing to her pulse, June said, "The pool is the only place where I can get my pulse rate up to 160 beats." Her stroke and rehabilitation reminded her of the importance of aerobic exercise. She now takes it very seriously, chiding me playfully during the interview, "Mary Pat, when were you last in the pool?" She sees herself competing in the Senior Olympics until she is 100 years old.

Expressing a concern about sedentary habits of young people today, she spoke of growing up in South Saint Louis in a German community where exercise was valued by the community and her family. Her whole family used to go to the Turnverein to work out. Using the parallel bars and broad jumping were a part of her grandparents' routine.

Maurine Lia

Maurine Lia, a vibrant sixty-nine-year-old and a three time national champion race walker, is full of energy and communicates an outer and inner beauty. She came in second place in the Mrs. Missouri contest. She spoke about the motivational speech she gave at the contest: "Life Begins After Fifty." She has had many accomplishments in her later years: a GED at fifty-eight, learning horseback riding at sixty, and competing in a worldwide event and winning first place in race walking at sixty-five. She feels she has become her own person now, with clear ideas about where she finds life.

WISE WOMEN PAST AND PRESENT

Elizabeth Cady Stanton and Susan B. Anthony

The Public Broadcasting Service documentary *Not for Ourselves Alone: The Story of Elizabeth Cady Stanton and Susan B. Anthony* is a powerful story. The writers of our history books have failed to give us a true picture of the courage and friendship of these two women. Stanton was a social reformer, a Quaker, a strategist, and a missionary who was on the road continually to promote her ideas about women's rights. Anthony was a mother of seven children, had an incisive mind, and wrote the *Women's Bible* as well as the original version of the Nineteenth Amendment that passed in Congress after seventy-two years of struggle for equality for women. Because they stood up for what they believed, they were considered bold and unladylike by many of the conservatives of their day. The issues for which they fought were (1) freedom to attend college (Elizabeth Cady Stanton had applied and was rejected because she was a woman), (2) freedom to own property, (3) political freedom to vote and to serve on a jury, and (4) religious freedom to preach and attend seminary.

Susan B. Anthony states her position well:

> I never felt I could give up my life of freedom to become a man's housekeeper. When I was young if a girl married poor she became a housekeeper and a drudge. If she married wealthy, she became a pet and a doll. Just think, had I married at twenty, I would have been a drudge or a doll for 55 years. Think of it![2]

The story of this great social transformation, through which women asserted their rights to be considered equal to men, is still untold history in many schools and homes.

Anita Hill

Anita Hill is a law professor from Oklahoma who charged that Clarence Thomas, a nominee for the Supreme Court, had engaged in sexual misconduct toward her when he was her boss ten years earlier at the Equal Employment Opportunities Commission. The hearings were held in September 1991. Hill's willingness to speak candidly in a public hearing encouraged other women to disclose sexual harassment, such as the Air Force women in the Tailhook case.

Gloria Steinem said it well:

> The Anita Hill hearing may be the first time in the history of the country that popular culture focused on women's experience in prime time for three days.[3]

Maya Angelou

Maya Angelou (b. 1928), American author, poet, and entertainer, is best known for her portrayals of strong African-American women. Born Marguerite Johns in Saint Louis, Missouri, Angelou spent most of her childhood living with her grandmother in rural Arkansas. She graduated with honors from Lafayette County Training School in 1940. At sixteen, she gave birth to her son, Guy. In the1950s she had work as a singer, dancer, actor, playwright, magazine editor, civil rights activist, poet, and novelist. Her works often express the themes of courage, perseverance, self-acceptance, and realization of one's potential. In 1998 Angelou made her directing debut with the release of the motion picture *Down in the Delta.*

WISE WOMEN WHO HAVE INFLUENCED ME

Rita C. Henehan

My mother died in November 1997. I admired her very much; she had a love for life I will always treasure. She raised five children, struggled through breast cancer and a history of sexual abuse, and suffered from diabetes and a stroke. She was supportive of me always. When I left religious life after twenty-five years, she said to me, "You have done your share." Her words meant a lot to me; I was feeling guilty about leaving the Daughters of Charity. I knew the lifestyle was oppressing me. Tension existed between my view of women's rights and the order to which I belonged. I wanted to study for a doctorate in ministry; I was told by my superiors in the order that I had no need for such a degree. My mother understood my decision to leave; she wrote me encouraging letters after I left. I was by her side when she had a cancerous breast tumor removed. I still recall her words to me as she was wheeled into surgery: "Everything will be all right; don't worry about me." She taught me that worry is a waste of energy.

Joan Marie Gleason

Joan Marie Gleason and I first met in 1971 at Saint Louis University. She had just finished her term as provincial. We both were enrolled in the Institute of Religious Formation. The year was a wonderful one for me, experiencing a sense of faith community as I never had before. A number of us in the program gave Joan Marie the title, "the godmother" not only because she was older than a few of us who were in our late twenties but also because her wisdom was evident. After we finished the program, she had asked me to do some discernment workshops with her in Augusta, Georgia. It was a joy to work with her. She possessed a gift for making you feel very comfortable in her presence. I asked if she would consider being my spiritual director, and she agreed to that role. I would meet with her twice a month, and I made some directed retreats with Joan Marie. It was wonderful to confide so much in her. I recall letting go of some old painful memories of a teacher who had been abusive to me. She hit my head against a blackboard in fourth grade because I was not working fast enough on a math problem. In contrast, Sister Joan Marie had a very healing presence. She assisted me in important decisions and affirmed leadership qualities that she saw in me.

Ann Marie Wrysch

Ann Marie Wrysch and I became friends when I was beginning my private practice as a psychotherapist. She had already been in practice for a while. Ann Marie was very willing to share her experience of being in business for herself. We attended a few meetings together on the subject of addictions and on nurse entrepreneurship. She, her husband, Lou, my husband, Jack, and I became close. We were in a marriage support group together. The wisdom I learned from Ann Marie was how to deal with suffering and loss. Her husband had undergone a kidney transplant but experienced many side effects from the medication; eventually his body rejected the transplanted kidney. We were privileged to stay in close contact throughout Lou's dying process. Lou invited my husband and me to conduct his wake service. Lou has been gone now for five years, and I see how well Ann Marie has adjusted to the terrible loss of someone she loved deeply.

Nancy Morrison

Nancy Morrison and I began doing joint marriage and family presentations together on the topic of "Aging Parents and Family Dynamics." Our discussions got me through one of the most difficult times in my life. My mother moved to St. Louis in need of care and communications with my brothers and sisters about my mother were strained. Nancy was also dealing with an aging parent, and our parents ended up at the same group home. We became an extended family of sorts. One time I visited my mom at the home late one evening and she was watching *I Love Lucy*. The group home had five residents at the time and they were all in their pajamas, eating popcorn, watching television together. I told Nancy the next day, "Our parents had a pajama party last night. They are enjoying life more than we are!"

Nancy invited me to teach a course for her. I had already been doing some supervision of the master's and doctoral students enrolled in the Counseling and Family Therapy Program at Saint Louis University. Nancy gave me a lot of help getting the course off the ground. I appreciated that she entrusted the students to me. She loves to teach, but her focus was redirected to administration when she was asked to chair the Department of Counseling and Family Therapy.

REFLECTION QUESTIONS

1. Name some wise women in your life. Describe their influence on you.
2. How do you feel about aging?
3. Name three habits you are developing to increase your vitality.
4. What women in history shine for you?
5. Name some goals you have for the next five years.
6. Break a few of these goals into manageable steps. When you take steps toward those goals, reward yourself.
7. Do you appreciate the friendships you have with women? Describe.
8. Who do you turn to for support?

Chapter 23

Croning of Women

Our culture has this belief that, starting at the age of 25, you begin to lose brain cells, and it's just a matter of time before you lose your mind and become a burden to society. What we do not understand is that what increases is the connections, so that there is a rich network of inner-neuron connections that never existed in a young person. It can only exist in an older person. That's how wisdom gets encoded in the brain.

Christiane Northrup
Women's Bodies, Women's Wisdom

I didn't prepare myself to be seventy-one. We should begin earlier to think about later on, because we are all living longer.

Lena Horne

Christella Carbaugh, who gives workshops titled *Crone Woman of Wholeness,* has a goal in life to change the definition of the word *crone.* Crone is defined as "an ugly, withered, witch-like, old woman." I support Carbaugh in her life's mission. I want to define the older woman the way the poet Jayne Relaford Brown does:

FINDING HER HERE

I am becoming the woman I've wanted,
gray at the temples, soft body, delighted,
cracked up by life, with a laugh that's known bitter
but, past it, got better.
Knows she's a survivor—
that whatever comes, she can outlast it.
I am becoming a deep weathered basket.

I am becoming the woman I've longed for
the motherly lover with arms strong and tender,
the growing up daughter who blushes surprises.
I am becoming full moons and sunrises.

I find her becoming this woman I've wanted
who knows she'll encompass, who knows she's sufficient.
Knows where she's going and travels with passion,
who remembers she's precious, but knows she's not scarce who
knows she is plenty, plenty to share.[1]

RESEARCH

Being fifty-nine years of age myself, I pay attention to messages
that I hear about women and aging. One of the more positive messages is from Tufts University's researcher Miriam Nelson, who has
proven the benefits of strengthening exercises. Her research demonstrates a hopeful message that you are never too old to benefit from
strengthening exercises, which build bone, improve balance and flexibility, and increase energy.[2] Muscle can be built at any age. Nelson
portrays women as strong—not fragile, as the media has a tendency
to do.

A challenge for us all is to distinguish constraining beliefs from facilitating beliefs about aging. Lorraine Wright and Jane Nagy, professors at the University of Calgary in Canada, write:

> Constraining beliefs arise from social, interactional, and cul-
> tural contexts. Constraining beliefs inhibit the autonomy of the
> individual and the family by restricting options for alternate so-
> lutions to problems. . . . Change occurs when there is a shift in
> the constraining beliefs.[3]

The team at Calgary, working with patients at the Family Nursing
Unit, makes an assumption: the belief about the problem is the prob-
lem. Epictetus, a first-century philosopher, had a similar approach.
He wrote:

Men (people) are not disturbed by things, but by the views which they take of things. Thus death is nothing terrible, but the terror consists in the notion of death, that it is terrible. When . . . disturbed or grieved, let us never impute it to others, but to ourselves—that is, to our own views.[4]

Wendy Watson, professor at Brigham Young, Salt Lake City, Utah, has also done research on beliefs about aging and how these constricting beliefs often cause barriers in the development of aging persons. She points out that changes take place with age, such as:

1. Increasing high-frequency deafness. Lower tones are easier to hear.
2. Changing visual acuity. The distinction between the colors blue and green becomes challenging for some people.
3. Changing sensitivity to heat and cold.
4. Increasing sensitivity to drugs.
5. Increasing sensitivity to sunlight. I once had a patient who kept her blinds down around the clock. Her family did not understand her behavior and believed she was trying to isolate herself. They did not understand this as an adaptive behavior.
6. Decreasing flexibility of the joints. The benefits of stretching become even more significant as we age.
7. Increasing caution.
8. Increasing duration of response to stimulus. For example, when interviewing, the interviewer needs to allow time between questions. It is as if a bell is rung, say after asking the first question, and silence is needed to provide for the vibrations of sound to disappear before going on to the second question.[5]

These changes are no excuse, however, for professionals to treat older persons as if they have no voice about their own care. Whenever I took my mother to the doctor, I was always surprised that he began talking to me rather than to her. Older women need to have a voice and feel visible in the health care system and in all aspects of their lives.

CULTURE

Our culture creates fears and constraining beliefs about aging by presenting images of drug-dependent aging persons daily in the media. Constraining beliefs limit our thinking about alternative choices. Facilitating beliefs lead to an "I can" attitude. (For instance, a constraining belief around aging would be: "I will get osteoporosis. I can do nothing to prevent it." A facilitating belief would be: "I can exercise and eat healthy for bone health as I grow older.") Television continues to present young, articulate anchorwomen whose jobs end when their wrinkles arrive. Gloria Steinem challenges the media in *Revolution from Within* when she discusses the media's obsession with her getting a face-lift.[6]

Constraining beliefs are created by our culture, yet there is a need for the gifts of older persons to be honored. When I consider the most important older women in my life, my mother and mother-in-law, they seem happy with who they are.

NARRATIVES OF WISE WOMEN

The Winter Guest (1997) is a movie rich with wonderful scenes. Emma Thompson plays the daughter, Frances. Thompson's mother, Phyllida Law, plays Elspeth, Frances's mother. The acting is wonderful and one wonders, since this is a real mother-daughter relationship, how much of it is acting. The Scottish mother, Elspeth, looks in the mirror one day and says, "I look old, but I feel young inside."[7]

The relationship between mother and daughter begins to get closer as the story unfolds. In a moving scene, Elspeth reminds her daughter that she had a name, Elspeth. She stood tall with dignity as she challenged her daughter's treatment of her. Finally, each holding the other's hand, they submitted to their need for mutual support.

This movie touched me deeply. I wept as I saw it. It reminded me of the wonderful opportunity I had to get close to my mother in her old age. We, too, needed each other in many ways. Time with my mother during the final years of her life is a memory I shall always treasure.

In his memoir, Frederick Buechner reveals another story of a wise woman following his father's death:

brightness and peace of the island we moved to were only the outward and visible signs of a brightness and peace that opened up inside my ten-year-old self. Naya came with us. Naya was the grandmother's name we gave to my mother's mother who was half French-Swiss and half old New England. She loved books and music and the French language and managed somehow to be so at peace inside herself that even when the heavens were falling, she could sit smoking a Chesterfield in a white paper holder and never turn a hair. She was my one true parent in the sense that she loved me . . .[8]

Betty Friedan, in *Life So Far: A Memoir,* points out there is much work to be done yet in shattering the age mystique. When she began looking at what courses on aging were being taught at Harvard, she found seminars on funeral services but nothing on the value of older people in society and their spiritual development.[9] There is a need to battle negative attitudes regarding aging in our culture.

CRONE ROLE MODELS

Golda Meir

Golda Meir, the first female prime minister of Israel, is another role model for older women. Known for her kitchen politics, Meir served honey cakes to U.S. senators as they talked about Israel's defense needs. Golda Meir had simple ways to renew herself. For instance, she would say, "I will think about that decision as I wash my hair."[10] Golda Meir considered polishing her teapot a stress reducer. She remained the leader of Israel into her seventies, through war to peace, and through her own struggle with cancer. Once, when Anwar al-Sadat of Egypt was visiting, she presented him with a gift for his granddaughter, using her thoughtfulness to build alliances.

Madeleine Korbel Albright

Madeleine Albright was the first female U.S. secretary of state who also chaired the Interagency Council on Women established in 1995 by President Clinton. This council was charged with implementing the platform for action adopted at Beijing for women around the world.

Albright also took leadership in attempting to stop sexual slavery, which has become a $9 billion business. Poverty makes young women vulnerable to the business of human trafficking. Often these young women are taken to a foreign country where they cannot speak the language and are unable to contact the police.[11]

Janet Reno

Born in 1938 in Miami, Florida (the town in which she began her career), Janet Reno was one of four children born to Henry, a Danish immigrant, and Jane. Her parents were reporters for the *Miami News*. It is thought that Janet Reno's self-confidence comes from her mother. With her own hands, Jane built the family home.

After graduating from law school, Reno worked several years in a private law practice. She then became the staff director of the Florida House Judiciary Committee in 1971. In 1978, she was appointed Florida's state attorney and was reelected five times. Following that, she became the first female U.S. attorney general. Her early days in office were concerned with settling the fatal standoff near Waco, Texas, between the Federal Bureau of Investigation and the Branch Davidians. Reno believed that children were being sexually abused inside the Waco compound. If Reno has a hot button to be pushed, it is the welfare of children.

Janet Reno has a good sense of humor and the ability to laugh at herself. She thought the frequent spoofs about her on *Saturday Night Live* were hilarious.

Bernice Neugarten

Betty Friedan wrote fondly of Bernice Neugarten in *The Fountain of Age*. Bernice began jogging at age sixty, opened a door in the academic setting she had been teaching in, and took on the leadership role of departmental chair. She is an example of an older woman acting on her facilitating beliefs that she can live a healthy lifestyle and use her talents in leadership and scholarship in an academic setting. Betty Friedan points out that older women often bring the wisdom of their lived experiences to the tasks at hand. Older women have a deep sense of intergenerational relationships.[12]

There are many wise women to write about. I hope you will continue to identify women who have inspired you in the reflection questions.

Each of us has a wise woman inside with whom we can consult. Following are some questions that assist us in hearing her wisdom. It has always been a delight to me that there is a whole book in the Old Testament called the Book of Wisdom (included in the Old Testament of the Catholic Bible, and in the Protestant Bible with the apocryphal literature), and the pronoun *she* used to refer to wisdom.

REFLECTION QUESTIONS

1. List three women who you wished you had met who are now deceased. Now list three women who you would like to hang out with for a while in eternity. What traits do you admire in these women that you can look for in your friends?
2. Describe yourself at eighty. What did you do after fifty that you enjoyed? Now, write a letter from you as an eighty-year-old to you at your current age. What will you tell yourself? What interests would you tell yourself to pursue?
3. What are your dreams? Be specific.
4. Reflect on the Book of Wisdom, specifically verse 10, chapter 10, "She guided the just in direct ways."
5. What are you doing to take care of your body? How often do you do strengthening exercises?
6. What are some constraining and facilitating beliefs you have about aging?
7. Write down what comes to mind when you read this quote by Susun Weed:

   > I am the Crone. I feel my way along paths following the energy and warmth that others have placed there. Trusting the dark, I am guided not by light, but by the flowing of movements I sense. I am like the water that follows, without sight or foreknowledge, the ancient river's channel.[13]

8. What are some ways that you can reduce stress in your life? List ten things you can do to take care of yourself when you experience stress.

Chapter 24

Spiritual Practices for Women

True life is lived when tiny changes occur.

Leo Tolstoy

Why are you so enchanted by the world when a mine of gold lies within you?

Rumi

It is good to have an end to journey toward; but it is the journey that matters, in the end.

Ursula K. Le Guin

This chapter examines spiritual practices for women: why they are important, what they look like in everyday life, and how to make them happen.

You might ask: Why is this necessary? Do men and women have different spiritual needs? I can best illustrate the importance of this point by sharing with you a piece of mail I recently received—an advent Jesus tree from a women's center in New Mexico. It lists important female ancestors of Jesus: Eve, Hagar, Sarah, Rebekah, Rachel, Leah, Tamar, Rahab, Naomi, Ruth, Bathsheba, and Mary. I have always found the family tree of Jesus fascinating. Jesus had some real characters in his family, just as we each have in ours. There was Rahab, by trade a harlot, whose bravery is recorded in the conquest of the promised land. There were Ruth and Naomi, daughter-in-law and mother-in-law, whose commitment to each other transformed the pain of the exile.[1] This spiritual practice of reflecting on the role of women before Christmas was new to me. After undertaking the reflection, I see how important it is. For me, it reversed some of the negative messages about women of the Bible that I had learned in my religious education. In this advent reflection, Eve is presented as the hand of original blessing rather than as the temptress.

VALIANT WOMEN LITANY

Reciting a litany of valiant women can be a wonderful spiritual exercise. I am Catholic and find that Mass lacks in feeding the feminine. There has been some progress in interfaith awareness. The acknowledgment of women from a variety of backgrounds is important as an expression of inclusiveness in this ritual. After reading Miriam Therese Winter,[2] I was inspired to write this litany to acknowledge the contributions of women through the ages:

> Hagar
> an Egyptian slave
> mother of Abraham's son, Ishmael
> You remind us that God hears and you give
> witness to the power of God who "makes
> a way out of no way."
>
> Hail, valiant woman!
>
> Judith
> heroine of the People of God
> warrior for justice
> you saved the city Bethulia from Holofernes
> you are not afraid of risking your life for good. (See Figure 24.1.)
>
> Hail, Brave woman!
>
> Lydia
> regarded in the early Church as a convener of prayer,
> a leader who proclaimed the Gospel side by side with Paul,
> a prosperous businesswoman who was a dealer of purple goods
> and made her home and
> resources available for the life of the early Christian Church.
>
> Hail, valiant woman!

FIGURE 24.1. Judith and Holofernes, 1554. Oil by Giorgio Varsari depicting the Old Testament story of the beautiful Jewish heroine. Note how Varsari conveys her bravery, faith, and virtue. Saint Louis Art Museum, Friends Fund, and funds given in honor of Betty Greenfield Grossman.

Fatimah
Mohammed's only surviving
daughter,
held in great esteem
by Muslims,
who supported her father
through his years of persecution.

Hail, valiant woman!

Bridget,
who founded Irish monastic
centers for men and women
in the fifth century,
leader in politics and ecclesiastical matters.

Hail, valiant woman!

Catherine of Alexandria,
who convinced fifty
Egyptian philosophers of the court
to convert to Christianity.
She inspires us with her story of the power
of one woman's wisdom. (See Figure 24.2.)

Hail, brave woman!

Wu Zi-Tien
the only woman Emperor
of China,
who reigned brilliantly and effectively
for forty years
late in the seventh century,
making Buddhism the state religion
and the Tang Dynasty a liberal interlude
for women.

Hail, valiant woman!

FIGURE 24.2. St. Catherine of Alexandria, 1525. Italian Sculpture by Antonello Gagini. This was a niche figure made for the Cathedral in Palermo. Spiritual grace of this wise woman is communicated by the artist. Saint Louis Art Museum, Purchase.

Catherine of Siena,
committed to self-knowledge, healing and counseling.
Doctor of the Church,
who convinced the Pope to return to Rome, and author of *The Dialogue,* her conversations with Christ. She died in 1380.

Hail, valiant woman!

Louise de Marillac,
born in 1591 in Paris, France,
was an inspired leader of women fighting for justice
for the poor. She had a radical spirit of service in the world,
"leaving God for God." She is the patroness of social workers and founded the Daughters of Charity and the Ladies of Charity with Vincent de Paul.

Hail, valiant woman!

Elizabeth Ann Seton
who in 1809
founded the Sisters of Charity and was the first American woman canonized by the Roman Catholic Church in the United States.

Hail, valiant woman!

Rosana Chouteau
North American Indian,
elected chief of the Osage Beaver Tribe
in 1875, the first female chief.

Hail, valiant woman!

Maud Booth,
bringing religion and rehabilitation to prisoners,
co-founder of the Salvation Army
in the United States in 1887.

Hail, valiant woman!

Pandita Ramabai,
a Sanskrit scholar
pilgrim and poet
who raised the status of women,
delegate to the Indian National Congress.

Hail, valiant woman!

Florence Nightingale
who raised up nursing to
a profession
in nineteenth-century England
and laid the foundation
for nursing as we know it today.

Hail, valiant woman!

Mary Baker Eddy,
author, founder, healer, and leader
of Christian Science
until her death in 1910,
established a metaphysical college
to teach spiritual healing.

Hail, wise woman!

Käthe Kollwitz,
artist and pacifist living in Berlin, Germany.
She died in 1945,
whose art portrayed aspects of maternal love, determination to
    protect the young, and the pain of not being able to feed chil-
    dren during the war.

Hail, wise woman!

Mother Jones,
Mary Jones,
organizer of the labor movement,

devoted to fostering the dignity
of the worker,
who died in 1930
at 100 years of age.

Hail, wise woman!

Mev Puleo,
witness of solidarity,
author and photographer,
bridge between the first world and the third world,
encouraging us to use the gift of wonder
and teaching us that life is short.
Died in 1996 at age thirty-two from cancer but lived fully her
    last years despite a deadly disease.

Hail, brave woman!

Venice Henehan,
mother and wife,
loving aunt and sister,
martyr from gun violence
who died unexpectedly
at Luby's Cafeteria, while
visiting Killeen, Texas, before her granddaughter's
wedding. Challenging us as a nation to
face needless deaths from gun violence.

Hail, brave woman!

What is at the heart of spiritual practices for women? These practices are about reclaiming self-esteem and restoring dignity, and the ability to reframe or free up new energy. Women acknowledged in historical writing have often been cast in a negative light. Eve is an example. Neither have we seen women's stories integrated into history. To be ignored and set aside is a terrible thing. Spiritual practices could take many forms. Spiritual exercises are discussed next to get you thinking of your own spiritual exercises and reflecting on why they are important to you.

MEDITATION

Some of these spiritual practices have preventive health and healing dimensions. Heart disease is the number one killer of women. Each year 250,000 women die of heart disease.[3] Angina, or heart pain, is caused by insufficient oxygen to the heart. Meditation can reduce the heart rate, and oxygen consumption can decrease 10 to 20 percent.

The following is an example of a meditation around the themes of heart health and loving spiritual connections:

1. Sit quietly for several minutes. Focus on your breathing. Feel the air coming through your nose and down into your lungs. Exhale. Repeat this several times. Say the phrase, "My body is calmed and relaxed" or "I am in the presence of God and safe."
2. Now focus your attention on the center of your upper chest, the area over your heart. Imagine a flower that represents love and compassion.
3. See this flower blooming as you breathe in and out.
4. Picture someone you care about. Now picture a beam of light as a manifestation of your loving energy that goes from your heart to the heart of this person.
5. Feel this loving energy in every cell of your body.
6. This can also be done by focusing on someone you do not like. See the divine presence in them.
7. Continue this meditation by refocusing on a dear friend with whom you wish to share the bond of compassion.
8. Close with one final, slow, deep breath, sending a ray of loving light to the other person and to yourself.[4]

Meditation has many advantages; one is the improvement of your health. In his research with cardiac and cancer patients, Dean Ornish recommends meditation to increase relaxation in the mind and body.[5] Meditation is recommended to promote digestive health by Elizabeth Lipski. She writes about the advantages of meditation for strengthening the immune system.[6] Herbert Benson recommends meditation for decreasing blood pressure. In his studies, he finds that meditation also reduces muscular tension in the body.[7]

Meditation is a way to connect with a deeper spiritual side of ourselves and our higher power. In my own life, when I take time to meditate I find myself calmer and I tend to be more centered. Because I grew up as the oldest daughter in a family of five siblings, meditation helps me maintain perspective: I do not have to be a caregiver all the time. I need time where I can let go and let God take over in my life. I need time to reflect on Scripture, or the beauty of nature, or how I feel God in my life through the kindness of a friend or the encouragement of my husband.

T'AI CHI

T'ai Chi Ch'uan is a spiritual practice that can assist you if you have a hard time sitting still to meditate. The classic Chinese practice is meditation in motion, graceful in movement, slow in tempo, and fluid in natural postures. T'ai Chi is a method of exercise for health, self-defense, and spiritual growth. For centuries it has been a part of Chinese culture for health and longevity. T'ai Chi harmonizes the energy processes within the body and integrates the mind and body within the natural order of the universe.[8]

COUNTING YOUR BLESSINGS

This exercise is at the heart of spirituality: expressing a grateful heart. The world is full of abundance. This is true only if we can take the time to see a smiling person, the beauty of a flower, and the freedom of a bird. To notice the understanding felt in a compassionate conversation, the good feeling when someone takes time to be with you, all these areas of life are the stuff of daily blessing. Every day can be a cause for Thanksgiving. If I bless the world, it also blesses me in return.[9]

MORNING PAGES

The morning pages that Julia Cameron recommends in *The Vein of Gold* are what she calls a Western form of meditation.[10] These exercises evolve from a stream of consciousness of longhand writing when you first get out of bed. The purpose is to clear and focus the mind. It allows prioritizing and alternative routing to solutions. Morning pages allow you to stand back and examine your thoughts and feelings. Often this helps you think of some other possibilities as you cope with situations in life.

IMAGING

Imaging helps to create a scene in the midst of your day. For example, while you are waiting for an elevator, you could get upset at the delay or you can use imaging to think about a comforting passage from Scripture. Imagine that you, at this moment, have a spiritual guide to shepherd you and lead you to restful waters. Through the use of imagery, you can recall a favorite vacation by the sea or a lake. Imaging a peaceful scene can help us focus and slow down in our hurried world.

CREATIVITY DATES

The practice of keeping artist dates can enhance your well-being. Julia Cameron[11] defines the practice as a weekly solitary experience with your "creative self" into new, interesting, and expansive territory. It might be a trip to an art museum, an aquarium, a secondhand record store, a concert, a drive in the country—anything that fills the artistic void. We may put off doing things that increase our imagination because we cannot find someone with a like interest or the time to go with us. Setting creativity dates pushes us to step out and experience these new situations by ourselves.

CHAKRA AWARENESS

The system of the chakra plays a role in Hinduism and in Buddhism. The word *chakra* means "wheel" or "circle," and it is used as a term for the centers of refined energy in the human body. There are seven chakras that transform and distribute the energy which streams through them. They are also points where the soul and the body connect with and penetrate each other. These points lie along the sushumna, the principal channel of subtle energy, located in the spinal column, through which the kundalina rises in the course of spiritual awakening. Each chakra corresponds to specific psychophysical properties, which are expressed through various symbols (such as color):

1. The lowest chakra is between the root of the genitals and the anus. The yogi who by spiritual practice penetrates this chakra conquers the earth and no longer fears death. Here the sins are wiped away. Here one knows the past, present, and future. Its color is yellow.
2. The second chakra lies in the energy at the root of the genitals. It controls the inner organs of elimination and procreation. Here the yogi acquires psychic powers and intuitive knowledge. The color is white.
3. The third chakra lies in the region of the navel. The yogi who concentrates on this chakra finds hidden treasures and knows fear of fire. The color is red.
4. The fourth chakra lies in the region of the heart. The yogi acquires in this center harmony and the ability to fly through the air and enter the bodies of others. Cosmic love and divine qualities come to the yogi. The color is grayish-blue.
5. The fifth chakra lies in the base of the throat; one who concentrates on this center will not perish even with the destruction of the cosmos. The color is white.
6. The sixth chakra is known as the "third eye" and is the space between the eyebrows. This center brings liberation; its color is milky white.
7. The seventh chakra is located above the crown of the head. This chakra radiates "like ten million suns." The yogi experiences supreme bliss and supreme knowledge. Here there is cosmic consciousness. It has no specific color.[12]

SABBATH OBSERVANCE

In a surprise best-seller of 1992, *The Overworked American*, economist Juliet Schor reported that work hours and stress are up and sleep and family time are down.[13] Wives working outside the home return to find a "second shift" of housework awaiting them. Dorothy Bass, a historian and author of American religion, suggests we return to observing the Sabbath—that we take a day of rest after six days of work. This practice is grounded in the biblical creation story.[14]

TREE PLANTING

Care of the earth is the responsibility of each of us. As we come to understand the reality that the quality of air is getting poorer and poorer, we need to take action. Plants increase the oxygen in the air. Thomas Berry points out the need to reclaim a reverence for the Earth and a spirituality of a new ecology that needs to begin to function with efficacy now.[15]

My husband and I began a Christmas ritual of planting a live tree in our yard. The trees serve as a wonderful reminder of the memories of the gathering of family. In addition, we help the environment. Earth Day presents another opportunity to plant.

A friend of mine plants a tree for each of her grandchildren. Consider a ritual that has meaning for you and helps improve the environment.

YES, NO

Just as we wish to protect, not destroy, the earth, we can learn to be less destructive in our relationships. Having healthy boundaries in our relationships allows us to say "yes" and to say "no." We need to say "yes" to life and "no" to destruction. The book of Deuteronomy (30:19) speaks of this practice:

> I have set before you life and death, blessings and curses,
> Choose life so that you and your descendants may live.

Many of us feel guilty when we say no. However, saying no may free us to focus on our existing commitments.

HOSPITALITY

Another important spiritual ritual is providing hospitality. None of us knows when we may be uprooted and cast on the mercy of others. This ritual affirms the rightness of taking people in and providing the basic need of human shelter. In the traditions shaped by the Bible, taking in a stranger or guest is a moral imperative.

MUSIC—LISTENING AND PERFORMING

I began looking at this spiritual practice with a reflection on Scripture. In the story of Exodus, we are told:

> "And Miriam sang to them: 'Sing to Yahweh who has triumphed gloriously; the horse and its rider thrown into the sea'." (15:21.2)

This is a wonderful practice she models for us, remembering through song the sacred history of a people and celebrating this liberation of the whole community.

Adding music to our world is a simple contribution. I play the hammered dulcimer and I see people's faces light up when they think of music. I recently played at a home for dementia patients, and their memories were stirred by the music. One of the residents is Jewish and the administrator was surprised when she sang along to "Silent Night."

INFORMATION FAST

A practice that can help us get inside ourselves and can give us more space to be creative is what I call an information fast. For one week take a vacation from e-mail, music, reading, radio, favorite talk shows, videos, and other television. We live in an age of information overload, and we can experience some relief by taking a break from technology. Emptying our minds of numbing chatter, we may find a deeper stream of ideas, insights, and recognitions. We encounter our authentic selves and understand our dreams with greater clarity.[16]

The following are some reflection questions on the practices presented in this chapter. I hope they encourage you to think of your own spiritual practices.

REFLECTION QUESTIONS

1. What spiritual exercises do you find helpful? Do you notice a difference in your life when you practice them?
2. Add to this chapter's litany the names and experiences of brave women who are important to you.
3. Can you think of some spiritual practices that you might begin to include in your lifestyle? What would the advantages be?
4. Take one day and begin to notice the blessings that are present. Begin a journal of thanksgiving.
5. Reflect on each chakra. Make note of any awarenesses you have as you pay attention to these seven areas of the body. Each chakra is like a computer disc with lots of information. For example, you might become aware of tendencies to control or fears that keep you from acting.
6. Do you take a day off and observe the Sabbath? Would it help our harried world? Can you rely on the bounty and goodness of God?
7. Do you have any practices you do that reverence the Earth? Describe.
8. Have you offered hospitality to someone in the past six months? Have you received hospitality? Describe these experiences. Were there spiritual elements of sharing, care, concern, and respect?
9. Write a paragraph about your weeklong information fast. What was your experience? Did you find you had more time? Were you more aware of your own thoughts? Did you have more fun? Were your sleep patterns different?

Appendix

Sources of Help

Organizational Support

American Association for Marriage and Family Therapy
1133 Fifteenth Street, NW, Suite 300
Washington, DC 20005
(202) 452-0109
<www.aamft.org> (Therapist locator is available.)

American Association of Pastoral Counselors
9504A Lee Highway
Fairfax, VA 22031-2303
(703) 385-6967

American Psychiatric Association
1400 K Street, NW
Washington, DC 20005
(202) 682-6000

The Center for Prevention of Sexual and Domestic Violence
2400 45th Street #10
Seattle, WA 98103
(206) 634-1903
<www.cpsdv.org>

National Institute of Mental Health
Information Resources and Inquiries Branch
Room 15C-05
5600 Fishers Lane
Rockville, MD 20857
(301) 443-4513

National Institute for Healthcare Research
6110 Executive Boulevard, Ste. 908
Rockville, MD 20852
Phone: (301) 984-7162
Fax: (301) 948-8143

Pact (Source of education and support for adoptive families, the name Pact was chosen because of the covenant to protect the child and adopted adults of color.)
1700 Montgomery St., Ste. 111
San Francisco, CA 94111
<www.pactadopt.org>

U.S. Masters Swimming, Inc.
2 Peter Avenue
Rutland, MA 01543
(508) 886-6265

Notes

Chapter 1

1. Ireland, M. (1993). *Reconceiving women: Separating motherhood from female identity.* New York: Guilford, pp. 1, 7.
2. Read, P. J. and Witlieb, B. L. (1992). *The book of women's firsts.* New York: Random House, pp. 381-382.
3. von Bingen, Hildegarde (1995). *Heavenly revelations.* Compact Disc Naxos. 8.550998.
4. Goleman, D. (1995). *Emotional intelligence.* Los Angeles, CA: Audio Renaissance Tapes.
5. Liswood, L.A. (1995). *Women world leaders: Fifteen great politicians tell their stories.* San Francisco, CA: HarperCollins, p. xi.
6. Progress in protecting women (editorial). (1998). *St. Louis Post-Dispatch,* October 11, p. B2.
7. Fortune, M.M. (1991). *Violence in the family: A workshop curriculum for clergy and other helpers.* Cleveland: Pilgrim Press, p. 109.
8. McGoldrick, M., Broken Nose, M.A., and Potenza, M. (1999). Violence and the family life cycle. In B. Carter and M. McGoldrick (Eds.), *The expanded family life cycle,* Third edition (p. 476). Boston: Allyn & Bacon.
9. Evans, K. (2000). *The lost daughters of China: Abandoned girls, their journey to America, and the search for a missing past.* New York: Putnam, p. 88.
10. Ibid., p. 2.
11. McGoldrick, M. (1999). Women through the family life cycle. In B. Carter and M. McGoldrick (Eds.), *The expanded family life cycle,* Third edition (pp. 106-121). Needham Heights, MA: Allyn & Bacon.
12. Lerner, H. G. (1988). *Women in therapy.* New York: Harper and Row, p. 170.
13. Stiver, I. (1991). Work inhibitions in women. In J.V. Jordan, A.G. Kaplan, J.B. Miller, I.P. Stiver, and J.L. Surrey (Eds.), *Women's growth in connection: Writings from the Stone Center.* New York: Guilford, p. 223.
14. Hochschild, A. R. (1997). *The time bind: When work becomes home and home becomes work.* New York: Owl Books, p. 147.
15. Whitney, C. (Ed.) (2000). *Nine and counting: Women of the Senate.* New York: William Morrow, p. 153.

Chapter 2

1. Satir, V. (1988). *The new peoplemaking.* Mountain View, CA: Science and Behavior Books, pp. 30-93.
2. Miller, M. A. (1995). Culture, spirituality, and women's health. *Journal of Obstetric, Gynecologic, and Neonatal Nursing* 24(3): 257-263.

3. Borysenko, J. (1997). *A woman's book of life: The biology, psychology, and spirituality of the feminine life cycle.* New York: Riverhead Books, pp. 1-9.

4. Gilligan, C. (1982). *In a different voice: Psychological theory and women's development.* Cambridge, MA: Harvard University Press.

5. Herman, M., producer, writer (1998). *Little voice.* Burbank, CA: Miramax video.

6. Armstrong, G. (1994). *Little women.* California: Columbia Pictures video.

7. Boysenko, *A woman's book of life.*

8. Tillman, G., producer, writer (1997). *Soul food.* 20th Century Fox video.

9. Koenig, H. (1999). *The power of faith in healing: Science explores medicine's last great frontier.* New York: Simon and Schuster.

10. Wright, L. (1999). Spirituality, suffering, and beliefs: The soul of healing with families. In F. Walsh (Ed.), *Spiritual resources in family therapy* (pp. 61-75). New York: The Guilford Press.

11. Carter, B. and McGoldrick, M. (1999). Self in context. In B. Carter and M. McGoldrick (Eds.), *The expanded family life cycle,* Third edition. Needham Heights, MA: Allyn & Bacon.

12. Borysenko, *A woman's book of life.*

13. Goldberger, N., Tarule, J., Clinchy, B., and Belenky, M. (Eds.) (1996). *Knowledge, difference, and power.* New York: Basic Books.

14. Carter, B. and McGoldrick, M. (1999), p. 33.

15. Cameron, J. (1992). *The artist's way: A spiritual path to higher creativity.* New York: Putnam, pp. 9-10.

16. Kriseman, N. and Claes, J. (1997). Gender issues and elder care. In T.D. Hargrave and S. Midori Hanna (Eds.), *The aging family: New visions in theory, practice and reality* (pp. 200-201). New York: Brunner/Mazel, Inc.

17. Carnes, P. (1993). *A gentle path through the twelve steps: The classic guide for all people in the process of recovery.* Minneapolis, MN: Compcare Publishers, p. 96.

Chapter 3

1. Ventura, M. (1996). The mission of memory. *The Family Therapy Networker,* 20(6): 22-28.

2. Carabatea, M. (1997). *Greek mythology.* Athens, Greece: Adams Editions.

3. Redmond, L. (1997). *When the drummers were women: A spiritual history of rhythm.* New York: Three Rivers Press.

4. Campbell, J. with Moyers, B. (1988). *The power of myth: Love and the goddess* (Program 5 Video). New York: Parabola.

5. Bolen, J. S. (1984). *Goddesses in everywoman: A new psychology of women.* New York: Harper and Row, p. 1.

6. Carter, B. and McGoldrick, M. (Eds.) (1999). *The expanded family life cycle: Individual, family, and social perspective,* Third edition. Needham Heights, MA: Allyn & Bacon, p. 78.

7. Nicolo, M., executive producer (1998). *A woman's place.* ph (212) 877-3253. Maryland Public Television video.

8. Ibid.

Chapter 4

1. Jampolsky, L. (1999). Healing the addictive mind. In O.J. Morgan and M. Jordan (Eds.), *Addictions and spirituality* (pp. 55-74). St. Louis: Chalice Press.

2. As cited in Flickstein, M. (1998). *Journey to the center: A meditation workbook.* Boston: Wisdom Publications.

3. Lerner, M. (2000). *Spirit matters: Global healing and the wisdom of the soul.* Charlottesville, VA: Hampton Roads Publishing Company, p. 35.

4. Conn, J.W. (Ed.) (1986). *Woman's spirituality.* New York: Paulist Press, p. 9.

5. Cited in Eisler, R. (1988). *The chalice and the blade: Our history, our future.* San Francisco: HarperSanFrancisco, pp. 12-13.

6. Leeming, D. and Page, J. (1998). *The mythology of native North America.* Norman: University of Oklahoma Press, p. 22.

7. Satir, V. (1988). *The new peoplemaking.* Mountain View, CA: Science and Behavior Books, Inc., p. 336.

8. Wigoder, G. (1974). *Encyclopedic Dictionary of Judaica.* New York: Leon Amiel Publisher, p. 548.

9. Whalen, M. (1999). In the company of women? The politics of memory in the liturgical commemoration of saints—male and female. *Worship, 73*(6): 482-504.

10. Daly, M. (1990). *Gyn/ecology: The metaethics of radical feminism.* Boston: Beacon Press, p. 183.

11. Barstow, A. (1995). *Witchcraze: A new history of the European witch hunts.* San Francisco, CA: Harper Collins, p. 15.

12. Roy, M. (Ed.) (1982). *The abusive partner.* New York: Van Nostrand Reinhold.

13. Anderson, S.R. and Hopkins, P. (1991). *The feminine face of God.* New York: Bantam, p. 18.

14. Woodward, K. (1997). Is God listening? *Newsweek,* March 31, pp. 57-64.

15. Wallis, C. (1996). Faith and healing: Can prayer, faith and spirituality really improve your physical health? *Time,* June 24, pp. 58-62.

16. Lunden, J. (1997). My survival secrets. *McCall's,* June, pp. 18-20.

17. Cooper-White, P. (1995). *The cry of Tamar: Violence against women and the church's response.* Minneapolis: Fortress Press.

18. Horwitz, S. (1999). Sexual politics: Theater women discuss sex and self-image on stage. *Back Stage,* November 19-25, p. 24.

19. Jordan, M. (1999). *Reclaiming your story: Family history and spiritual growth.* Louisville, KY: Westminster John Knox Press, p. 91.

20. Wright, W. (1999). The charism of parenting. In D. Donnelly (Ed.), *Retrieving charisms for the twenty-first century* (pp. 85-101). Collegeville, MN: The Liturgical Press.

Chapter 5

1. Jacobs, R. (1996). Remember the ladies. Vol. 1 in *Women: First and foremost.* Hosted by Moreno, R. and Stone, D. W. CA: Monterey Home Video.

2. Zagano, P. (1993). *Woman to woman: An anthology of women's spirituality.* Collegeville, MN: The Liturgical Press, p. 97.

3. Lerner, H. G. (1988). *Women in therapy.* New York: Harper and Row.

4. Chodorow, N. (1990). *Feminism and psychoanalytic theory.* New Haven: Yale University Press.

5. Benjamin, J. (1988). *The bonds of love: Psychoanalysis, feminism, and the problem of domination.* New York: Pantheon Books, p. 156.

6. Kasl, C. (1999). Many roads, one journey: One woman's path to truth. In O. J. Morgan and M. Jordan (Eds.), *Addictions and spirituality.* St. Louis, MO: Chalice Press, p. 118.

7. Ibid., p. 130.

8. Grinnan, J., McCarthy, M.R., Mitrano, B., Muschal-Reinhardt, R. (1997). *Sisters of the thirteen moons: Rituals celebrating woman's lives.* Webster, NY: The Prism Collective, p. 21.

9. Carnes, P. (1993). *A gentle path through the twelve steps: The classic guide for all people in the process of recovery.* Minneapolis, MN: Compcare Publishers, p. 15.

10. Gilligan, C., Lyons, N., and Hanmer, T. (Eds.) (1990). *Making connections: The relational worlds of adolescent girls at Emma Williard School.* Cambridge, MA: Harvard University Press.

11. Estes, C.P. (1992). *Women who run with the wolves: Myths and stories of the wild woman archetype.* New York: Ballantine Books, p. 80.

12. D'Angelo, M.R. (1995). Veils, virgins, and the tongues of men and angels: Women's heads in early Christianity. In H. Eilberg-Schwartz and W. Doniger (Eds.), *Off with her head! The denial of women's identity in myth, religion, and culture.* Berkeley: University of California Press, p. 131.

Chapter 6

1. Carter, B. and McGoldrick, M. (Eds.) (1999). *The expanded family life cycle: Individual, family, and social perspectives,* Third edition. Needham Heights, MA: Allyn & Bacon, p. 112.

2. Avis, J. (1985). The politics of functional family therapy: A feminist critique. *Journal of Marital and Family Therapy* 11(2): 127-138.

3. Carter and McGoldrick, *The expanded family,* p. 113.

4. Lim, S. (1996). *The nature of healing.* Part 3 Movement Video, Landmark Media Inc. (800) 342-4336.

5. McDougall, J. (1989). *Theaters of the body: A psychoanalytic approach to psychosomatic illness.* New York: W.W. Norton, p. 28.

6. Hinton, C. (1982). *Small happiness: Women of a Chinese village.* Documentary film shown at St. Louis Art Museum, February 29, 2000.

7. Simon, R. (1997). The family unplugged: An interview with Mary Pipher. *The Family Therapy Networker* 21(1): 24-33.

8. Wilder, L. (1999). *7 steps to fearless speaking.* New York: John Wiley and Sons, Inc., p. 38.

9. Griffith, J. and Griffith, M. (1994). *The body speaks: Therapeutic dialogues for mind-body problems.* New York: Basic Books.

10. Northrup, C. (1994). *Women's bodies, women's wisdom: Creating physical and emotional health and healing.* New York: Bantam Books, p. 11.

11. Lerner, H.G. (1988). *Women in therapy.* New York: Harper and Row, pp. 201-226.

12. Cited in Saussy, C. (1995). *The gift of anger: A call to faithful action.* Louisville, KY: Westminster John Knox Press, p. 23.

13. Cited in Tavris, C. (1989). *Anger: The misunderstood emotion.* New York: Touchstone, p. 302.

Chapter 7

1. Weingarten, K. (1994). *The mother's voice: Strengthening intimacy in families.* New York: Guilford, p. 63.

2. Silverstein, S. (1964). *The giving tree.* New York: HarperCollins.

3. Weingarten, *The mother's voice.*

4. Northrup, C. (1994). *Women's bodies, women's wisdom: Creating physical and emotional health and healing.* New York: Bantam. p. 178.

5. Alexie, S. (1993). *The Lone Ranger and Tonto fistfight in heaven.* New York: The Atlantic Monthly Press, p. 33.

6. Hassani, R. (1998). *Fresh air.* Interview by Terry Gross. National Public Radio, December 10.

7. Buechner, F. (1991). *Telling secrets: A memoir.* New York: HarperCollins, pp. 8, 75.

8. Simon, R. (1997). The family unplugged: An interview with Mary Pipher. *The Family Therapy Networker,* January/February, p. 29.

9. Brown, E. (1999). *Affairs: A guide to working through the repercussions of infidelity.* San Francisco: Jossey-Bass, p. 93.

10. Gottman, J. (1994). *Why marriages succeed or fail: And how you can make a difference.* New York: Simon and Schuster.

11. Laird, J. (1993). Women's secrets—women's silences. In E. Imber-Black (Ed.), *Secrets in families and family therapy,* pp. 241-267. New York: W.W. Norton.

Chapter 8

1. Northrup, C. (1994). *Women's bodies and women's wisdom: Creating physical and emotional health and healing.* New York: Bantam Books, p. 4.

2. Levy, H. (1966). *Chinese foot binding: The history of a curious erotic custom.* New York: Walton Rawls, p. 219.

3. Jackson, B. (1997). *Splendid slippers: A thousand years of an erotic tradition.* Berkeley, CA: Ten Speed Press.

4. Daly, M. (1990). *Gyn/ecology: The metaethics of radical feminism.* Boston: Beacon Press, pp. 155-156.

5. Dorkenoo, E. (1994). *Cutting the rose: Female genital mutilation: The practice and prevention.* London: Minority Rights Publications, p. 25.

6. Walker, A. and Parmar, P. (1993). *Warrior marks: Female genital mutilation and the sexual blinding of women.* New York: Harcourt Brace and Company.

7. Dorkenoo, E. *Cutting the Rose.*

8. Cited in Sinacore-Guinn, D. (1998). U.S. ban on female circumcision raises threat of further harm. *The Park Ridge Center Bulletin,* May/June, p. 6.

9. Johnson, R. (1998). A world apart. *Vogue,* June, pp. 251-252.

10. Wassef, N. (1998). Masculinities and mutilations: Female genital mutilation in Egypt. *Middle East Women's Studies,* XIII (2): 1-3.

11. Walker, A. and Parmar, P., *Warrior Marks,* p. 326.

12. Narayanan, V. (1999). Brimmin with *Bhakti,* embodiments of *Shakti:* Devotee, deities, performers, reformers, and other women of power in the Hindu tradition. In A. Sharma and K. Young (Eds.), *Feminism and world religions* (pp. 25-77). Albany, NY: State University of New York Press.

13. Stark, E., Flitcraft, A., Zucherman, D., et al. (1981). *Wife abuse in the medical setting: An introduction for health personnel.* Monograph Series No. 7. National Clearinghouse on Domestic Violence. Washington, DC: U.S. Government Printing Office, April.

14. Fortune, M. (1991). *Violence in the family: A workshop curriculum for clergy and other helpers.* Cleveland, OH: The Pilgrim Press.

15. Conran, T., Robinson, M. L., and Russell, A. (1997). *Tamar's plea: A guide to prayer, worship and liturgy for family violence prevention.* St. Louis, MO: Care and Counseling.

16. Goodrich, T. J. (Ed.) (1991). *Woman and power: Perspectives for family therapy.* New York: W.W. Norton.

Chapter 9

1. McGrath, E., Keita, G.P., Strickland, B.R., and Russo, N.F. (1990). *Women and depression: Risk factors and treatment issues.* Washington, DC: American Psychological Association.

2. Hemphill, H. and Haines, R. (1997). *Discrimination, harassment, and the failure of diversity training.* Westport, CT: Quorum Books.

3. Bellafante, G. (1998). Feminism, *Time,* June 29, p. 58.

4. Hass, S. (1997). Presentation on sexual harassment at St. Anthony's Hospital, St. Louis, MO, June.

5. Cooper-White, P. (1995). *The cry of Tamar: Violence against women and the church's response.* Minneapolis, MN: Fortress Press, p. 59.

6. Stoodley, E. (1998). Presentation on violence to Employee Assistance Professionals, St. Louis, MO, June 17.

7. Meltzer, T. (1999). Understanding and managing anger. Unpublished presentation. Saint Anthony's Medical Center, St. Louis, MO.

8. Dutton, D. (1998). *The abusive personality: Violence and control in intimate relationships.* New York: Guilford.

9. Kindlon, D. and Thompson, M., with Barker, T. (1999). *Raising Cain: Protecting the emotional life of boys.* New York: Ballantine Books, p. 219.

10. Hallowell, E. (1999). *Connect: 12 vital ties that open your heart, lengthen your life, and deepen your soul.* New York: Random House.

11. Wallace, H. (1999). *Family violence: Legal, medical, and social perspectives,* Second edition. Needham, MA: Allyn & Bacon, p. 295.

Chapter 10

1. Kilbourne, J. (1999). *Deadly persuasion: Why women and girls must fight the addictive power of advertising.* New York: The Free Press, p. 80.

2. Ibid., pp. 96, 103.

3. Ibid., p. 104.

4. Ibid., pp. 46-47.

5. Echevarria, P. (1998). *For all our daughters: How mentoring helps young women and girls master the art of growing up.* Worcester, MA: Chandler House Press, p. 12.

6. Cited in Kilbourne, *Deadly persuasion,* p. 253.

7. Ibid.

8. Borysenko, J. (1990). *Guilt is the teacher, love is the lesson: A book to heal you, heart and soul.* New York: Warner Books, pp. 35-43.

9. Nathanson, D. (1992). *Shame and pride: Affect, sex, and the birth of the self.* New York: W.W. Norton.

10. Caplan, P.J. (1989). *Don't blame mother: Mending the mother-daughter relationship.* New York: Harper and Row.

11. Dweck, C.S. and Licht, B. G. (1980). Learned helplessness and intellectual achievement. In M. Seligman and Garber, J. (Eds.), *Human helplessness: Theory and research* (pp. 197-221). New York: Academic Press.

Chapter 11

1. Lerner, H. G. (1993). *The dance of deception: Pretending and truth-telling in women's lives.* New York: HarperCollins Publisher, p. 121.

2. Viscott, D. (1991). *The winning woman: Understanding your feelings of anger and guilt.* Chicago, IL: Nightingale-Conant Corporation, audiotape, 1-800-323-5552.

3. Shinkle, F. (1999). Women in the vote: St. Louis suffragists helped pave the way with their "Golden Lane" demonstration in 1916. *St. Louis Post-Dispatch,* February 14, p. A12.

4. Woods, H. (2000). *Stepping up to power: The political journey of American women.* Boulder, CO: Westview Press, pp. 138-139.

5. Discussed in Saussy, C. (1995). *The gift of anger: A call to faithful action.* Louisville, KY: Westminster, p. 75.

6. Cited in Scarf, M. (1995). *Intimate worlds: Life inside the family.* New York: Random House, pp. 23-36.

7. Rosenberg, M. (1999). *Nonviolent communication: A language of compassion.* Del Mar, CA: PuddleDancer Press.

Chapter 12

1. Imber-Black, E. (1998). *The secret life of families: Truth-telling, privacy and reconciliation in a tell-all society.* New York: Bantam Books.

2. Thornton, B. B. and Epperson, T. (1996). *A family thing.* United Artists Video.

3. Leigh, M., producer (1996). *Secrets and lies.* 20th Century Fox.

4. Gitai, A. (1999). *Kadosh* (Sacred). Produced by Agav Hafakot, M.P. Productions, and Le Studio Canal.

5. Cameron, J. (1996). *The vein of gold: A journey to your creative heart.* New York: Putnam Books, pp. 13-17.

6. Allen, W. (1998). *Deconstructing Harry.* New Line Home Video.

7. Dutton, D. (1998). *The abusive personality: Violence and control in intimate relationships*. New York: Guilford.

8. Hartman, A. (1993). Secrecy in adoption. In E. Imber-Black (Ed.), *Secrets in families and family therapy* (pp. 86-105). New York: Norton.

9. Wright, L. and Nagy, J. (1993). Death: The most troublesome family secret of all. In E. Imber-Black (Ed.), *Secrets in families and family therapy* (pp. 121-137). New York: Norton.

10. "Heroes and icons: The fifth in a series of special issues on the most influential people of the century." (1999). *Time,* 153(23), June 14, p. 30.

11. Imber-Black, E. (1998), p. 104.

Chapter 13

1. Frymer-Kensky, T. (1992*). In the wake of the goddesses: Women, culture, and biblical transformation of pagan myth*. New York: The Free Press.

2. Hirshfield, J. (Ed.) (1994). *Women in praise of the sacred: 43 centuries of spiritual poetry by women*. New York: HarperCollins, p. 4.

3. Gottman, J. (1998). *Scientifically based workshop on marital therapy*. St. John's Hospital, St. Louis, MO, April.

4. Cleary, T. (Ed.) (1996). *Immortal sisters: Secret teachings of Taoist women*. Berkeley: North Atlanta Books.

5. Leeming, D. and Page, J. (1994). *Goddess: Myths of the female divine*. New York: Oxford University Press, p. 76.

6. Gross, T. (1998). *Fresh air*. National Public Radio interview with Pat Schroeder, May.

7. Gilligan, C. (1982). *In a different voice: Psychological theory and women's development*. Cambridge, MA: Harvard University Press, p. 18.

8. Ibid., p. 67.

9. Gilligan, C., Rogers, A., and Tolman, D. (Eds.) (1991). *Women, girls and psychotherapy: Reframing resistance*. Binghamton, NY: The Haworth Press, Inc.

10. Goldberger, N., Tarule, J., Clinchy, B., and Belenky, M. (Eds.) (1996). *Knowledge, difference, and power*. New York: Basic Books.

11. Holohan, M. (1998). *Left out by Rosie*. Wilmette, IL: The Broadway Ballplayers, Inc.

12. Graham, K. (1997). *Personal history*. New York: Random House.

Chapter 14

1. Sadler, M. and Sadler, D. (1994). *Failing at fairness: How America's schools cheat girls*. New York: Charles Scribner's Sons.

2. *Shortchanging girls, shortchanging America*. (1991). Washington, DC: Commissioned by American Association of University Women and researched by Greenberg-Lake: The Analysis Group.

3. Borysenko, J. (1996). *A woman's book of life: The biology, psychology, and spirituality of the feminine life cycle*. New York: Riverhead Books, pp. 64-65.

4. *Hostile hallways: Bullying, teasing, and sexual harassment in school*. (1991). Washington, DC: Report by the American Association of University Women Educational Foundation.

5. Woods, H. (2000). *Stepping up to power: The political journey of American women*. Boulder, CO: Westview Press.

6. Ibid., p. 105.

7. Rehm, D. (1999). *Finding my voice*. New York: Knopf.

8. Pipher, M. (1994). *Reviving Ophelia: Saving the selves of adolescent girls*. New York: Putnam.

9. Pittman, F. (1989). *Private lies: Infidelity and the betrayal of intimacy*. New York: W.W. Norton and Company.

10. Barnes, D. and Earle, R. (1998). *Healing conversations: Therapy and spiritual growth*. Downers Grove, IL: InterVarsity Press, p. 141.

11. hooks, b. (2000). *all about love: new visions*. New York: William Morrow and Company, Inc.

Chapter 15

1. Hillesum, E. (1984). *An interrupted life, the diaries of Etty Hillesum 1941-1943* (Arno Pomerans, Trans.). New York: Pantheon Books (Original work published in 1984), p. 129.

2. Ellsberg, R. (1997). *All saints: Daily reflections on saints, prophets, and witnesses for our times*. New York: Crossroads, p. 523.

3. Hillesum, *An interrupted life,* p. 130.

4. Ochs, C. and Olitzky, K. (1998). *Jewish spiritual guidance: Finding our way to God*. San Francisco: Jossey-Bass Publishers, p.16.

5. Kearns, M. (1976). *Käthe Kollwitz: Woman and artist*. New York: The Feminist Press, p. 82.

6. Cuchel, K. (1988). *Notes on Käthe Kollwitz*. The Saint Louis Art Museum.

7. Klein, M.C. and Klein, H. A. (1972). *Käthe Kollwitz: Life in art*. New York: Holt, Rinehart and Winston, p. 85.

8. Steere, D. (1984). *Quaker spirituality: Selected writings*. New York: Paulist Press, p. 248.

9. Julian of Norwich (1978). *Showings*. New York: Paulist Press, p. 295.

10. Ibid., p. 299.

11. Ellsberg, R. *All saints,* p. 448.

12. Zagano, P. (1993). *Woman to woman: An anthology of women's spiritualities*. Collegeville, MN: The Liturgical Press, pp. 105-106.

Chapter 16

1. Lesyk, J. (1998). *Developing sport psychology within your clinical practice: A practical guide for mental health professionals*. San Francisco: Jossey-Bass, p. 141.

2. Stiver, I. (1991). Work inhibitions in women. In Jordan, J.V., Kaplan, A.G., Miller, J.B., Stiver, I.P., and Surrey, J.L. (Eds.), *Women's growth in connection: Writings from the Stone Center*. New York: Guilford, p. 225.

3. Olson, D. (1998). The use of assessments in pre-marital therapy. 56th AAMFT Annual Conference.

4. Vaughan, S. (2000). *Half empty half full: Understanding the psychological roots of optimism*. New York: Harcourt, Inc., p. 49.

5. Heller, N. G. (1997). *Women artists: An illustrated history,* Third edition. New York: Abbeville Press, pp. 58-61.

6. Winfrey, O. (2000). Women who broke barriers. Chicago: NBC Television, April 25.

7. Switzer, K. (1998). *Running and walking for women over 40: The road to sanity and vanity.* New York: St. Martin's Press.

8. Interview by Oprah Winfrey, April 25, 2000.

9. Ryan, T. (1986). *Wellness, spirituality and sports.* New York: Paulist Press, p. 43.

10. Falk, M. (1989). Notes on composing new blessings: Toward a feminist-Jewish reconstruction of prayer. In J. Plaskow and C. Christ (Eds.), *Weaving the visions: New patterns in feminist spirituality.* New York: HarperCollins, p. 134.

11. Scherman, Rabbi N. (1990). *The complete artscroll Siddur.* New York: Mesorah Publications, p. 19.

12. Mitchell, R. C. and Ricciuti, G. A. (1991). *Birthings and blessings: Liberating worship service for the inclusive church.* New York: Crossroad.

13. Robinson-Walker, C. (1999). *Woman and leadership in health care: Journey to authenticity and power.* San Francisco: Jossey-Bass Publishers, p. 149.

Chapter 17

1. Jordan, M. (1999). *Reclaiming your story: Family history and spiritual growth.* Louisville, KY: Westminster John Knox Press, p. 50.

2. McGuire, M. and Klein, J. (1999). *The interactive focusing process.* Canada: Nada Lou Productions. Video requests contact Dr. Janet Klein at (561) 540-2687.

3. Yapko, M. (1999). *Hand me down blues: How to keep depression from spreading in families.* New York: Golden Books.

4. Rosenberg, M. (1999). *Nonviolent communication: A language of compassion.* Del Mar, CA: PuddleDancer Press, p. 2.

5. Katherine, A. (1991). *Boundaries: Where you end and I begin.* New York: Simon and Schuster.

Chapter 18

1. Quinn, S. (1995). *Marie Curie: A life* (pp. 351-375). New York: Simon and Schuster.

2. Dally, P. (1999). *The marriage of heaven and hell: Manic depression and the life of Virginia Woolf.* New York: St. Martin's Press.

3. Schlessinger, A. (1995). *Wilma Rudolph: American women of achievement.* Schlessinger Video Productions.

4. Heller, N. G. (1997). *Women artists: An illustrated history,* Third edition. New York: Abbeville Publishers, p. 29.

5. Woodruff, J. (1996). *Women world leaders.* New Dimension Media, Inc. Video. ph (217) 243-4567.

6. Lessa, C. (1998). *Stories of triumph, women who win in sport and in life.* New York: Universe, p. 71.

7. Ibid., p. 142.

8. Ibid., p. 149.

9. Henehan, M. P. and Herning, P. (1999). Strong minds strong bodies. Unpublished research. Saint Louis, MO: Counseling and Educational Associates, Inc.

10. Ibid.

11. Weger, L. (1995). Christmas reflection. Unpublished, p. 1.

12. Cochran, J. and Brinley, M.B. (1987). *Jackie Cochran: An autobiography.* New York: Bantam Books.

13. Randle, N. (1999). In 1942, for the first time, chicks took wing on military mission for the U.S. *St. Louis Post-Dispatch,* May 24, p. E3.

Chapter 19

1. Wilder, M., music, and Coats, P., producer (1998). *Mulan.* CA: Walt Disney Production. Buena Vista Video.

2. Read, P.J. and Witlieb, B.L. (1992). *The book of women's firsts: Breakthrough achievements of almost 1,000 American women.* New York: Random House.

3. Sicherman, B. (1984). *Alice Hamilton: A life in letters.* Cambridge, MA: Harvard University Press.

4. Proud Deer, N. (2000). Chief among us. *St. Louis Times,* May, pp. 16-17. Reprinted with permission.

5. Ibid.

6. Mankiller, W. and Wallis, M. (1993). *Mankiller: A chief and her people.* New York: St. Martin's Griffin, pp. 12, 16.

7. Siggins, L. (1997). *Mary Robinson: The woman who took power in the park.* Edinburgh: Mainstream Publishing Company, p. 210.

8. Dorcey, M. (2001). Irish women poets. Presentation at International Studies, University of Missouri, St. Louis, MO.

Chapter 20

1. Walsh, F. (1998). *Strengthening family resilience.* New York: Guilford.

2. Lelwica, M. M. (1999). *Starving for salvation: The spiritual dimensions of eating problems among American girls and women.* New York: Oxford, p. 125.

3. Dorcey (2001). *Like joy in season, like sorrow.* Cliffs of Mohr, Co. Clare, Ireland: Salmon Publishing Ltd., pp. 8-9.

4. Bishop, E. (2001). *Geography III* (Twenty-first printing). New York: Farrar, Straus and Giroux.

5. cummings, e. e. (1972). *Complete poems 1913-1962.* New York: Harcourt Brace Jovanovich, p. 682.

6. Grizzle, A. (1992). Family therapy with the faithful: Christians as clients. In L. A. Burton (Ed.), *Religion and the family: When God helps* (pp. 139-162). Binghamton, NY: The Haworth Pastoral Press.

7. Wallis, J. (2000). *Faith works: Lessons from the life of an activist preacher.* New York: Random House, p. 23

Chapter 21

1. Benson, H. (1997). *Spirituality and healing.* Harvard MED-CME Video. P.0. Box 825, Boston, MA 02117-0825.

2. Gelenberg, A., Lydiard, R. B., Rudolph, R., Aguiar, L., Haskins, J.T., and Salinas, E. (2000). Efficacy of Velafaxine Extended-Release capsules in non-depressed outpatients with generalized anxiety disorder. *JAMA* 283(23): 3082-3088.

3. Fraser, L. (1997). *Losing it: America's obsession with weight and the industry that feeds on it.* New York: Dutton.

4. Lesyk, J. (1998). *Developing sport psychology within your clinical practice.* San Francisco, CA: Jossey-Bass.

5. Jackson, P. and Delehanty, H. (1995). *Sacred hoops: Spiritual lessons of the hardwood warrior.* New York: Hyperion.

6. Morrison, T. (1987). *Beloved.* New York: Knopf, p. 88.

7. Cameron, J. (1996). *The vein of gold: A journey to your creative heart.* New York: Putnam Books, p. 99.

8. Borysenko, J. (1994). *The power of the mind to heal: Renewing body, mind, and spirit.* New York: Simon and Schuster, Inc.

9. Roth, G. with Loudon, J. (1998). *Maps to ecstasy: A healing for the untamed spirit.* Novato, CA: New World Library, p. 3.

10. Ingerman, S. (1991). *Soul retrieval: Mending the fragmented self.* New York: HarperCollins, p. 40.

Chapter 22

1. Henehan, M.P. and Herning, M. (1999). Strong minds, Strong bodies. Unpublished research. St. Louis, MO: Counseling and Educational Associates, Inc.

2. Burns, K. (1999). *Not for ourselves alone: The story of Elizabeth Cady Stanton and Susan B. Anthony.* Alexandria, VA: PBS Video, November 7-8.

3. Woods, H. (2000). *Stepping up to power: The political journey of American women.* Boulder, CO: Westview Press, p. 149.

Chapter 23

1. Relaford Brown, J. (1994). Finding her here. In S. Haldeman Martz (Ed.), anthologies, *I am becoming the woman I have wanted.* Watsonville, CA: Paper-Mache Press, p. 1. Reproduced with permission of the author.

2. Nelson, M. with Wernick, S. (1998). *Strong women stay slim.* New York: Bantam.

3. Wright, L. and Nagy, J. (1993). Death: The most troublesome family secret of all. In E. Imber-Black (Ed.), *Secrets in families and family therapy.* New York: W.W. Norton, p. 123.

4. Higginson, J. (1948). *Epictetus, the enchiridion.* New York: Macmillan, p. 19.

5. Watson, W. (1995). *Aging families and beliefs.* AAMFT Annual Convention audio tapes. ph 1-800-241-7785.

6. Steinem, G. (1992). *Revolution from within: A book of self-esteem.* Beverly Hills, CA: Dove Audio.

7. Mac Donald, S. and Richman, A. (1997). *The winter guest* (screenplay). Fine Line Feature Video.

8. Buechner, F. (1991). *Telling secrets: A memoir.* New York: HarperCollins, p. 69.

9. Friedan, B. (2000). *Life so far: A memoir.* New York: Simon and Schuster.

10. Gast, H. and Gethers, S. (1982). *A woman called Golda.* Paramount Home Video.

11. Dateline Special (2001). Human trafficking. March 18. Video. ph (800) 420-2626.

12. Friedan, B. (1993). *The fountain of age.* New York: Audioworks, Simon and Schuster.

13. Weed, S. (2002). *New menopausal years the wise woman way.* Woodstock, NY: Ash Tree Publishing, p. xiii. Reprinted with permission.

Chapter 24

1. Berlin, D. (1992). *Reclaiming advent.* Calendar. Rio Rancho, New Mexico: Friends of Women.

2. Winter, M.T. (1990). *Woman prayer woman song.* New York: Crossroad.

3. Diethrich, E. and Cohan, C. (1992). *Women and heart disease.* New York: Random House.

4. Seaward, B. (1997). *Stand like mountain, flow like water.* Deerfield Beach, FL: Health Communications, Inc.

5. Ornish, D. (1982). *Stress, diet, and your heart.* New York: Signet.

6. Lipski, E. (1996). *Digestive wellness.* New Canaan, CT: Keats, p. 97.

7. Benson, H. with Klipper, M. (1975). *The relaxation response.* New York: HarperTorch.

8. Dunn, T. (1989). *T'ai Chi for health.* Healing Arts Home Video.

9. Cameron, J. (1998). *Blessings.* New York: Tarcher/Putnam, p. 64.

10. Cameron, J. (1996). *The vein of gold: A journey to your creative heart.* New York: Tarcher/Putnam.

11. Cameron, J. (1992). *The artist's way: A spiritual path to higher creativity.* New York: G. P. Putnam's sons.

12. Schuhmacher, S. and Woerner, G. (1989). *The encyclopedia of Eastern philosophy and religion.* Boston: Shambhala, pp. 58-61.

13. Schor, J. (1992). *The overworked American: The unexpected decline of leisure.* New York: Basic Books.

14. Bass, D. (Ed.) (1997). *Practicing our faith: A way of life for a searching people.* San Francisco: Jossey-Bass.

15. Berry, T. (1988). *The dream of the earth.* San Francisco: Sierra Club Books, p. 119.

16. Bryan, M. with Cameron, J. and Allen, C. (1998). *The artist's way at work.* New York: William Morrow and Company, Inc.

Bibliography

Alexie, S. (1993). *The Lone Ranger and Tonto fistfight in heaven*. New York: The Atlantic Monthly Press.

Allen, W. (1998). *Deconstructing Harry*. New Line Home Video.

Allende, I. (1998). *Aphrodite: A memoir of the senses*. New York: HarperCollins.

Anderson, S. R. and Hopkins, P. (1991). *The feminine face of God: The unfolding of the sacred in women*. New York: Bantam.

Aponte, H. J. (1994). *Bread and spirit: Therapy with the new poor*. New York: W.W. Norton.

Armistead, M. (1995). *God-images in the healing process*. Minneapolis: Fortress Press.

Armstrong, G. (1994). *Little women*. California: Columbia Pictures video.

Avis, J. (1985). The politics of functional family therapy: A feminist critique. *Journal of Marital and Family Therap*y 11(2): 127-138.

Barnes, D. and Earle, R. (1998). *Healing conversations: Therapy and spiritual growth*. Downers Grove, IL: InterVarsity Press.

Barstow, A. (1995). *Witchcraze: A new history of the European witch hunts*. San Francisco, CA: HarperCollins.

Bass, D. (Ed.). (1997). *Practicing our faith: A way of life for a searching people*. San Francisco: Jossey-Bass.

Bateson, Mary Catherine (1989). *Composing a life*. New York: The Atlantic Monthly Press.

Becvar, D. (1997). *Soul healing*. New York: Basic Books.

Bellafante, G. (1998). Feminism. *Time,* June 29, p. 58.

Benjamin, Jessica (1988). *The bonds of love: Psychoanalysis, feminism, and the problem of domination*. New York: Pantheon Books.

Benson, H. (1997). *Spirituality and healing*. Harvard MED-CME Video. P.O. Box 825, Boston MA 02117-0825.

Benson, H. and Klipper, M. (1975). *The relaxation response*. New York: HarperTorch.

Berlin, D. (1992). *Reclaiming advent*. Calendar Rio Rancho, NM: Friends of women.

Berry, T. (1988). *The dream of the earth*. San Francisco: Sierra Club Books.

Berry, T. (1999). *The great work: Our way into the future*. New York: Bell Tower.

Bishop, E. (2001). *Geography III* (Twenty-first printing). New York: Farrar, Straus and Giroux.

Bolen, J. (1984). *Goddesses in everywoman: A new psychology of women.* New York: Harper and Row.

Bolman, L. G. (1995). *Leading with soul: An uncommon journey of spirit.* San Francisco: Jossey-Bass Publishers.

Borysenko, J. (1990). *Guilt is the teacher, love is the lesson: A book to heal you, heart and soul.* New York: Warner Books.

Borysenko, J. (1997). *A woman's book of life: The biology, psychology, and spirituality of the feminine life cycle.* New York: Riverhead Books.

Boscolo, L. and Cecchin, G. (1987). *Master series: What to call it?* Washington, DC: American Association of Marriage and Family Therapy.

Brown, E. (1999). *Affairs: A guide to working through the repercussions of infidelity.* San Francisco: Jossey-Bass.

Bryan, M. with Cameron, J. and Allen, C. (1998). *The artist's way at work.* New York: William Marrow and Co. Inc.

Buechner, F. (1991). *Telling secrets: A memoir.* New York: HarperCollins.

Burns, K. (1999). *Not for ourselves alone: The story of Elizabeth Cady Stanton and Susan B. Anthony.* Alexandria, VA: PBS video, November 7-8.

Burton, L. A. (Ed.) (1992). *Religion and the family: When God helps.* Binghamton, NY: The Haworth Pastoral Press.

Cameron, J. (1992). *The artist's way: A spiritual path to higher creativity.* New York: Putnam.

Cameron, J. (1996). *The vein of gold: A journey to your creative heart.* New York: Putnam Books.

Cameron, J. (1998). *Blessings.* New York: Tarcher/Putnam.

Campbell, J. with Moyers, B. (1988). *The power of myth: Love and the goddess* (Program 5 video). New York: Parabola.

Caplan, P. (1989). *Don't blame mother: Mending the mother-daughter relationship.* New York: Harper Row.

Carabatea, M. (1997). *Greek mythology.* Athens, Greece: Adams Editions.

Carnes, P. (1993). *A gentle path through the twelve steps: The classic guide for all people in the process of recovery.* Minneapolis, MN: Compcare Publishers.

Carter, B. and McGoldrick, M. (Eds.) (1999). *The expanded family life cycle: Individual, family, and social perspectives,* Third edition. Needham Heights, MA: Allyn & Bacon.

Chodorow, N. (1990). *Feminism and psychoanalytic theory.* New Haven: Yale University Press.

Cleary, T. (Ed.) (1996). *Immortal sisters: Secret teachings of Taoist women.* Berkeley: North Atlanta Books.

Clinton, H. R. (1996). *It takes a village: And other lessons children teach us.* New York: Simon and Schuster.

Cochran, J. and Brinley, M. B. (1987). *Jackie Cochran: An autobiography.* New York: Bantam Books.

Conn, J. W. (Ed.) (1986). *Woman's spirituality.* New York: Paulist Press.

Conran, T., Robinson, M. L., and Russel, A. (1997). *Tamar's plea: A guide to prayer, worship, and liturgy for family violence prevention.* St. Louis, MO: Care and Counseling.

Cooper-White, P. (1995). *The cry of Tamar: Violence against women and the church's response.* Minneapolis: Fortress Press.

Cousins, N. (1989). *Head first: The biology of hope.* New York: E.P. Dutton.

Cuchel, K. (1988). *Notes on Käthe Kollwitz's work.* St. Louis, MO: Art Museum.

cummings, e. e. (1972). *Complete poems 1913-1962.* New York: Harcourt Brace Jovanovich.

Dally, P. (1999). *The marriage of heaven and hell: Manic depression and the life of Virginia Woolf.* New York: St. Martin's Press.

Daly, M. (1990). *Gyn/ecology: The metaethics of radical feminism.* Boston: Beacon Press.

Diethrich, E. and Cohan, C. (1992). *Women and heart disease.* New York: Random House.

Doherty, W. (1995). *Soul searching: Why psychotherapy must promote moral responsibility.* New York: Basic Books.

Donnelly, D. (1999). *Retrieving charisms for the twenty-first century.* Collegeville, MN: The Liturgical Press.

Dorcey, M. (2001). Irish women poets. Presentation at International Studies, The University of Missouri, St. Louis, MO.

Dorcey, M. (2001). *Like joy in season, like sorrow.* Cliffs of Mohr, Co. Clare, Ireland: Salmon Publishing Ltd.

Dorkenoo, E. (1994). *Cutting the rose: Female genital mutilation: The practice and prevention.* London: Minority Rights Publications.

Dossey, L. (1993). *Healing words.* New York: HarperCollins.

Dossey, L. (1996). *Prayer is good medicine.* New York: HarperCollins.

Dunn, T. (1989). *T'ai Chi for health.* Healing Arts Home Video.

Dutton, D. (1998). *The abusive personality: Violence and control in intimate relationships.* New York: The Guilford Press.

Dweck, C. S. and Licht, B. G. (1980). Learned helplessness and intellectual achievement. In M. Seligman and J. Garber (Eds.), *Human helplessness: Theory and research* (pp. 197-221). New York: Academic Press.

Echevarria, P. (1998). *For all our daughters: How mentoring helps young women and girls master the art of growing up.* Worcester, MA: Chandler House Press.

Eilberg-Schwartz, H. and Doniger, W. (Eds.) (1995). *Off with her head: The denial of women's identity in myth, religion, and culture.* Berkeley: University of California Press.

Eisler, R. (1988). *The chalice and the blade: Our history, our future.* San Francisco, CA: HarperSanFrancisco.

Ellsberg, R. (1997). *All saints: Daily reflections on saints, prophets, and witnesses for our times.* New York: Crossroads.

Estes, C. P. (1992). *Women who run with the wolves: Myths and stories of the wild woman archetype.* New York: Ballantine Books.

Eyler, A. A., Brownson, R. C., Brown, D., Donatelle, R. J., Heath, G. (1997). Physical activity and women in the United States: An overview of health benefits, prevalence, and intervention opportunities. *Women and Health* 26(3), 27-49.

Falk, M. (1989). Notes on composing new blessings: Toward a feminist-Jewish reconstruction of prayer. In J. Plaskow and C. Christ (Eds.), *Weaving the visions: New patterns in feminist spirituality* (pp. 128-138). New York: HarperCollins.

Fiorenza, E. S. (1985). *In memory of her: A feminist reconstruction of Christian origins.* New York: Crossroad.

Fiorenza Schussler, E. (1994). *Searching the scriptures: A feminist commentary,* Volume two. New York: Continuum.

Fiorenza Schussler, E. (1994). *Searching the scriptures: A feminist introduction.* New York: Continuum.

Flickstein, M. (1998). *Journey to the center: A meditation workbook.* Boston: Wisdom Publications.

Fortune, M. (1991). *Violence in the family: A workshop curriculum for clergy and other helpers.* Cleveland, OH: The Pilgrim Press.

Fraser, L. (1997). *Losing it: America's obsession with weight and the industry that feeds on it.* New York: Dutton.

Friedan, B. (1993). *The fountain of age.* New York: Audioworks, Simon and Schuster.

Friedan, B. (2000). *Life so far: A memoir.* New York: Simon and Schuster.

Frymer-Kensky, T. (1992). *In the wake of the goddesses: Women, culture, and biblical transformation of pagan myth.* New York: The Free Press.

Gast, H. and Gethers, S., writers (1982). *A woman called Golda.* Paramount Home Video.

Gelenberg, A., Lydiard, R. B., Rudolph, R., Aguiar, L., Haskins, J. T., and Salinas, E. (2000). Efficacy of Velafaxine Extended-Release capsules in non-depressed outpatients with generalized anxiety disorder. *JAMA* 283(23): 3082-3088.

Gilligan, C. (1982). *In a different voice: Psychological theory and women's development.* Cambridge, MA: Harvard University Press.

Gilligan, C., Lyons, N., and Hammer, T. (Eds.) (1990). *Making connections: The relational worlds of adolescent girls at Emma Williard School.* Cambridge, MA: Harvard University Press.

Gilligan, C., Rogers, A. and Tolman, D. (Eds.) (1991). *Women, girls and psychotherapy.* Binghamton, NY: The Haworth Press.

Gitai, A. (1999). *Kadosh* (Sacred). Produced by Agav Hafakot, M. P. Productions, and Le Studio Canal.

Goldberger, N. R., Tarule, J. M., Clinchy, B. M., Belenky, M. F. (Eds.) (1996). *Knowledge, difference, and power.* New York: Basic Books.

Goleman, D. (1995). *Emotional intelligence.* Los Angeles, CA: Audio Renaissance Tapes.

Goodrich, T. J. (Ed.) (1991). *Woman and power: Perspectives for family therapy.* New York: W.W. Norton.

Gottman, J. (1994). *Why marriages succeed or fail: And how you can make a difference.* New York: Simon and Schuster.

Gottman, J. with Silver, N. (1994). *Why marriages succeed or fail.* New York: Simon and Schuster.

Grace, M. and J. (1980). *A joyful meeting.* St. Paul, MN: International Marriage Encounter.

Graham, K. (1997). *Personal history.* New York: Random House.

Griffith, J. and Griffith, M. (1994). *The body speaks: Therapeutic dialogues for the mind-body problems.* New York: Basic Books.

Grinnan, J., McCarthy, M. R., Mitrano, B., Muschal-Reinhardt, R. (1997). *Sisters of the thirteen moons: Rituals celebrating women's lives.* Webster, NY: The Prism Collective.

Grizzle, A. (1992). Family therapy with the faithful: Christians as clients. In L. A. Burton (Ed.), *Religion and the family: When God helps* (pp. 139-162). Binghamton, NY: The Haworth Pastoral Press.

Gross, D. (1999). Take it from the top. *Working woman.* July/August. New York: MacDonald Communication Center.

Gross, T. (1998). *Fresh air.* Interview of Rana Hassoni. New York and Washington, DC: National Public Radio, December 10.

Habito, R. L. F. (1993). *Healing breath: Zen spirituality for a wounded earth.* Maryknoll, NY: Orbis.

Hallowell, E. (1999). *Connect: 12 vital ties that open your heart, lengthen your life, and deepen your soul.* New York: Random House.

Hargrave, T. and Hanna, S. (Eds.). (1997). *The aging family: New visions in theory, practice, and reality.* New York: Brunner/Mazel.

Hartman, A. (1993). Secrecy in adoption. In E. Imber-Black (Ed.), *Secrets in families and family therapy* (pp. 86-105). New York: Norton.

Hassani, R. (1998). *Fresh Air.* Interview by Terry Gross. National Public Radio, December 10.

Hay, L. L. (1982). *Heal your body.* Carson, CA: Hay House, Inc.

Heller, N. (1997). *Women artists: An illustrated history,* Third edition. New York: Abbeville Press.

Hemphill, H. and Haines, R. (1997). *Discrimination, harassment, and the failure of diversity training.* Westport, CT: Quorum Books.

Henehan, M. P. and Herning, P. (1999). Strong minds, strong bodies. Unpublished research, Saint Louis, MO: Counseling and Educational Associates, Inc.

Herman, M., writer, director (1998). *Little voice.* Burbank, CA: Miramax video.

Higginson, J. (1948). *Epictetus, the enchiridion.* New York: Macmillan.

Hillesum, E. (1984). *An interrupted life, the diaries of Etty Hillesum 1941-1943.* (Arno Pomerans, Trans.). New York: Pantheon Books (original work published in 1984).

Hinton, C. (1982). *Small happiness: Women of a Chinese village*. Documentary film shown at St. Louis Art Museum, February 29, 2000.

Hirschfield, J. (Ed.) (1994). *Women in praise of the sacred: 43 centuries of spiritual poetry by women*. New York: HarperCollins.

Hochschild, A. R. (1997). *The time bind: When work becomes home and home becomes work*. New York: Owl Books.

Holohan, M. (1998). *Left out by Rosie*. Wilmette, IL: The Broadway Ballplayers, Inc.

hooks, b. (2000). *all about love: new visions*. New York: William Morrow and Company, Inc.

Horacek, B. (1980). Life review: A pastoral counseling technique. In J. A. Thorson and T. C. Cook (Eds.), *Spiritual well-being of the elderly* (pp. 100-107). Springfield, IL: Thomas Books.

Imber-Black, E. (Ed.) (1993). *Secrets in families and family therapy*. New York: W.W. Norton.

Imber-Black, E. (1998). *The secret life of families: Truth-telling, privacy and reconciliation in a tell-all society*. New York: Bantam Books.

Ingerman, S. (1991). *Soul retrieval*. New York: HarperCollins.

Ireland, M. S. (1993). *Reconceiving women*. New York: Guilford.

Jackson, B. (1997). *Splendid slippers: A thousand years of an erotic tradition*. Berkeley, CA: Ten Speed Press.

Jackson, P. and Delehanty, H. (1995). *Sacred hoops: Spiritual lessons of the hardwood warrior*. New York: Hyperion.

Jacobs, R. (1996). Remember the ladies. Vol. 1 in *Women: First and foremost*. Hosted by Moreno, R. and Stone, D. W. CA: Monterey Home Video.

Johnson, R. (1998). A world apart. *Vogue,* June, pp. 251-252.

Jordan, J. V., Kaplan, A., Miller, J. B., Stiver, I., and Surrey, J. L. (1991). *Women's growth in connection: Writings from the Stone Center*. New York: Guilford.

Jordan, M. (1999). *Reclaiming your story: Family history and spiritual growth*. Louisville, KY: Westminster John Knox Press.

Julian of Norwich (1978). *Showings*. New York: Paulist Press.

Kasl, C. (1999). Many roads, one journey: One woman's path to truth. In O. J. Morgan and M. Jordan (Eds.), *Addictions and spirituality* (pp. 111-135). St. Louis, MO: Chalice Press.

Katherine, A. (1991). *Boundaries: Where you end and I begin*. New York: Simon and Schuster.

Kearns, M. (1976). *Käthe Kollwitz: Woman and artist*. New York: The Feminist Press.

Kilbourne, J. (1999). *Deadly persuasion: Why women and girls must fight the addictive power of advertising*. New York: The Free Press.

Kindlon, D. and Thompson, M. (1999). *Raising Cain: Protecting the emotional life of boys*. New York: Ballantine Books.

Klein, M. C. and Klein, H. A. (1972). *Käthe Kollwitz: Life in art.* New York: Holt, Rinehart, and Winston.

Koenig, H. G. (1994). *Aging and God: Spiritual pathways to mental health in midlife and later years.* Binghamton, NY: The Haworth Pastoral Press.

Koenig, H. G. (1999). *The healing power of faith: Science explores medicine's last great frontier.* New York: Simon and Schuster.

Lahs-Gonzales, O. and Lippard, L. (1997). *Defining eye: Women photographers of the 20th century.* Saint Louis: Saint Louis Art Museum.

Laird, J. (1993). Women's secrets—women's silences. In Evan Imber-Black (Ed.), *Secrets in families and family therapy* (pp. 241-267). New York: W.W. Norton.

Leeming, D. and Page, J. (1994). *Goddess: Myths of the female divine.* New York: Oxford University Press.

Leeming, D. and Page, J. (1998). *The mythology of native North America.* Norman, OK: University of Oklahoma Press.

Leigh, M., producer (1996). *Secrets and lies.* 20th Century Fox Video.

Lelwica, M. M. (1999). *Starving for salvation: The spiritual dimensions of eating problems among American girls and women.* New York: Oxford.

Lerner, H. G. (1988). *Women in therapy.* New York: Harper and Row.

Lerner, H. G. (1993). *The dance of deception: Pretending and truth-telling in women's lives.* New York: HarperCollins Publisher.

Lerner, M. (2000). *Spirit matters: Global healing and the wisdom of the soul.* Charlottesville, VA: Hampton Roads Publishing Company.

Lessa, C. (1998). *Stories of triumph: Women who win in sport and in life.* New York: Universe.

Lesyk, J. (1998). *Developing sport psychology within your clinical practice: A practical guide for mental health professionals.* San Francisco: Jossey-Bass.

Levy, H. (1966). *Chinese foot binding: The history of a curious erotic custom.* New York: Walton Rawls.

Lim, S. (1996). *The nature of healing.* Part 3, movement video, Landmark Media Inc. (800) 342-4336.

Lipski, E. (1996). *Digestive wellness.* New Canaan, CT: Keats.

Liswood, L. A. (1995). *Women world leaders: Fifteen great politicians tell their stories.* San Francisco, CA: HarperCollins.

MacDonald, S. and Richman, A. (1997). *The winter guest* (screenplay). Fine Line Feature Video.

Magida, A. (1996). *How to be a perfect stranger: A guide to etiquette in other people's religious ceremonies.* Woodstock, VT: Jewish Light Publishing.

Mankiller, W. and Wallis, M. (1993). *Mankiller: A chief and her people.* New York: St. Martin's Griffin.

Mason, M. J. (1991). *Making our lives our own: A woman's guide to the six challenges of personal change.* New York: HarperCollins.

McDougall, J. (1989). *Theaters of the body: A psychoanalytic approach to psychosomatic illness.* New York: W.W. Norton and Company.

McGrath, E., Keita, G. P., Strickland, B. R., and Russo, N. F. (1990). *Women and depression: Risk factors and treatment issues.* Washington, DC: American Psychological Association.

McGuire, M. and Klein, J. (1999). *The interactive focusing process.* Canada: Nada Lou Productions. Video contact Dr. Janet Klein at (561) 540-2687.

McMahon, E. M. (1993). *Beyond the myth of dominance: An alternative to a violent society.* Kansas City, MO: Sheed and Ward.

Meier, P. (1993). *Don't let jerks get the best of you.* Nashville: Thomas Nelson Publishers.

Miller, M. A. (1995). Culture, spirituality, and women's health. *J O G N N* 24(3): 257-263.

Mitchell, R. C. and Ricciuti, G. A. (1991). *Birthings and blessings: Liberating worship services for the inclusive church.* New York: Crossroad.

Mollenkott, V. R. (1989). *The divine feminine: The biblical imagery of God as female.* New York: Crossroad.

Moore, T. (1992). *Care of the soul: A guide for cultivating depth and sacredness in everyday life.* New York: HarperCollins.

Morgan, O. and Jordan, M. (Eds.) (1999). *Addictions and spirituality: A multi-disciplinary approach.* St. Louis, MO: The Chalice Press.

Morrison, T. (1987). *Beloved.* New York: Knopf.

Myss, C. (1996). *Anatomy of the spirit: The seven stages of power and healing.* New York: Three Rivers Press.

Narayanan, V. (1999). Brimmin with *Bhakti,* embodiments of *Shakti:* Devotee, deities, performers, reformers, and other women of power in the Hindu tradition. In A. Sharma and K. Young (Eds.), *Feminism and world religions* (p. 33). Albany, NY: State University of New York Press.

Nathanson, D. (1992). *Shame and pride: Affect, sex, and the birth of self.* New York: W.W. Norton.

Nelson, M. with Wernick, S. (1998). *Strong women stay slim.* New York: Bantam.

Northrup, C. (1994). *Women's bodies, women's wisdom: Creating physical and emotional health and healing.* New York: Bantam Books.

Ochs, C. (1983). *Women and spirituality.* New Jersey: Roman and Allanheld.

Ochs, C. and Olitzky, K. (1998). *Jewish spiritual guidance: Finding our way to God.* San Francisco: Jossey-Bass.

Ornish, D. (1982). *Stress, diet, and your heart.* New York: Holt, Rinehart and Winston.

Ornish, D. (1993). *Eat more, weigh less.* New York: HarperCollins.

Peck, M. S. (1993). *Further along the road less traveled.* New York: Simon and Schuster.

Pelletier, K.R. (1977). *Mind as healer, mind as slayer.* New York: Dell.

Pipher, M. (1994). *Reviving Ophelia: Saving the selves of adolescent girls.* New York: Putnam.

Pipher, M. (1996). *The shelter of each other: Rebuilding our families.* New York: Putnam.

Pittman, F. (1989). *Private lies: Infidelity and the betrayal of intimacy.* New York: W. W. Norton.

Proud Deer, N. (2000). Chief among us. *St. Louis Times,* May, pp. 16-17.

Quinn, S. (1995). *Marie Curie: A life.* New York: Simon and Schuster.

Randle, N. (1999). In 1942, for the first time, chicks took wing on military mission for the U.S. *Saint Louis Post Dispatch,* May 24, p. E3.

Read, P. J. and Witlieb, B. L. (1992). *The book of women's firsts.* New York: Random House.

Redmond, L. (1997). *When the drummers were women: A spiritual history of rhythm.* New York: Three Rivers Press.

Rehm, D. (1999). *Finding my voice.* New York: Knopf.

Relaford Brown, J. (1994). Finding her here. In S. Haldeman Martz (Ed.), anthologies, *I am becoming the woman I have wanted* (p. 1). Watsonville, CA: Paper-Mache Press.

Renard, J. (1996). *Seven doors to Islam: Spirituality and the religious life.* Berkeley: University of California.

Robinson-Walker, C. (1999). *Woman and leadership in health care: Journey to authenticity and power.* San Francisco: Jossey-Bass Publishers.

Rosenberg, M. (1999). *Nonviolent communication: A language of compassion.* Del Mar, CA: PuddleDancer Press.

Roth, G. with Louden, J. (1998). *Maps to ecstasy: A healing for the untamed spirit.* Novato: CA: New World Library.

Roy, M. (Ed.) (1982). *The abusive partner.* New York: Van Nostrand Reinhold.

Ryan, T. (1986). *Wellness, spirituality, and sports.* New York: Paulist Press.

Sadler, M. and Sadler, D. (1994). *Failing at fairness: How America's schools cheat girls.* New York: Charles Scribner's Sons.

Satir, V. (1988). *The new peoplemaking.* Mountain View, CA: Science and Behavior Books.

Saussy, C. (1995). *The gift of anger: A call to faithful action.* Louisville, KY: Westminister John Knox Press.

Scarf, M. (1995). *Intimate worlds: Life inside the family.* New York: Random House.

Schenckel, S. (1991). *Giving away success.* New York: Random.

Scherman, N. (1990). *The complete artscroll Siddur.* New York: Mesorah Publications.

Schipper, M. (1991). *Source of all evil: African proverbs and sayings on women.* Chicago: Ivan R. Dee, Inc.

Schlessinger, A. (1995). *Wilma Rudolph: American women of achievement.* Schlessinger Video Productions.

Schor, J. (1992). *The overworked American: The unexpected decline of leisure.* New York: Basic Books.

Schuhmacher, S. and Woerner, G. (1989). *The encyclopedia of eastern philosophy and religion*. Boston: Shambhala.

Seaward, B. L. (1997). *Stand like mountain, flow like water: Reflections on stress and human spirituality*. Deerfield Beach, FL: Health Communications, Inc.

Seligman, M. and Garber, J. (Eds.) (1980). *Human helplessness: Theory and research*. New York: Academic Press.

Sharma, A. and Young, K. (Eds.) (1999). *Feminism and world religion*. New York: New York State University.

Shomer, E. (2001). *Stars at noon: Poems from the life of Jacqueline Cochran*. Fayetteville: The University of Arkansas Press.

Sicherman, B. (1984). *Alice Hamilton: A life in letters*. Cambridge, MA: Harvard University Press.

Siegel, B. (1995). Love: The work of the soul. In R. Carlson and B. Shield (Eds.), *Healers on healing* (pp. 48-52). Los Angeles: Jeremy P. Tarcher.

Siggins, L. (1997). *Mary Robinson: The woman who took power in the park*. Edinburgh: Mainstream Publishing Company.

Silverstein, S. (1964). *The giving tree*. New York: Harper Collins.

Simon, R. (1997). The family unplugged: An interview with Mary Pipher. *The Family Therapy Networker* 21(1): 24-33.

Sinacore-Guinn, D. (1998). U.S. ban on female circumcision raises threat of further harm. *The Park Ridge Bulletin*, May/June, p. 6.

Stark, E., Flitcraft, A., Zucherman, D., et al. (1981). *Wife abuse in the medical setting: An introduction for health personnel*. Monograph Series No. 7, National Clearinghouse on Domestic Violence. Washington, DC: U.S. Government Printing Office, April.

Steere, D. (1984). *Quaker spirituality: Selected writings*. New York: Paulist Press.

Steinem, G. (1992). *Revolution from within: A book of self-esteem*. Beverly Hills, CA: Dove Audio.

Stiver, I. (1991). Work inhibitions in women. In *Women's growth in connection: Writing's from the Stone Center* (pp. 223-236). New York: Guilford.

Switzer, K. (1998). *Running and walking for women over 40: The road to sanity and vanity*. New York: St. Martin's Press.

Tavris, C. (1989). *Anger: The misunderstood emotion*. New York: Touchstone.

Teresa of Avila (1979). *The Interior Castle* (Kavanaugh, K. and Rodriguez, O. Trans.). New York: Paulist Press.

Thornton, B. B. and Epperson, T. (1996). *A family thing*. United Artists Video.

Tillman, G., producer, writer (1997). *Soul food*. 20th Century Fox video.

Tooker, E. (Ed.) (1979). *Native North American spirituality of the eastern woodlands: Sacred myths, dreams, visions, speeches, healing formulas, rituals and ceremonials*. New York: Paulist Press.

Vaughan, S. (2000). *Half empty half full*. New York: Harcourt, Inc.

Ventura, M. (1996). The mission of memory. *The Family Therapy Networker* 20(6): 22-28.

Viscott, D. (1991). *The winning woman: Understanding your feelings of anger and guilt.* Chicago, IL: Nightingale-Conant Corporation, audiotape (800) 323-5552.

Vohra, P. (1998). *A woman's place.* Maryland: Public Radio video. Contact Maria Nicolo (212) 877-3253.

Walker, A. and Parmar, P. (1993). *Warrior marks: Female genital mutilation and the sexual blinding of women.* New York: Harcourt Brace and Company.

Wallace, H. (1999). *Family violence: Legal, medical, and social perspectives,* Second edition. Needham, MA: Allyn & Bacon.

Wallis, J. (2000). *Faith works: Lessons from the life of an activist preacher.* New York: Random House.

Walsh, F. (1998). *Strengthening family resilience.* New York: Guilford.

Walsh, F. (Ed.) (1999). *Spiritual resources in family therapy.* New York: Guilford.

Wassef, Nadia (1998). Masculinities and mutilations: Female genital mutilation in Egypt. *Middle East Women's Studies,* 13(Summer/2): 1-3.

Watson, W. (1995). *Aging families and beliefs.* AAMFT Annual Convention Audiotape, ph. (800) 241-7785.

Weed, S. (2002). *New menopausal years the wise woman way.* Woodstock, NY: Ash Tree Publishing.

Weil, A. (1995). *Spontaneous healing.* New York: Alfred A. Knopf.

Weingarten, K. (1994). *The mother's voice: Strengthening intimacy in families.* New York: Guilford.

Whalen, M. D. (1999). In the company of women? The politics of memory in the liturgical commemoration of saints—male and female. *Worship* 73(6): 482-504.

White, M. and Epston, D. (1990). *Narrative means to therapeutic ends.* New York: Norton.

Whitney, C. (Ed.) (2000). *Nine and counting.* New York: William Morrow.

Wigoder, G. (1974). *Encyclopedic dictionary of Judaica.* New York: Leon Amiel Publisher.

Wilder, L. (1999). *7 steps to fearless speaking.* New York: John Wiley and Sons, Inc.

Wilder, M., music, and Coats, P., producer (1998). *Mulan.* CA: Walt Disney Production Buena Vista Video.

Winter, M. T. (1990). *Woman prayer woman song.* New York: Crossroad.

Woodruff, J. (1996). *Women world leaders.* New Dimension Media, Inc. Video. ph (217) 243-4567.

Woods, H. (2000). *Stepping up to power: The political journey of American women.* Boulder, CO: Westview Press.

Wright, L. and Nagy, J. (1993). Death: The most troublesome family secret of all. In E. Imber-Black (Ed.), *Secrets in families and family therapy* (pp. 121-136). New York: Norton.

Wright, W. (1999). The charism of parenting. In D. Donnelly (Ed.), *Retrieving charisms for the twenty-first century* (pp. 85-101). Collegeville, MN: The Liturgical Press.

Yapko, M. (1999). *Hand me down blues: How to keep depression from spreading in families*. New York: Golden Books.

Zagano, P. (1993). *Woman to woman: An anthology of women's spiritualities*. Collegeville, MN: The Liturgical Press.

Zagano, P. (1996). *Ita Ford: Missionary martyr*. New York: Paulist Press.

Zimmerman, J. and Dickerson, V. (1996). *If problems talked: Narrative therapy in action*. New York: Guilford.

Web Sites

Adoption in General:
  <http://www.adoptioninstitute.org>

The Anxiety Disorders Association of America:
  <http://www.adaa.org>

Congregational Resources:
  <http://www.congregationalresources.org>

Holistic Childbirth Lessons and Feminine Wisdom:
  <http://www.motherhealth.com>

Prayer, Spirituality:
  <http://www.cdc.gov/nccdphp/dash/presphysactrpt/index.htm>

Research by the American Association of University Women
  <http://www.aauw.org>

Index

SPECIAL 25%-OFF DISCOUNT!
Order a copy of this book with this form or online at:
http://www.haworthpressinc.com/store/product.asp?sku=4689

INTEGRATING SPIRIT AND PSYCHE
Using Women's Narratives in Psychotherapy

_____in hardbound at $29.96 (regularly $39.95) (ISBN: 0-7890-1209-X)

_____in softbound at $18.71 (regularly $24.95) (ISBN: 0-7890-1210-3)

Or order online and use Code HEC25 in the shopping cart.

COST OF BOOKS_____

OUTSIDE US/CANADA/
MEXICO: ADD 20%_____

POSTAGE & HANDLING_____
(US: $5.00 for first book & $2.00
for each additional book)
Outside US: $6.00 for first book
& $2.00 for each additional book)

SUBTOTAL_____

IN CANADA: ADD 7% GST_____

STATE TAX_____
(NY, OH & MN residents, please
add appropriate local sales tax)

FINAL TOTAL_____
(If paying in Canadian funds,
convert using the current
exchange rate, UNESCO
coupons welcome)

☐ **BILL ME LATER:** ($5 service charge will be added)
(Bill-me option is good on US/Canada/Mexico orders only;
not good to jobbers, wholesalers, or subscription agencies.)

☐ Check here if billing address is different from
shipping address and attach purchase order and
billing address information.

Signature_____

☐ **PAYMENT ENCLOSED: $**_____

☐ **PLEASE CHARGE TO MY CREDIT CARD.**

☐ Visa ☐ MasterCard ☐ AmEx ☐ Discover
☐ Diner's Club ☐ Eurocard ☐ JCB

Account # _____

Exp. Date_____

Signature_____

Prices in US dollars and subject to change without notice.

NAME_____

INSTITUTION_____

ADDRESS_____

CITY_____

STATE/ZIP_____

COUNTRY_____ COUNTY (NY residents only)_____

TEL_____ FAX_____

E-MAIL_____

May we use your e-mail address for confirmations and other types of information? ☐ Yes ☐ No
We appreciate receiving your e-mail address and fax number. Haworth would like to e-mail or fax special
discount offers to you, as a preferred customer. **We will never share, rent, or exchange your e-mail address
or fax number.** We regard such actions as an invasion of your privacy.

Order From Your Local Bookstore or Directly From
The Haworth Press, Inc.
10 Alice Street, Binghamton, New York 13904-1580 • USA
TELEPHONE: 1-800-HAWORTH (1-800-429-6784) / Outside US/Canada: (607) 722-5857
FAX: 1-800-895-0582 / Outside US/Canada: (607) 722-6362
E-mailto: getinfo@haworthpressinc.com
PLEASE PHOTOCOPY THIS FORM FOR YOUR PERSONAL USE.
http://www.HaworthPress.com   BOF02